LIFE STORIES
PERSONAL CONSTRUCT THERAPY
WITH THE ELDERLY

WILEY SERIES IN
PSYCHOTHERAPY AND
COUNSELLING

SERIES EDITORS
Franz Epting, *Dept of Psychology, University of Florida, USA*
Bonnie Strickland, *Dept of Psychology, University of Massachusetts, USA*
John Allen, *Dept of Community Studies, University of Brighton , UK*

Self, Symptoms and Psychotherapy
Edited by Neil Cheshire and Helmut Thomae

Beyond Sexual Abuse: Therapy with Women who were Childhood Victims
Derek Jehu

Cognitive-Analytic Therapy: Active Participation in Change: A New Integration in Brief Psychotherapy
Anthony Ryle

The Power of Countertransference: Innovations in Analytic Technique
Karen J. Maroda

Strategic Family Play Therapy
Shlomo Ariel

The Evolving Professional Self: Stages and Themes in Therapist and Counselor Development
Thomas M. Skovholt and Michael Helge Rønnestad

Feminist Perspectives in Therapy: An Empowerment Model for Women
Judith Worell and Pam Remer

Counselling and Therapy with Refugees: Psychological Problems of Victims of War, Torture and Repression
Guus van der Veer

Psychoanalytic Counseling
Michael J. Patton and Naomi M. Meara

Life Stories: Personal Construct Therapy with the Elderly
Linda L. Viney

Further titles in preparation

LIFE STORIES
PERSONAL CONSTRUCT THERAPY WITH THE ELDERLY

Linda L. Viney

University of Wollongong, Australia

John Wiley & Sons

Chichester • New York • Brisbane • Toronto • Singapore

Other Wiley Editorial Offices

John Wiley & Sons, Inc., 605 Third Avenue,
New York, NY 10158-0012, USA

Jacaranda Wiley Ltd, G.P.O. Box 859, Brisbane,
Queensland 4001, Australia

John Wiley & Sons (Canada) Ltd, 22 Worcester Road,
Rexdale, Ontario M9W 1L1, Canada

John Wiley & Sons (SEA) Pte Ltd, 37 Jalan Pemimpin #05-04,
Block B, Union Industrial Building, Singapore 2057

British Library Cataloguing in Publication Data

A catalogue record for this book is available from the British Library

ISBN 0-471-93867-X (paper)

Typeset in 10/12pt Times from author's disks by Text Processing Department,
John Wiley & Sons Ltd, Chichester
Printed and bound in Great Britain by Biddles Ltd, Guildford, Surrey

Contents

vi   Contents

Series preface

The Wiley Series in Psychotherapy and Counselling is designed to advance the science and practice of professional psychology. One of the areas of development focuses on new and innovative approaches to the treatment of specific groups or populations. Certainly a book focused on the elderly could rival any other named group in terms of importance. Given the sizable increase in the population of elderly in the world, no other group has a better claim for sustained professional attention. In the United States alone it is now estimated that there are approximately 50 000 people who have lived a full century. Dr Viney has provided an excellent opportunity for the series to move into this most important area.

Her approach is most engaging because she has elected to tap the power of the personal narrative in providing the substance of her work with the elderly. The richness this provides enables the reader to grasp the personal experiences of the participants in a most direct fashion. This is then complemented by providing a theoretical framework for understanding these experiences. Using personal construct theory and therapy for this purpose gives the total enterprise a coherence and provides a way for the reader to take up this position and use it. It provides a way to examine the lived experience of the elderly as they encounter difficulties and as they attempt to empower themselves for further growth and development. She also includes themes which relate to significant age-related events such as retirement, illness, bereavement and dying. Reading and using her book should prove to be most rewarding for both the professional worker in this field as well as the general reader who wishes to understand the events in aging from the viewpoint of the reported direct experience of the elderly. The book is well documented with suggested readings at the end of chapters and a list of definitions of some personal construct theory terms at the end of the volume. The book is positioned to make a significant contribution to the therapeutic literature on the elderly by providing an access to the elderly as persons, and is a most welcome addition to the series.

Franz R. Epting
Series Editor

Preface

Why would anyone working professionally with the elderly want to read a book entitled *Life Stories*? The elderly themselves? Or their families? You may have noticed that elderly people do tell a lot of stories. In fact, sometimes those stories, especially when they are told slowly or repetitively, may seem to get in the way of achieving professional goals. Yet I believe that these stories, and the reactions of others to them, are of central importance to the elderly. Such stories maintain or threaten their personal well-being. It follows, then, that understanding the many roles these stories play for them can enhance the impact that nurses, welfare workers, physiotherapists, social workers, psychologists and physicians can have on the lives of the elderly. That same understanding can also be of use to people who themselves are elderly. It can help them to make sense of some of their more puzzling and frightening, as well as their more enjoyable, experiences. This understanding can also be useful to the families of elderly family members.

In this book, I assume that we all make sense of our current experiences and even anticipate the future through meanings we have built up from our past experiences. These meanings, or personal constructs, guide and limit our actions. Each system of inter-related meanings developed by every one of us is unique. However, because we have many experiences in common, we also have meanings in common. We use these meanings to create stories about events in our lives, especially those that are very important to us. Having our stories told provides confirmation of those meanings for us. If these stories provide difficulties for us, we can choose to retell them. Elderly people have built up often very complex systems of meaning during their long lives. These meanings guide and limit their actions. The elderly tell stories about events that are important to them, but they rarely hear their stories told. Some of these stories are self-promoting and need to be encouraged, while others are self-limiting and need to be retold so as to ease the constraints they impose. Psychotherapy with the elderly can be seen as providing opportunities for them to both tell and retell their stories.

There are three other aspects of this book on which I want to comment. The first is that, in order to protect the confidentiality of the elderly clients discussed here, I have disguised any information that could have identified them or their families. I have also chosen, given the large literature on the elderly to which I have access, to be selective in the reading I recommend at the end of each of its chapters. These readings are identified by raised numbers in the text. The other aspect is the choice I have made of words to describe people at the latter end of their life span. "Older person" may be politically correct in the nineties. I have preferred to use the word "elderly" to show my own respect for these people. For me, "elderly" is linked with the role of church and tribal "elders" in society, and concepts such as "the wisdom of the elderly".

Linda L. Viney,
Austinmer, 1992.

Acknowledgements

My thanks must first go to these courageous clients who kindly shared their personal and private stories with us. Acknowledgement is next owed to the two therapists who worked most with me and these clients, Yvonne Benjamin and Carol Preston. Both of these therapists taught me much about therapy with the elderly. Yvonne Benjamin and Alex Clarke have been very helpful in commenting critically on this manuscript as it has developed. Franz Epting has also been a most supportive and yet thoughtful editor for my contribution to this series of books on personal construct therapy. Dayna Meades has, as usual, produced an impeccable final manuscript. Lastly, I should like to thank the Commonwealth Department of Community Services and Health who funded the development of therapy with the elderly that is reported here, as well as its evaluation.

1 The power of stories about the elderly

We are all trying to make sense of ourselves and our worlds. As we do so, we create our own accounts of events. One of our favourite accounts is the story. In a story, a sequence of meanings comes together to form a theme. We all think, feel, act, make our judgements about ourselves and others, and in fact live our lives, in terms of stories. Some of these stories are personal accounts. Others are shared by groups of people who agree, not only on the content of their shared stories, but on the rules that govern their development. The responses of the world to the elderly, then, are determined by the stories we all tell about them. Medical practitioners tell certain kinds of stories; nurses tell others; and social workers and occupational therapists tell yet others. However, in this book I shall focus mostly on the stories about being elderly told by elderly people themselves.

What is a story?

What do I mean when I use this concept of story? A story enables people to link together the events they experience, using their customary ways of viewing things, or their personal constructs,[1] to do so. This linking often occurs over time.[2,3] Integration is therefore a defining characteristic of stories, or narratives, but it can vary from being tight and inflexible to loose and easily changed over time.[4] Good or bad stories can be identified, not so much in terms of the degree of integration they provide but in terms of the paths of living that they open or close for those who tell them. Another important aspect of the story is its context. Each story has a story teller who chooses to tell a particular story from a number usually available, in a particular way, to a particular person and in a particular setting.

2 Life stories: personal construct therapy with the elderly

The stories that are important to understanding the elderly are centred primarily on the self, but they also help to make sense of other people in relation to the self.[5] There are therefore personal, social and cultural aspects to each one. The personal aspects of stories include the presentation of self to others, as well as of the events which are most important to them. They also meet some psychological needs, such as preserving self-esteem or allocating responsibility. Stories also have implications for emotion and action, and the linking of present and past in order to anticipate the future. The most important social aspects of the story are its context, the sources of confirmation or validation for it and how it allocates power to the teller and to other people. Its major cultural aspects lie in the information which is shared through it and the values which are implicit in it.

Our stories have at least four major implications for how we live our lives. First, and perhaps most important, they help us to develop and maintain a sense of identity.[6] We know best who we are when we tell stories in which we play active roles. These stories help to fill out the many different ways in which we can live, and they can remind us of our own resources. Yet important, too, is the hearing of stories about ourselves from other people, or at least stories that could be ours. To live in a culture in which none of our stories were told would be to very soon lose any sense of identity.[7]

Second, stories provide us with guidance by which to live our lives. They enable us to recognise our own existences, unleash our abilities and continue to broaden our focus on the world. They also give us opportunities to acknowledge and make use of our similarities to others, while maintaining our sense of uniqueness. They permit us to prepare for the future. It is when people's stories no longer provide them with this guide, that problems in living become apparent.[8,9] Elderly people who are depressed are an example. Their view of themselves, as presented in their stories, is mainly negative and self-critical. Their focus on the world has narrowed. They feel helpless and alienated from others. They are hopeless and therefore unable to plan effectively for the future. Such stories make living very difficult indeed.

Third, our stories enable us to place order on the sometimes chaotic events of our lives. They hold our experiences in sequences for us, so that we can move in a planned fashion through them and are not overwhelmed by them. They also give us the opportunity to link present, past and future events together. Such sequencing provides the chance to reflect on what we have done, and to draw more general conclusions from it. Psychologists have paid particular attention to the stories people develop to account for why events occur as they do. There is, however, a much wider range of accounts available from people than those simply dealing with mechanical causality. For example, some stories focus on the purposes and goals of people in their causal explanations.

Fourth, when we are able to get others to listen to our stories, this gives us more power than we might otherwise have.[10,11] This is partly because the narrator's role is one of active agent and because of the personal resources of which they remind us.[12] But it is also because of the social contexts in which these stories are heard. When people are invited to tell their stories, this is often an indication that they have sufficient power to ensure that the invitation occurs. Moreover, when their story is listened to, it opens up many opportunities for contributions from them to the shared interpretation of events that occurs in that social context. People whose stories are heard within a culture contribute to framing how that culture sees itself and its problems. That is why there is so much competition for a voice in newspapers, radio and television. People whose stories are not heard are those who lack influence. If they seek more power, it can come, in part, through their stories being heard.

We need, then, to have our stories told and heard. Our listeners are often family and friends, but sometimes we need a professional or wider community audience. This depends on the content of our stories and their implications for us and others. This story-telling leads to support from others as well as to action. People can gain power through the telling and hearing of their stories, especially when choice between alternative courses of action follows. Some such stories can be too self-defeating and alienating; and these need to be retold. The depressive story sketched earlier needs to be retold, for example, so as to find alternatives to so much self-criticism, helplessness and hopelessness. Such retelling can be achieved in counselling or psychotherapy. Other stories that need some retelling include those that show much isolation. They need to be told and retold among small, supportive groups of people. Yet other stories are those which show much alienation; and they need to be retold in the wider community. Of course therapists, too, have their own stories: about themselves as therapists and about how therapy works.[13]

Stories about the elderly

Accounts of being elderly are constructed, much as accounts of any other events are, in the form of stories. This means that people who are older think, feel, act and indeed live their lives in terms of their own and other people's stories about the elderly. So do the health and welfare professionals who work with them, and so do all of us who belong to communities with elderly members. There are many different stories available. It is useful to remember, however, that each account of being elderly is a story in itself, whether it be a journalistic story or a medical one. Personal construct psychology provides a perspective on being elderly that acknowledges and values alternative accounts of it.

It is particularly important to the elderly to hear, and of course tell, stories about people like themselves. They have a special need to maintain their identities in the face of less and less confirmation for them.[14] For example, many isolated elderly people enjoy going through their family photograph album and benefit from telling the stories associated with it. This process is also prompted by the loss of spouses and old friends, with which they have to contend. This is why, when dealing with the loss of their own abilities resulting from, for example, a stroke, they will give the same account of that stroke over and over again. The elderly also need their own stories in the face of the stigma which their communities often place on them in other relevant stories, and by their exclusion from power in those same communities.

Stories about elderly people as competent are particularly important to them.[15] For example, 74-year-old Mr D often told the story of how he was known as "Big John" among the other members of his club, because of his reputation for "defending the ladies". Telling stories about themselves as "old" has been shown to have affected the elderly badly.[16] Conversely, being able to see themselves as mutually involved in helping relationships is of great value to them.[17] Mrs J, 71, with a leg amputated because of diabetes, was able to feel both competent and useful as she told her story of still being able to help other ill people with the massage techniques by which she had earned her living for so long.

Some often repeated stories about the elderly which interfere with their psychological functioning are highly questionable, in terms of their accuracy, and so should be discarded for that reason. One such story assumes that, as people grow older, they become isolated from family and friends.[18,19] This is not necessarily so; although physical disability and increasing fragility can impair their ability to be with others.[20-22] Another such story is that with increasing age comes increasing dependence on others, which is, again, not necessarily the case.[19,23] This story seems to be important to our Western culture, as does the third questionable story, which is potentially the most damaging. In it, the psychological functioning of the elderly is seen as taking the same course as their physical development, that is, one of decline. Some diseases of the elderly do lead to brain damage and subsequent deterioration of cognitive functioning. However, there is increasing evidence that cognitive functioning does not necessarily decline with increasing age, especially if tests appropriate for the elderly are used.[24,25] Psychologists are now learning more about the emotional and social development of the elderly; it goes beyond and even transcends what we, earlier in our life spans, experience. In the next chapter, I shall examine some of these aspects in more detail.

What kinds of stories about the elderly, then, are found in newspapers and on television? My own survey of newspapers, conducted while I was writing this book, showed them to be horrifyingly barren of stories serving as sources of identity and self-esteem for the elderly. The national and metropolitan papers gave no space to stories about the elderly, unless someone had died. There was no mention of them in the international or local news, entertainment, sports sections or even in the advertisements. It was only in the free local papers, supported completely by advertising, that some stories about the elderly appeared. In these papers, the news included the one hundredth anniversary of the Soccer Club reunion of old members and a community-based programme to provide a bridge between young and old. The entertainment sections provided, for example, accounts of the Combined Pensioners' Card Day. However, it was the advertisements that included the greatest number of stories about the elderly: investment opportunities, building "granny flats", holiday travel and special hairdressing rates for pensioners. Their often meagre financial resources are still sought after, it seems.

The only story I could find which showed the elderly in an active rather than passive, accepting role involved a recently set-up Grandmothers' Club. Its aim was to build friendships with disabled children. Only in this were the elderly portrayed as competent. Much broader and more rigorous surveys of the papers, magazines and television by others have also found references to the elderly to be very rare.[26-29] They have reported that those media provide many hints to the elderly that they are excluded from their story telling.[30] Even when a story about an elderly person who is competent and happy is told, it is presented in such a way as to make it both uncommon and unexpected. For example, the headline "Life is Great at 98!" contrives to imply that it ought not to be.

Sadly, some of the most demeaning and psychologically disabling stories about the elderly are told by the elderly themselves. "I'm not up to it now, you know, at my age." "When you're older, you can't learn anything new like you used to." "Old people aren't much use to anybody, you know." Happily, there are some elderly people who manage to communicate their stories which contain more hope. One example of published work comes from the autobiography of a 71-year-old retired school teacher who was confined to bed in a nursing home. In her book, *This bed my centre*,[31] Elizabeth Newton wrote: "Everyone who lives grows older. The majority don't grow soured and helpless or bitter and irresponsible, simply because the passing years slow down their tempo of living." The psychotherapist, Carl Rogers, when in his eighties, also optimistically entitled an article "Growing old—or older and growing?"[32]

The power of stories about the elderly

Because all stories about the elderly are created by people, each of us is able to choose which of them he or she tells to others or to ourselves. Different stories are created by different groups in our communities,[33] and, again, each of us is able to choose to which of these he or she subscribes. In this book, I want to help people who work with the elderly to become aware of their roles as creators and tellers of stories about them. I also want to help the elderly themselves to recognise the importance of telling their own stories, as well as some of the implications these stories have, and to support them in doing this. My other aim is to make available to them and to therapists who work with them some alternative stories; that is, to give them a greater range of choices.

Psychotherapy with the elderly can be very useful. There is research evidence to show that it is effective in terms of improving both their psychological functioning and the quality of their lives.[34,35] In these ways, elderly clients have, because of their many losses, the social stigma they often suffer and their exclusion from power in our culture, an otherwise unmet need to tell their own stories in therapy and to receive support and validation of them.[36,37] Because of the lack of stories about people like them, they need to hear such stories told by therapists.[38,39] They also need to retell some of their own stories, especially the questionable ones that they have accepted within our culture, as well as their own stories which are psychologically undermining.

Personal construct therapists work with the goal of helping their clients to explore their ways of viewing their worlds and the implications of those constructs for the courses of action they can take. With elderly clients, the exploration of their stories in this way is particularly important.[40,41] Alternative stories are tried out. "When you're elderly, you can't learn anything new" can become, if only for a brief trial period, "I think I'll try that Day Centre. It'd be nice to be with people my own age sometimes." "Old people aren't much use to anybody" can become "I was a good mother when the children were young. Maybe I can now help out with those disabled children." So not only are a firmer sense of identity and greater self-esteem apparent, but also more courses for action become available. Therapy with many other elderly people will now be explored.

The other chapters in the present section of this book serve, like this one, as introductions to personal construct concepts useful for working therapeutically with the elderly. In Chapter 2, I shall provide an account of the personal construct approach to their psychological functioning. Chapter 3 deals with the assessment of that functioning in elderly clients, especially in terms of the stories they tell. Chapter 4 is concerned with how their stories can be retold in therapy. In the next section I address the implications of three common and self-limiting stories told by the elderly: "Sometimes I feel as if life isn't worthwhile" (Chapter 5), "I worry about the future" (Chapter 6), and "I don't want to be a burden to anyone" (Chapter 7). In the following section, I examine some unfortunately not so common but self-empowering stories of the elderly: "It is marvellous, being able to do what I want to do when I want to do it" (Chapter 9), "I enjoy myself these days" (Chapter 8), and "I have a wonderful relationship with my grandchildren" (Chapter 10). The themes I have used as titles of Chapters 5–10 point to each set of stories but, of course, cannot express them fully. It is in these chapters, hopefully, that the roles played by their stories in the life of the elderly become apparent. In them, the voices of many different elderly people are heard; but in the next section, I shall describe only one client and the retelling of his or her story in each chapter. Each chapter will focus on an age-related event: retirement (Chapter 11), illness (Chapter 12), bereavement and loss (Chapter 13) and dying (Chapter 14). Perhaps the most important message of this book is that we therapists have much to learn from our elderly clients. In the last chapter of the book, then, I shall move from the telling and retelling of the stories of clients, to the much-needed telling and retelling of the stories of therapists (Chapter 15).

Suggested reading

● *What is a story?*

1. Kelly, G.A. (1955). *The psychology of personal constructs*, Vols 1 & 2. New York: Norton.
2. Cohler, B.J. (1982). Personal narrative and life course. In P. Baltes & O.G. Brim (Eds.), *Life span development and behaviour*, Vol. 4. New York: Academic Press.
3. Sarbin, T. (Ed.) (1986). *Narrative psychology: The storied nature of human conduct.* New York: Praeger.
4. Britton, B. & Pellergrini, I.D. (1990). *Narrative thought and narrative language.* Hillsdale, New Jersey: Erlbaum.
5. Dennett, D.C. (1983). The self as a centre of narrative gravity. In D.L. Johnson & P.M. Cole (Eds.), *Consciousness and self.* New York: Praeger.
6. White, H. (1980). The value of narrativity in the representation of reality. *Critical Inquiry*, **7**, 5–28.
7. Mair, J.M.M. (1990). Telling psychological tales. *International Journal of Personal Construct Psychology*, **3**, 27–36.
8. Sontag, S. (1977). *Illness as metaphor.* London: Allen Lane.
9. Viney, L.L. (1989). *Images of illness.* Florida: Krieger, Second edition.
10. McAdams, D.P. (1985). *Power, intimacy and the life story.* Homewood, Illinois: Dorsey Press.
11. Rowe, D. (1982). *The construction of life and death.* New York: Wiley.
12. Berger, J.W. (1989). Developing the story in psychotherapy. *American Journal of Psychotherapy*, **43**, 248–259.
13. Mair, J.M.M. (1988). Psychology as story telling. *International Journal of Personal Construct Psychology*, **1**, 125–137.

● *Stories about the elderly*

14. Unruh, D.R. (1983). *Invisible lives: Social worlds of the aged.* New York: Sage.
15. Cooper, J. & Goethals, G.R. (1981). The self concept and old age. In S.B. Kiesler, J.N. Morgan & U.K. Oppenheimer (Eds.), *Ageing: Social change.* New York: Academic Press, pp. 431–452.
16. Carp, F.M. & Carp, A. (1981). Mental health characteristics and acceptance/rejection of old age. *American Journal of Orthopsychiatry*, **5**, 230–241.

17. Frogatt, A. (1985). Listening to the voices of older women. In A. Butler (Ed.), *Ageing: Recent advances and creative responses*. London: Croom Helm.
18. Shanass, E. (1979). Social myth as hypothesis: The case of the family relations of old people. *The Gerontologist*, **19**, 3–9.
19. Townsend, P. (1981). The structured dependency of the elderly: A creation of social policy in the twentieth century. *Ageing and Society*, **1**, 5–28.
20. Brody, H. (1987). *Stories of sickness*. New Haven: Yale.
21. Kleinman, A. (1988). *The illness narratives*. New York: Basic Books.
22. Russell, C. (1981). *The ageing experience*. Sydney: Allen & Unwin.
23. Walker, A. (1980). The social creation of poverty and dependency in old age. *Journal of Social Policy*, **9**, 49–75.
24. Avorn, J. (1983). Biomedical and social determinants of cognitive impairment in the elderly. *American Geriatrics Society Journal*, **31**, 137–143.
25. Henig, R.M. (1981). *The myth of senility*. New York: Anchor.
26. Berman, L. & Sokowska-Ashcroft, I. (1986). The old in language and literature. *Language and Communication*, **6**, 139–144.
27. Loupland, N., Couplan, J. & Giles, H. (Eds.) (1991). *Sociolinguistics and the elderly: Discourse, identity and ageing*. Oxford: Blackwell.
28. Rosenthal, M. (1984). Geriatrics: A selected up-to-date bibliography. *American Geriatrics Society Journal*, **32**, 64–79.
29. Ward, R.A. (1984). The marginality and salience of being old: When is age relevant? *Gerontologist*, **24**, 227–237.
30. Giles, H. (1991). "Gosh, you don't look it!" A sociolinguistic construction of ageing. *The Psychologist*, **4**, 99–119.
31. Newton, E. (1979). *This bed my centre*. Melbourne: McFee Gribble.
32. Rogers, C.R. (1980). Growing old—or older and growing. *Journal of Humanistic Psychology*, **20**(4), 5–16.

● *The power of stories about the elderly*

33. Ferraro, K.F. (1992). *Gerontology: Perspectives and issues*. New York: Springer.
34. Marmar, G.R., Gaston, L. & Gallagher, D. (1989). Absence and outcome in late life depression. *Journal of Nervous and Mental Disease*, **177**, 464–472.
35. Viney, L.L., Benjamin, Y.N. & Preston, C.A. (1989). An evaluation of personal construct therapy for the elderly. *British Journal of Medical Psychology*, **62**, 35–41.
36. Fitting, M.D. (1984). Professional and ethical responsibilities for psychologists working with the elderly. *The Counselling Psychologist*, **12**, 69–78.
37. Plank, W. (1989). *Gulag 65: Towards a humanistic perspective in gerontology*. Frankfurt: Lang.
38. Nash, C. (Ed.) (1990). *Narrative in culture*. New York: Routledge, Chapman & Hall.
39. Salmon, P. (1985). *Living in time*. London: Dent.
40. Leitner, L.M. (1982). Literalism, perspectivism, chaotic fragmentalism and psycho-therapy techniques. *British Journal of Medical Psychology*, **55**, 307–317.
41. Viney, L.L. (1987). Psychotherapy in a case of physical illness. In G.J. & R.A. Neimeyer (Eds.), *A casebook for personal construct theory*. New York: Plenum.

2 A personal construct approach to the elderly

The personal construct approach to the elderly views them as having built up complex sets of personal meanings to deal with the many events in their long lives. They are likely, because they experience new events continually, still to be changing some of those constructs. They are also seen like all adults, as, actively handling their own flows of experience, and as being able to reflect on that process and to recognise that they are, themselves, agents of it. They are also able to integrate separate aspects of this experience over time in the stories they construct, and to reintegrate it, when events make such change appropriate, by retelling their stories. This active flexibility of elderly people, psychologically, is sometimes in direct contrast to their passive rigidity, physically, as a result of frailness and disability.

The personal construct view of psychological development

The personal construct view of the psychological development of adults provides an account of our changing experiences. We interpret and reinterpret events continuously throughout our lives.[1] It is important, therefore, to find out how such continually changing individuals as ourselves make sense of our past, present and future.[2] How do we construe and incorporate them? We use constructs which are identified as having two poles to provide two choices.[3] Yet even with this complex form of construing, we are not always able to incorporate our experiences through reinterpretation as soon as we need to. This can be stressful. Such blocks to incorporation occur when we experience life transitions.[4] The latter are times of great personal vulnerability, but also of great potential for growth. More commonly, however, our continuing psychological development is ensured by a never-ending cycle of validation–invalidation, by others and by events, of the constructs we use in order to make sense of ourselves and our worlds.[5,6]

The personal construct approach even identifies a range of clues that tell us when we need to change our ways of viewing our worlds.[3] Those worlds may include objects, events or other people. This is apparent in the personal construct account of how we make these changes. Impending change in our construct systems are signalled to us by a range of emotions, most of them unpleasant. When our constructs do not work well as predictors, anxiety or hostility, for example, can result. When we feel anxiety, we are recognising that the events we experience are outside the range of our construct systems. When we feel hostility, we make annoyed and often blind probes for evidence in support of our invalidated constructs. We can also react, on the other hand, with a non-hostile but assertive aggression, which leads to a more functional and less blind acting on our worlds.

The personal construct view of psychological functioning in the elderly

The first of four assumptions of this personal construct account of psychological functioning in the elderly is that we all try to make sense of what is happening to us now and what will happen in the future. We do so by building up a system of constructs, on the basis of our past experiences, through which we interpret our own behaviour and that of others. This assumption, like the three to follow, is as true of the elderly as it is of any other age group. Such a psychology must be a psychology of changing experiences.[7] The second assumption is that both the internal, subjective as well as the external, objective perspective is accepted as important. The third assumption follows from the first two assumptions. Psychological development occurs where we interpret and reinterpret our experiences, in a process that can be described as serial reconstruction.[8] The fourth assumption is that the integration of these reinterpretations is the primary characteristic of psychological development. This is especially important for our more central, core constructs about ourselves, and less so for our more peripheral constructs.

The ongoing series of psychological changes, or transitions, which the elderly experience are set off by events that invalidate some of their constructs; that is, they disconfirm their expectations.[9] The events most likely to do this fall into four categories. The first of these are the body–related changes of old age, including tiredness and lack of energy, illness and disability, and the physiological antecedents of death.[10,11] The second category consists of self-related changes, including memory lapses, depression and the anticipation of the death of the, until now, actively construing self. The third category includes interpersonal losses by the elderly, of spouse, family and friends, as well as so many others of their own age group.[12] The former losses are immediately more distressing; but the latter can eventually lead to the alienation of the elderly from their communities. Both types of interpersonal losses are losses of sources of validation for their construct systems. The fourth type of loss consists of changes in social roles, such as retirement from paid work or from work in voluntary organisations.

The content of the constructs employed by elderly people takes an important role in this account. These constructs can be viewed as attempts to make sense of events in the four areas that have been described: body-related changes, self-related changes, interpersonal losses and changes in social roles.[9] When validation of their most central expectation about how they relate to others is available, the elderly will experience love and happiness. When this occurs, body-transcendent constructs are also likely to be voiced; for example, "I get a little bit tired these days, but I still enjoy life". When invalidation, or disconfirmation of expectations based on their deepest beliefs about themselves as social beings occurs, threat and fear are experienced by the elderly and they are more likely to use body-preoccupied constructs, for example, "I can't walk as far as the bus stop any more. My leg stops me." With validation, in contrast, more self-transcendent constructs are likely to be used by the elderly, for example, "*I* won't go on forever, but the family name will go on". With invalidation, self-preoccupied constructs are more likely, for example, "I don't remember things as well as I used to". With validation, interpersonally-related constructs occur more frequently, for example, "My grandchildren mean a lot to me"; but with invalidation, socially isolated constructs are used, for example, "No-one even says 'hello' these days". When validation of the central core expectations of the elderly is available, their constructs indicate an integration of new social roles into their construct systems, for example, "I never had friends before; now I've time for friendships". When they experience invalidation they use constructs that are preoccupied with old roles, for example, "I was a good foreman. The young blokes still tell me that".

The personal construct account also deals with forms of construing by the elderly that differ according to whether validation or invalidation of their most central expectations of themselves are experienced. Broadly speaking, when validation occurs, the strategies used by the elderly to cope with these changes are flexible and adaptive. However, when invalidation of those constructs is experienced, such strategies become rigid and self defeating. With validation of their most central role expectations, then, the elderly move easily between tight and loose construing. In other words, they move easily between stable and more varying anticipations of events, an important flexibility of construing for dealing with change. With invalidation, the construing of the elderly can be either too loose, sometimes resulting in confusion, or too tight, sometimes resulting in their repeated and inappropriate blaming of others. With validation of their role expectations, the elderly are able to develop new constructs and alter old ones. Yet with invalidation, they can become trapped by their own constructs, and that can result in apathy. With continuing validation of their self-related constructs, the elderly can remain actively seeking both alternate views of events and solutions to problems. With continuing invalidation, they are more likely to be passive, resulting often in withdrawal. Finally, experiencing predominantly invalidation of their expectations is linked by the elderly with anxiety and anger. These occur in response to the inevitable invalidations experienced by the elderly when they construe so many areas of their lives.

Other accounts of the psychological functioning of the elderly

The most influential accounts of the psychological functioning of the elderly have focused on them in their social context.[13-20] Disengagement theory[21] sees them as withdrawing more and more from their friends and family, and so is based on one of the sometimes misleading stories about the elderly that I identified in Chapter 1. Many other approaches to development, such as those of Carl Jung,[22] Erik Erikson[23] and Bernice Neugarten,[24] have, in contrast, much in common with the personal construct approach, especially in the identification of the special strength of the elderly as being their ability to integrate their personal meanings into some coherent whole. For Erikson, for example, the integrity or wholeness of elderly people is based firmly on their earlier mastery of the tasks they faced when they were younger, such as developing trust, autonomy, competence, closeness to others, a sense of identity and an ability to care for others.[25-27] To elderly people with such integrity, and the inner certainty it gives, Erikson says come also courage, faith, grace, perseverance and understanding.[28]

Current psychological accounts of purely cognitive processing and of the making of moral judgements are also compatible with this personal construct emphasis on the integration and reintegration of personal meanings by the elderly. For example, those of us in our middle years tend to function with only a single abstract system to guide our actions. In contrast, the elderly tend to operate with an inter-related set of abstract systems.[29] They use these systems to integrate their own identities over their lifetime with those of others specifically, and with those of their culture more generally, to form meaningful wholes. The moral reasoning of the elderly has also been seen as following this pattern, although not necessarily as being on a higher level than that of other adults.[30] Judgement about moral issues made by the elderly are said to involve capacity for reflection which is focused on others rather than self, and a sense of being part of the whole of life.

The elderly and their families

For the personal construct approach to families there is a continuing interaction between families and their actual worlds, which are always changing. Families create constructs to represent those worlds.[31] If they create these constructs, they can also change them. They differ in how well they can interpret and anticipate the actual world, in part according to the looseness, or intuitiveness, and tightness, or precision, of their construing. These interpretations or constructs are confirmed or validated by other family members or others outside the family.[32] There are potentially as many ways to construe an event as there are people to construe it. Family members, however, tend to use a set of common constructs to interpret the events they share, although individual construing and shared construing involving only part of the family are both also possible. Of course, family construct systems govern how individual family members act.

Families that have elderly members are different from other families in certain specific ways; for example, they are three- or four-generation families. There is also the increasing fragility and disability of those elderly members, leading to role changes for them and therefore for other family members as well. The support of their families has been shown to make less severe the effects of medical conditions as varied as cardiac disease, cancer, multiple sclerosis and rheumatoid arthritis.[33-34] Families can, in fact, help their ill members to reconstrue that illness more effectively, maintain their good feelings about themselves and minimise their distress. Such chronic illness does, however, create stress for all the family members, as research on the burden on family care-givers has shown.[35-37]

This personal construct account of family functioning with an elderly family member is concerned with the viewpoint of the perceiving participants rather than the viewpoint of any objective observer. This account deals, also, with events, construct content, forms of construing and outcomes, as does this approach to the psychological functioning of the elderly individual. However, the events are those relating to the family members, the construct content is for family construct systems and the forms of construing are shared by all family members.[32] The events relating to the elderly family member which affect the family system are dealt with before the family construct system itself is considered. These events, in four categories, parallel the major losses experienced by elderly individuals: body-related, and self-related, as well as interpersonal and social role losses. They include the physical needs of the elderly, as well as their psychological needs. Disruption of family inter-relationships by the elderly may also occur. There is, too, the need for the role changes of the elderly family member and so for changes within the family construct system.

The content of the construct systems of families with elderly members differs according to how effectively the families function.[32] Fully functioning families have constructs which show respect for their elderly member, whereas poorly functioning families show a lack of respect. Fully functioning families have constructs which show acceptance of their elderly member, whereas poorly functioning families show rejection. Such acceptance or rejection may be directed towards, for example, the moral values of the elderly, which can be different and even alien from those of later generations of the family. Similarly, fully functioning families see their elderly member as having roles within the family, while poorly functioning families do not. The family itself is also viewed differently in the two types of families. The family is seen as open to change by the former and at least partially closed to change by the latter.

Uncovering these shared family constructs which, before therapy are often unrecognised by the family, offers family members a choice as to whether to keep them or change them. Mr M, now 76 years old, repeatedly stated to his therapist "I'm a Scot and Scots do not forget". His children showed a strong sense of responsibility for Mr M's physical welfare but also a thinly veiled hostility toward him. Mr M was able to review his anger and unforgiving attitude with his therapist. She helped him to see it as a stance that he had maintained as a young man, with his own father as the source of its validation, which was no longer appropriate. He then wanted to show his affection and gratitude to his family. But at first one of his daughters said "If he's going to do that, then I won't even come to see him again. He didn't show us any affection when we were children and I won't take it now." Family therapy, on which I write more in Chapter 4, was necessary to work on this impasse.

Elderly people as story tellers

The fully functioning elderly, then, are able to integrate many of the events they have experienced into their current lives. They do this using the personal constructs they have built up. Because of the many threatening events they experience towards the end of their life span, such as illness, disability, loss and approaching death, their personal meanings are often invalidated. When invalidation occurs, unpleasant emotions, such as anxiety and anger, result, and some reinterpretation and reintegration of those meanings are needed. Their construing does not operate in a social vacuum but often occurs in relation to other people. One of the most important groups of relevant people are the families of the elderly. Families have their own shared personal meanings, which may or may not be revised. It makes considerable sense, then, to see the elderly as story tellers, integrating those all important personal meanings. And they can retell those stories too. The elderly can be seen as describing the history of their own development. They both reflect on their past and anticipate their future, and the stories that result provide them with much else as well. For example, they help to maintain meaningfulness, and a sense of identity and continuity across many different types of situations. Elderly people are believed, within this personal construct perspective, still to be growing psychologically. This growth is achieved because they continue the life-long human attempt not only to understand and anticipate events but also to construct a satisfying story about them.

Eighty-one years old, active and successful, Mrs D was such a story teller. Her husband of 62 years had died recently. She had finally, after many attempts to remain independent, gone to live in her daughter's home. She originally found life at her daughter's "very different, but I must be grateful and adjust". However, she was gradually able to negotiate with her daughter some useful jobs to do and so now had a role in her new household. "My husband and I had a good life", she was proud to be able to reflect, and she went on to find some experiences that could be integrated in that life story, that is, "reading, crochet and friendships". "People are more important, you know, than places or things", she concluded. She was also able to anticipate the future in her story: "Death is to be expected and accepted". She was even able to make meaningful the loss of her husband: "I'm glad now that I didn't go first and leave him alone to grieve".

In this and the next two chapters, I have chosen to refer only rarely to such elderly clients to illustrate my points. In the bulk of the book, however, I shall do so much more often.

Suggested reading

- *The personal construct view of psychological development*

    1. Feffer, M. (1988). *Radical constructivism: Rethinking the dynamics of development.* New York: New York University Press.
    2. Hermans, H.J.M., Kempen, H.J.G. & Van Loon, R.J.P. (1992). The biological self: Beyond individualism and rationalism. *American Psychologist*, 47, 23–32.
    3. Kelly, G.A. (1955). *The psychology of personal constructs.* New York: Norton.
    4. Viney, L.L. (1980). *Transitions.* Sydney: Cassell.
    5. Bannister, D. & Fransella, F. (1985). *Inquiring man.* Beckenham: Croom Helm.
    6. Keating, D.P. & Rosen, H. (1991). *Constructivist perspectives on developmental psychopathology and atypical development.* Hillsdale, New Jersey: Erlbaum.

- *The personal construct view of psychological functioning in the elderly*

    7. Viney, L.L. (1987). A sociophenomenological approach to lifespan development complementing Erikson's psychodynamic approach. *Human Development*, 30, 125–136.
    8. Fransella, F. (1984). Kelly's constructs and Durkheim's representations. In R. Farr & S. Moscovici (Eds.), *Social representations.* Towerbridge: Redwood Burn.
    9. Viney, L.L., Benjamin, Y.N. & Preston, C. (1990). Personal construct therapy for the elderly. *Journal of Cognitive Psychotherapy*, 4, 211–224.
    10. Viney, L.L. (1983). Experiencing chronic illness: A personal construct commentary. In J. Adams Webber & J.C. Mancuso (Eds), *Applications of personal construct theory.* London: Academic Press.
    11. Viney, L.L. (1989). *Images of illness*, Florida: Krieger, Second edition.
    12. Viney, L.L. (1990). The construing widow: Dislocation and adaptation in bereavement. *The Psychotherapy Patient*, 3, 202–207.

- *Other accounts of the psychological functioning of the elderly*

13. Belsby, J.K. (1990). *The psychology of ageing: Theory, research and intervention.* California: Brooks Cole.
14. Cytrynbaum, S., Blum, L., Patrick, R., Stein, J., Wadner, D. & Wilk, C. (1980). Midlife development: A personality and social systems perspective. In L.W. Poon (Ed.), *Ageing in the 1980s.* Washington, DC: American Psychological Association.
15. Gould, R.L. (1978). *Transformations.* New York: Simon & Schuster.
16. Hildebrand, H.P. (1982). Psychotherapy with older patients. *British Journal of Medical Psychology*, **55**, 19–28.
17. Levinson, D.J. (1978). *The seasons of a man's life.* New York: Ballantine.
18. Marshall, V.W. (1980). *A sociology of ageing and dying.* Belmont, California: Wadsworth.
19. Riegel, K.F. (1975). Adult life crises: A dialectic interpretation of development. In N. Datan & L.H. Ginsberg (Eds.), *Life-span development psychology: Normative life crises.* New York: Academic Press, pp. 99–128.
20. Starr, J.W. (1983). Toward a social phenomenology of ageing: Studying the self process in biographical work. *International Journal of Ageing and Human Development*, **16**, 255–270.
21. Cumming, E. & Henry, W.E. (Eds.) (1961). *Growing old: The process of disengagement.* New York: Basic Books.
22. Jung, C. (1934). *The development of personality.* Princeton, NJ: Princeton University Press.
23. Erikson, E.H. (1982). *The life cycle completed.* New York: Norton.
24. Neugarten, B.L., Havighurst, R.J. & Tobin, S.S. (1968). Personality and patterns of ageing. In B.L. Neugarten (Ed.), *Middle age and ageing.* Chicago: University of Chicago.
25. Erikson, E.H. (1950). Transactions of June 8–9, 1950 meeting. In M.J.E. Senn (Ed.), *Symposium on the healthy personality.* New York: Macey Foundation, pp. 15–90.
26. Erikson, E.H. (Ed.) (1978). *Adulthood.* New York: Norton.
27. Wagner, K.D., Lorion, R.P. & Shipley, T.E. (1983). Insomnia and social crises: Two studies of Erikson's developmental theories. *Journal of Consulting and Clinical Psychology*, **51**, 595–603.
28. Erikson, E., Erikson, J.M. & Kivnick, H.Q. (1986). *Vital involvement in old age.* London: Norton.
29. Fischer, K.W. (1980). A theory of cognitive development: The control and construction of hierachies of skills. *Psychological Review*, **87**, 427–431.
30. Kohlberg, L. (1973). Stages and ageing in moral development—some speculations. *Gerontologist*, **13**, 497–502.

- *The elderly and their families*

31. Reiss, D. (1981). *The family's construction of reality.* Cambridge: Harvard University Press.
32. Viney, L.L., Benjamin, Y.N. & Preston, C. (1988). Constructivist family therapy with the elderly. *Journal of Family Psychology*, **2**, 241–258.
33. Bloom, J.R. & Spiegel, D. (1984). The relationship of two dimensions of social support to the psychological well-being and social functioning of women with advanced breast cancer. *Social Science and Medicine*, **19** (8), 831–837.

34. Radley, A. & Green, R. (1986). Bearing illness: Study of couples where the husband awaits coronary graft surgery. *Social Science and Medicine,* 23, 577–585.
35. Kendig, H.L. (Ed.) (1986). *Ageing and families: A support networks perspective.* Sydney: Allen & Unwin.
36. Mace, N. & Rabins, P.U. (1981). *The 36-hour day.* Baltimore: Johns Hopkins.
37. Thompson, L.W., Breckenridge, J.N., Gallagher, D & Peterson, J, (1984). Effects of bereavement on self perceptions of physical health in elderly widows and widowers. *Journal of Gerontology,* 39, 309–314.

3 Listening to the stories of the elderly in therapy

Regarding elderly people as story tellers can be helpful, for the purposes of using personal construct therapy with them. However, it is important that their stories are listened to with an open but evaluating ear. Therapists need to be able to decide which stories are going to be helpful to their clients and which are not. They need to see the effects that such stories are having on the lives of the tellers. If some stories seem problematic, then the relative importance of those stories to the tellers and the extent to which they are holding on to certain outcomes of them should both be assessed. Therapists also need some general standards to refer to when listening to the stories of their clients.

A change of focus and values becomes important to therapists who are beginning work with the elderly. There are also some problems that can occur in interaction with the elderly which need to be acknowledged. I discuss these issues at the start of this chapter and then consider some general criteria for the assessment of the stories of clients. These criteria are described in terms of both the functions they fulfil and the implications for living of their content. Then a number of self-limiting content areas for the stories of the elderly are examined: physical and cognitive functioning, depression, suicide, drugs (including prescription drugs and alcohol), lack of sexual activity and the very fast pace of change they experience. In contrast, I then identify some self-empowering content of such stories. These include the general competence and abilities of the elderly, their capacity to self-actualise, the support and inspiration often offered to them by religious beliefs and the helpful roles played by their families and friends. Then follows an introduction to some personal construct tools for better listening to clients: the traditional techniques from personal construct therapy and the more recent techniques developed to supplement them. The final section of this chapter focuses on client myths about ageing, and acknowledgement and understanding of them.

Problems in the assessment of the elderly for therapy

Problems in the assessment of the elderly abound across the health and welfare professions.[1-3] In clinical psychology, for example, the profession which may be said to specialise in the use of tests to evaluate clients, assessment of the elderly is carried out with confidence only in limited areas such as cognitive malfunctioning. Even in this area there are difficulties in distinguishing, for the elderly, whether such malfunctionings are due to break-down of physiological functioning or to grief-related depression.[4] Also, the standardised questionnaires designed to measure depression in adults do not always work well with the elderly.[5] Insights from literature about being elderly can be added to those from the professions trying to help them. There is a need for cooperative multi-pronged assessment for the elderly, reaching into all the areas of their lives and involving them in a more active role in the assessment process.

Changes are also needed in the values of therapists who are preparing to work with the elderly.[6,7] Is autonomy of the client still an appropriate central value with which to approach an elderly client? Is there scope for exploring the implications of prizing sociality and spirituality in them? There are also some obstacles that may impede some therapists who really try to understand the world of elderly clients. Deafness in clients, for example, can make it difficult to create communication effective enough for assessment. Then there may be another kind of deafness in the would-be therapists, whose mixed feelings about their own ageing process can interfere with listening properly to the stories of elderly people. There is a need to become aware of the stories therapists themselves tell about the elderly, especially those that involve self-deception. However, there are ways in which therapists can set aside these deceptionss, take an appropriate ethical stance and come to listen respectfully to their elderly clients. I shall deal with some of these strategies in Chapter 15.

General criteria for the assessment of stories

Two sets of criteria are useful in listening evaluatively to the stories of clients. They have to do with the functions they fulfil and their content.[8] A story provides a sequence of personal constructs that together form a theme. Stories integrate different constructs and events to achieve a whole; and that overriding whole has a meaning different from its separate constructs. First, then, stories should integrate or pull together separate elements. Second, stories should be internally consistent and cohesive. Third, they should provide this integration of constructs and events over time, in order to give their teller a sense of continuity. A story should integrate present, past and future. However, the content of the stories of clients is also important. Their content needs to include predictions about the outcomes of actions which are precise and feasible enough to make appropriate action by clients possible. They also need to be optimistic enough to make it possible. Stories without hope make life for those who tell them very difficult.

Some self-limiting story content from the elderly

There is, unfortunately, much in the lives of the elderly that can lead to hopelessness and so to stories that are self-limiting for their tellers. Such self-limiting content needs to be listened to by therapists when assessing clients prior to therapy. For example, their physical functioning is often not as good as it used to be, even if this has resulted only in tiredness and lack of energy. Their cognitive functioning is different from when they were younger: slower than it was and perhaps less organised, because of their less organised life style. Depression has been considered a frequent problem for them, and suicide can be associated with this. Elderly people can also have problems with drugs—through taking many medications simultaneously and underestimating the effects alcohol will have on them as they age, especially if alcohol is taken with medication so that the two interact. Many elderly people lack partners for sexual activities. This can be another source of hopelessness. So, too, can the pace of change be. These likely sources of self-defeating stories of the elderly will now be considered. Others—retirement, illness, bereavement and dying—will be dealt with in the chapters about retelling the stories of clients who are dealing specifically with these events (Chapters 11–14).

The physical functioning of the elderly

Ill health is not a necessary accompaniment of ageing, even for people in their eighties and nineties; yet very large numbers of elderly people use drugs available only on prescription from medical practitioners. They have a larger share of chronic illness, such as coronary conditions, hypertension and rheumatism than the rest of the population, and also a considerable share of accidents in the form of hip and other fractures.[9] Yet they can also suffer from ataxia, constipation, over sedation and even hypotension as a result of some of their non-steroidal anti-inflammatory, anti-hypertensive, diuretic and psychotropic drugs.[9] Current life events, such as bereavement, have also been linked with greater illness in the elderly.[10]

There is also a more general physical condition which the elderly experience, that of having less energy, and some may even feel quite lethargic. This, and their chronic problems, together with fractures, can interfere with their ability to look after themselves. So, too, can loss, even if partial, of sight or hearing. All prospective elderly clients should be assessed in terms of their capacity to carry out the normal tasks of everyday living: dressing, eating and keeping self and surroundings clean, as well as the appropriate indoor and outdoor chores, including meal preparation. For all this, it is important for elderly clients and their therapists alike to remember that being elderly is not a medical condition, even though it may seem so, but an expected turn in the path of life.

Cognitive functioning

While I have criticised the notion that the cognitive functioning of all elderly people is necessarily inferior to that of people who are younger, I must also acknowledge that there are physical conditions to which some elderly people are prone, involving brain damage, which can cause them great confusion. These are referred to as dementias, and the most feared of these is Alzheimer's disease, which leads to great distress to the sufferers, their families and their friends. However, there is also evidence that the cognitive processing of the elderly is different from that of younger people: it focuses as much on the distant and near past as the here and now.[11] This difference has probably been experienced by any reader of this book over the age of 14. The short-term memory, for telephone and pin numbers, for example, has been declining since that age. This may well be because early in our lives we needed short-term memory to build up our developing systems of knowledge. The elderly have, of course, already built up their systems and so need short-term memory less than the long-term memory that allows them to access those systems.

Depression

Elderly people who are depressed look tired and apathetic and may report having little appetite and much disturbance of their sleep. They may be sad and weepy, but also angry and sullen. They often feel lonely. Elderly people have been thought to be at greater risk of depression than any other age group.[12–14] This epidemiological finding has been accepted as appropriate and even inevitable, because, from the vantage point of younger people, they seem to suffer so many losses of people and situations. Recent research, however, has indicated that people in their twenties and thirties are now at greatest risk.[15, 16] The earlier findings may have been due to a cohort effect, holding only for that group of people born at the beginning of this century. They experienced at the beginning of their working lives the great losses of the economic Depression, as well as of the two World Wars. Bereavement is associated not only with poor health, but also with depression in the elderly. Also, the financial status of more recent cohorts of elderly may be more secure, providing more protection from some losses.

For the personal construct therapist, the grip of depressed elderly people on their worlds has become more constricted or limited in focus. This constriction is apparent both in the content of the stories they tell and the way in which they apply them to living. The constructs they use in their stories emphasise the negative and exclude the positive, and they see themselves of course negatively but also as alienated from others. They have difficulty in anticipating any future for themselves, and, when they do, that is negatively toned and pessimistic as well. Attempts to get them to acknowledge that there are other, more positive outcomes for their stories are rejected. However, therapeutic work is possible using this approach, as will be shown in later chapters.

Suicide

A small proportion of elderly people try to commit suicide.[17] If they do so, they are more likely to succeed than younger people. Assessing the potential suicide risk of elderly clients can be an important aspect of preparation for therapy. Risk of suicide attempts can be assessed using the same criteria that have proved useful with younger clients: severity of losses and readiness of means. Severity of loss can be considered in terms of both number of losses sustained by clients and their significance to them. Number of losses needs extensive interviewing to elicit, but the most difficult task is to ascertain their personal significance. A dead cat on the road can be well handled by an elderly woman who is very emotionally close to her children and their families who live nearby. Another dead cat could mean the loss of one's last friend to a lonely elderly woman living far from her family and friends and too poor to visit them. In regard to the other criterion of assessment, the readiness of the means of suicide refers to both how specific the proposed procedures are, and how readily available they are to the elderly person.

Drugs

There are two major drug-related areas that require assessment in elderly clients: use of prescription drugs and alcohol. Their use of prescription drugs may be problematic because of the potential side effects noted already.[18] However, there is also the problem of multiple scripts being used, so that unintended interaction of drugs may occur.[19] Women and people living in institutions are most likely to be involved in inappropriate drug use,[20] which makes elderly women living in hostels and nursing homes doubly likely to be so. Also, it takes elderly people longer to clear drugs from their physical systems than it does for those who are younger.[18] This is true of alcohol as it is of prescription drugs. This means that elderly people who continue to drink as much as they did when middle-aged will find that both the short-term and long-term effects on their bodies will be greater than they used to be.[21]

Loss of sexual activity

Many elderly people, when sexual activity is mentioned to them, claim total abstinence and seem to believe that this is appropriate for people of their age. Many young people also believe that sex is their own prerogative, hence the term "dirty old man". However, there is increasing evidence that people can be sexually active into their nineties, so long as suitable partners are available.[22] There seem to be at least three impediments to this; they apply particularly if previous sexual partners are lost through death or divorce, and it becomes necessary to find new ones. These are embarrassment at having a body which may not seem as attractive as it once did, fears about not being able to perform effectively and guilt over quite normal but strong sex feelings. Of course these reactions identified so far, like the epidemiological findings for depression, may change as new cohorts of elderly people become available. Elderly people were brought up in a sexually repressed era. Later cohorts, for example those growing up in the sixties and seventies, may be able to remain sexually active without such shame and guilt.

Pace of technological change

Elderly people experience so much change, not only in their losses of families, friends, pets, houses and neighbourhoods, but also in the new values, information and technology with which they are faced. People who are elderly today have moved all the way from crystal radios to colour televisions and "fax" machines, for example, with all the changes in values and information which have accompanied them. It is as if they are continually in transition or even crisis.[23,24] It is important to assess how well elderly people are dealing with such crisis in order to plan effective therapy for them.[25] They need to separate to some extent from their past, and they may find difficulties in doing this. They may also experience problems in deciding, when new paths need to be taken, on what is best for them. They may also have trouble in carrying out decisions once they are made and in weathering the period of adjustment that necessarily follows. Each elderly person will vary in the extent to which they follow this self-defeating content in their stories.

Some self-empowering story content from the elderly

There are, however, other areas of content in the stories of elderly clients for which therapists can listen to find answers to the self-defeating content that has been described. These are areas of self-empowering content, of which there are four. Firstly, acknowledgement by elderly people of their own control, competence and other abilities often gives evidence of capacity to cope effectively with whatever assails them. Secondly, so too does self-actualisation, in its capacity for growth, finding of the meaning in life, and establishment of the identity and integrity of the self. Thirdly, religious beliefs are another source of self-empowering stories. Fourthly, there are family and friends who, at many degrees of intimacy and geographical closeness, provide support for and confirmation of many of these stories.

Competence, control and humour

Feeling in control is as important to the elderly as it is to people in any other age group. For example, in facing the possible physical pain, threat to self-esteem and the unavoidable uncertainty of life after death, the elderly have been shown to use, as well as prayer[26,27] and social support,[28,29] an internalised self-control.[30,31] Some elderly face the wider range of adjustment in store for them by holding on or constricting or becoming apathetic and disorganised, yet many are able to reorganise and refocus with a resulting complexity of integration that is not found in younger people.[32] They can also use humour effectively, which gives them a useful perspective on themselves and events.[33] Joking, often in an ironic way, can help give a reminder that age-related events can always be reconstrued. For example, an elderly man using many prescription drugs for his daily ills would say "I'm taking so many pills now, that I reckon that if you shook me I'd rattle!"

Self-actualisation

The later years can also be a time for people to become more fully themselves and expand their horizons. The kinds of activities that are meaningful to them begin to change.[34-36] Achievement no longer seems so important and is supplanted by intellectual pursuits, creativity and finding joy in relationships, for example with grandchildren. Personal interests are transcended and yet there is increased awareness of the uniqueness of the individual.[37-39] Wisdom is gained. The central issue of this period of life is how to maintain self-actualisation.[40] This to-be-envied state involves a sense of the identity of the self, knowing who I am and what I stand for. Then there is the continuity of the self, knowing that who I am today is who I was yesterday and for many years before. Finally, there is the integrity of the self, knowing that the incredibly complex person I have become over the years will hold together in responding to future events.

Religious beliefs

Believing in a God who is good and has some plan for the universe seems to be a help to many elderly people in dealing with their losses and the approach of their own death.[27] They report prayer as an important way of coping, whether they see their relationship with a loving God who provides companionship or with a ruling God who declares what is lawful. There is also evidence that church attendance is linked to greater expression of satisfaction with life.[26] Of course there are some elderly people who grasp desperately for some ray of hope during their depressed moods, and then drop their faith when no longer feeling cornered. People do this at all ages. Many elderly people do develop religious faith and go no further than a simple undifferentiated, infinite grasp of it. Others may be quite literal in their belief systems. Many others develop their faith into a universalising way of life which has much in common with the other aspects of psychological functioning of the elderly I have described. The faith of a person with integrity can be extremely powerful.[41]

Family and friends

Any assessment before and during therapy of the functioning of elderly people should view them in their proper context of family and friends. Families are important to them, both the family they grew up in and the family they reared themselves. Elderly people do not suddenly change into new people when they age. They continue to construe the world in some of the ways they learned during infancy and childhood in their family of origin. These shared family constructs were, of course, shaped by historical circumstances at the time they are developed, such as the presence of healthy, loving grandparents. Yet these constructs can still affect, for example, how positively elderly people view the process of ageing in themselves.

As people get older, of course, the family they created, the family of procreation, becomes more important to them. Some wonderfully rewarding relationships between grandparents and grandchildren can develop, when grandparents do not need to take on the disciplinary role they held as parents. Grandparents have been described as "the family watchdogs".[42] It is necessary, too, for therapists to assess not only the roles filled by elderly people in the families of procreation, but also the stories the family members are telling, their constructs and expectations.[43] These also need to be monitored as therapy progresses. As elderly people aged and needed more help from their families, families used to function well as support systems. However, because of the smaller number of children in families, changes in the roles of women and changes to the economic structure so that the elderly no longer have so much control of family finances, this source of support has dwindled. Elderly people now need to look to meals and cleaning services provided by Health and Welfare Departments and, if they have the finances, private organisations, as well as to their neighbours and friends. Many of them form mutually supportive "families" of friends of different ages, who can take on the "parental" roles as it becomes needed.

In their relationships with both family and friends, the elderly like to feel that they are reciprocal, that what is done for them by others is repaid by them in some way.[44] This reciprocity has often been important to them throughout their life span; and then it seems to be associated with successful ageing. At the same time, the elderly are often freer of role stereotypes, giving them a wider range of ways of relating to others than were available to them when they were younger. Being perceived as attractive to others, however, seems to continue to be important as age increases. This is because the relationships provided by this attractiveness, which includes but transcends the physical, promote self-esteem and allow more practice of interpersonal skills, which in turn lead to more interpersonal attractiveness. The stories these people tell express this. Elderly people who have not much of this quality think little of themselves and relate to others poorly, which can help to maintain their lack of attractiveness and consequent social isolation.[45] Their stories show this lack too.

I have described how all of us, including people in the last part of their life span, need to hear their own stories told. We also need confirmation of our stories from others; and family and friends, as well as the wider community, can provide this confirmation. With the losses of friends and family the elderly have experienced, and their frequent isolation from their ever-changing community, they have relatively fewer sources of confirmation. This seems to be one reason why they often reminisce, spending hours telling with great clarity and detail stories from their earlier lives. They are seeking validation for their view of the world; and in the absence of much support from others, they use themselves as sources of validation.[46] This process can be used therapeutically with the elderly, as I shall show in the next chapter. Yet, for the purpose of assessment, these stories have much to tell about elderly clients.

Some personal construct tools for better listening

The personal construct view of the psychological functioning of the elderly and their families, which I presented in Chapter 2, provides a useful framework for assessing elderly clients. The elderly build their own systems of constructs but are continually changing some of these constructs as they deal with new events. The major events for the elderly are considered to be body-related and self-related changes, interpersonal losses and changes in social roles. There are three groups of personal construct tools for better listening to the stories of the elderly. They included the traditional techniques as proposed by George Kelly,[47] as well as some new ones designed to supplement the originals, by either encouraging a vaguer, more intuitive approach or by tightening and making greater cognitive specificity possible. An exploration of myths, or culturally shared stories, about the elderly also seems appropriate here, to help therapists become more sensitive to how they affect the elderly.

Traditional personal construct tools for listening

There is evidence that when most elderly people tell their stories they use constructs with content that differs from that of younger people.[48] For example, they express both integrity and despair, and both generativity and stagnation, while younger people express both social embeddedness and isolation and both some sense of identity and identity diffusion. Of course the elderly continue to use some construct content from their earlier years. The balances need to be considered. Is there a balance of new to old construct content and is it predominantly positive or negative in tone? There are also questions to be asked about the internal consistency of their construct systems and their ability to interpret and anticipate effectively. Also, stories that necessarily employ constructs can be evaluated by these criteria.

Self-characterisation and the Role Construct Repertory Technique have been applied for these purposes traditionally. Self-characterisation[49] involves asking clients to write a character sketch of themselves as if they were a character in a play. There are, of course, no right or wrong responses to this request. Clients are asked to write about themselves from the outside, so as to reduce the threat of self-reflection as much as possible. Some elderly people, when they have lost much of the self-consciousness which is the burden of the young, do not need this protection. The constructs found in their stories of reminiscence serve this purpose as well. Both forms of material can be checked for recurring themes, and this process often reveals constructs that are important to them. Missing content is also of interest. When an elderly client does not refer to sharing events with others, for example, is this because he is actually isolated or because he construes himself to be so?

The Role Construct Repertory Technique[47] involves an increasingly structured series of steps, not all of which need to be taken with elderly clients. It provides information not only about the content of the client's constructs but also about how they are related to one another. It also shows how the constructs are used to make sense of people and events. When the interpersonal relationships of the elderly client are of interest, the important people in the client's lives are compared, three at a time, in such a way as to provide descriptions of both poles of their bipolar constructs. For example, "Think of your mother, your father and your sister. How are two of them alike and one of them different?" Jean replied: "Mother and sister were warm and easy to be with, but my father was so irritable." A sheet for recording the answers needs to be filled in, either by the therapist or the client. This rather formal procedure, and especially the full Repertory Grid, with a grid of ratings of each of the people on each of the constructs that emerges, often proves not to be suitable for the elderly. With the elderly, a selection of these triadic comparison questions can be raised in the course of a more flexible assessment interview schedule.

Other personal construct tools for listening

As noted earlier, the tools that have been developed to supplement these two basic techniques provide a loosening, for freer, more intuitive construing, and a tightening, for greater predictive power.[50-55] Both loosening and tightening of construing should still be possible for the elderly. The main loosening technique has been relaxation, of a systematic kind, in which the tension in certain muscle groups is relaxed in the client in a standard order; and this order is followed when she practices it at home. Dreams can also show evidence of this loosening, as can free associations, drawing, painting and clay modelling. Some loosening techniques can also be used to gain access to the core, most central constructs of clients. For example, when clients talk about the most significant events in their lives as they reflect on them, their core constructs will emerge.[56] Similarly, encouraging clients to talk about their religious beliefs and how they relate them to the problems they are having can also reveal core constructs. Therapists need to identify the most central, self-descriptive constructs, because they will be particularly resistant to change.

Several effective tools for tightening the construing of the elderly client are also available. Constructs can be concrete or abstract. Those that are abstract are more general and less related to the physical world of these clients. They also have a higher level of conceptualisation, which can often be helpful in therapy, when clients are struggling to understand the meanings of the complex and interrelated events in their lives. Their construing becomes more concrete as it becomes more particular, more related to the physical world, with a lower level of conceptualisation. This construing enables them to understand individual events. Both types of construing are important. Abstraction is encouraged by the techniques of laddering.[50] This technique involves asking clients "why" they use a construct. Esmé spoke of some of her friends as "clean" or "dirty". In laddering, the therapist would pick the positive pole of this construct to ask, "And why is it important to you that they be clean?" Esmé might then reply, "Because they have good manners." The laddering would continue with "why" asked until Esmé had reached a more abstract and possibly more influential construct, such as "They are kind and considerate." This may also be a tightening technique for arriving at more concrete constructs. Pyramiding works in the opposite direction to help understand how clients are using particular constructs in particular concrete situations. The questions asked then are "what?" and "how?" rather than "why?"

The ABC Model[50] is another technique that helps to tighten construing, this time by providing information for therapists about which constructs of their clients are likely to change and which not, and which stories may change their outcomes and which will not. Although it may be used at the beginning of therapy, it is often employed later when therapy seems blocked. It enables clients to explore the implications of moving from one construct pole to its opposite when construing themselves. It refers to this construct with A_1 as the pole presently in use and A_2, the opposite pole, B_1 and C_1 then represent the disadvantages of each pole and B_2 and C_2, the advantages. June was a 65-year-old smoker whose sister had died of lung cancer recently. She wanted to stop smoking for the sake of her health, but no effort of hers to do so succeeded. The ABC model of her construing of herself as smoker or non-smoker follows.

A_1 Smoker.	A_2 Non-smoker.
B_1 Husband nags me. Could use the extra money.	B_2 Please my husband. We could spend more when we go to the club.
C_1 My nerves would be bad. I'll feel deprived. I'll put on weight.	C_2 Cuts the tension. Like to give a little some- thing to myself now and then.

Smoking was, she was able to then tell her therapist, keeping at bay anxiety and depression, and giving it up could lead to her becoming less physically attractive. With such a story about smoking, it was not surprising that she did not stop.

There is also a technique called narrative analysis that enables therapists to take the long and complex entwined stories of clients and analyse them in order to arrive at a core narrative.[57] This method summarises some of the many themes that have emerged, preferably using the client's own words so as to be likely to be using their constructs rather than the therapist's own. Elaborations of this core story are stripped away to reveal the bones of it. Of course, therapists do not stop when they write down the results of that narrative analysis in their case notes. Rather they go back to the client to check that their interpretation and expression of this core story are acceptable to the client. If not, further negotiation takes place between client and therapist to arrive at an agreed version. The implications of this core story for the life of clients is then explored.

Myths about the elderly

There are many myths about the elderly that influence how they see themselves and how the other members of their community see them.[58] Many communities tend to see the elderly as having decreased strength, as well as reduced economic productivity and power. Benign stereotypes of this kind are expressed in phrases like "little old lady" and "old fellah", and many myths underlying these phrases show the triumph of young over old age. However, there are other myths, Jung would call them archetypes, in which special properties of knowledge and caring are linked with old age. For example, "the old, wise woman", and "the old man". I shall later argue, in agreement with at least one other therapist,[59] the importance of therapists who work therapeutically with the elderly examining the myths that influence them. For now, it is sufficient to point to the need for elderly clients to become aware of the myths, a specially powerful kind of story, they espouse, and to see how they affect them. Such myths can be revised using informed analysis together with intuition. They can also be brought to bear more effectively on the lives of clients.

Which clients benefit most from therapy?

Certain types of elderly clients seem likely to benefit more from psychotherapy than others and to be easier to work with. A list of suggested client selection criteria for personal construct therapists to use follows. Prospective clients should have:

1. some physical energy, although not necessarily physical mobility;
2. some intact cognitive capacities;
3. evidence of being able to relate closely to the therapist, if not immediately, at least later, in therapy;
4. evidence of being able to be interested in other people;
5. at least a few self-empowering stories;
6. some self-limiting stories; and
7. an ability to not be totally overwhelmed by confusion, depression or helplessness.

Listening to the stories of the elderly

In this chapter I have acknowledged the poor state of the tools available for assessing elderly clients. Sad though this is, it contrasts with this concept of story which can be used so effectively to understand both the experiences and actions of elderly clients. Some general criteria for assessing stories have been provided, focusing on the structures of the stories of the elderly and their content. Possible areas of problematic story content were then considered: physical and cognitive functioning, depression, suicide, drugs, loss of sexual activity and the pace of technological change. This self-limiting content of stories which elderly people may tell was then contrasted with some potentially self-empowering content that can be searched for during assessment. This included the sense of control and competence, self-actualisation, religious beliefs and relationships with family and friends. I finally introduced some personal construct tools for listening better to the stories of the elderly. These consisted of the more traditional tools of self-characterisation and a revision of the Role Construct

Repertory Technique, the more recently developed wide range of tools to loosen and tighten their construing, and the myths about ageing which the elderly themselves and others subscribe to.

There is much in the stories of elderly clients for therapists to listen for with care. Both the structure of the tales and their content are important. Much of this assessment needs to be made before therapy begins, but some still continues during therapy. The listening task for therapists working with elderly clients is harder than it might at first appear. Assumptions should not be made, expectations should be set aside, and then truly open listening becomes possible. The task is also difficult because it varies so much between clients, each of whom has a unique life and a unique view of it. It is important, too, to watch the balance between the positive and the negative that clients express, and what traps their stories set for them.

One way of identifying these traps is to analyse them in terms of the personal, social and cultural implications of the stories of elderly clients. These analyses will be carried out for some of their common stories in Chapters 5–10. The personal implications include their presentation of themselves and the age-related events they experience in their stories, the psychological functions their stories fulfil for them and the story's influence on their emotions and actions, as well as the way in which it links their present, past and future. The social implications of a story include its interpersonal context, who confirms it and to whom or what it gives power. The cultural implications of their stories include the information that they share with their audiences and the values on which they are based. All of these aspects of the stories of clients need to be considered before therapy can begin. An introduction to how such therapeutic retelling of their stories is accomplished is provided in the next chapter.

Suggested reading

● *Problems in the assessment of the elderly*

1. Charatan, F.B. (1986). An overview of geriatric psychiatry. *New York State Journal of Medicine*, **86**, 630–634.
2. Kane, R.A. & Kane, R.L. (1981). *Assessing the elderly*. Lexington, Massachusetts: Heath.
3. Woods, R.T. & Britton, P.G. (1985). *Clinical psychology with the elderly*. Beckenham: Croom Helm.
4. Taylor, C. (1984). *Growing on: Ideas about ageing*. New York: Van Nostrand.
5. Dunn, U.K. & Sacco, W.P. (1989). Psychiatric evaluation of the Geriatric Depression Scale and the Jung Self-Rating Depression Scale using an elderly community sample. *Psychology and Ageing*, **4**, 125–126.
6. Fitting, M.D. (1986). Ethical dilemmas in counselling elderly adults. *Journal of Counselling and Development*, **64**, 325–327.

7.   Spielman, B.J. (1986). Rethinking paradigms in geriatric ethics. *Journal of Religion and Health*, **25**, 142–158.

● *General criteria for the assessment of stories*

8.   Viney, L.L. (1989). Psychotherapy as shared reconstruction. *International Journal of Personal Construct Psychology*, **3**, 423–442.

● *Some self-limiting story content from the elderly*

9.   Wattis, J. & Church, M. (1986). *Practical psychiatry of old age*. London: Croom Helm.
10.   Thompson, L., Breckenridge, J.N., Gallagher, D. & Peterson, J. (1984). Effects of bereavement of self-perceptions on health in elderly widows and widowers. *Journal of Gerontology*, **39**, 309–314.
11.   Hess, T.M. (1990). *Ageing and cognition*. New York: North Holland.
12.   Goldstein, S.E. (1979). Depression in the elderly. *Journal of the American Geriatrics Society*, **27**, 38–42.
13.   Newman, J., Engel, R. & Jensen, J. (1990). Depressive symptom patterns among older women. *Psychology and Ageing*, **5**, 101–118.
14.   Gilewski, M.J., Farberow, N.L., Gallagher, D. & Thompson, L.V. (1991). Interaction of depression and bereavement on mental health in the elderly. *Psychology and Ageing*, **6**, 67–75.
15.   Blazer, D.G. (1989). Current concepts: Depression in the elderly. *New England Journal of Medicine*, **320**, 164–166.
16.   Blazer, D.G. (1989). The epidemiology of depression in later life. *Journal of Geriatric Psychiatry*, **22**, 35–52.
17.   Templer, D.I. & Cappelle, Y.G. (1986). Suicide in the elderly: Assessment and intervention. *Clinical Gerontologist*, **5**, 475–487.
18.   Powell, J.E. (in press). Literature review: Alcohol and drug use by elderly people. *Australian Psychologist*.
19.   German, P.S. & Burton, C.C. (1989). Clinicians, the elderly and drugs. *Journal of Social Issues*, **19**, 221–243.
20.   Harper, C.M., Newton, P.A. & Walsh, J.R. (1989). Drug-induced illness in the elderly. *Postgraduate Medicine*, **86**, 245–256.
21.   Curtis, J.R., Geller, G., Stokes, E.J., Levine, D.M. & Moore, R.D. (1989). Characteristics, diagnosis, and treatment of alcoholism in the elderly. *Journal of the American Geriatric Society*, **37**, 310–316.
22.   Renshaw, D.C. (1984). Geriatric sex problems. *Journal of Geriatric Psychiatry*, **17**, 123–138.
23.   Golan, N. (1981). *Passing through transitions*. New York: Free Press.
24.   Victor, C.R. (1991). Continuity or change: Inequalities in health in later life. *Ageing and Society*, **11**, 23–39.
25.   Aguilera, D., Messick, J.M. & Farrell, M.S. (1970). *Crisis intervention*. St. Louis: Mosby.

● *Some self-empowering story content from the elderly*

26.   Markides, K.S. (1983). Aging, religiosity and adjustment: A longitudinal analysis. *Journal of Gerontology*, **38**, 621–625.

27. Meissner, W.W. (1987). *Life and faith*. Washington, DC: Georgetown University Press.
28. McLeish, J.A.P. (1983). *The challenge of ageing*. Toronto: Douglas and McIntyre.
29. Specht, R. & Craig, G.J. (1982). *Human development: A social work perspective*. New Jersey: Prentice Hall, 1982.
30. Fry, P.S. (Ed.) (1989). *Psychological perspectives of helplessness and control in the elderly*. New York: North Holland.
31. Fry, P.S. (1990). A factor analytic investigation of home-bound elderly individuals' concern about death and dying, and their coping responses. *Journal of Clinical Psychology*, **46**, 737–748.
32. Erikson, E.H. (1964). *Insight and responsibility*. New York: Norton.
33. Nahemow, L., McCluskey-Fawcett, K.A. & McGee, P.E. (1981). *Humour and ageing*. New York: Academic Press.
34. Neugarten, B.L., Havighurst, R.J. & Tobin, S.S. (1968). Personality and patterns of ageing. In B.L. Neugarten (Ed.), *Middle age and ageing*. Chicago: University of Chicago Press.
35. Levinson, D.J. (1978). *The seasons of a man's life*. New York: Ballantine.
36. Lieberman, M.A. (1978). Adaptive processes in later life. In N. Datan & L.H. Ginsberg (Eds.), *Life span developmental psychology*. New York: Academic Press.
37. Hareven, T. & Adams, K. (1982). *Ageing and life course perspectives*. London: Tavistock.
38. Kuypers, J.A. (1974). Ego functioning in old age: Early adult life antecedents. *International Journal of Ageing and Human Development*, **5**, 157–179.
39. Lieberman, M.A. & Tobin, S.S. (1983). *The experience of old age*. New York: Basic Books.
40. Leslie, R.N. (1982). Counselling the aged. *International Forum for Geriatric Therapy*, **5**, 47–52.
41. Rogers, D. (1982). *The adult years: An introduction to ageing*. Englewood Cliffs, New Jersey: Prentice Hall.
42. Brubaker, T.H. (Ed.) (1983). *Family relationships in later life*. Beverly Hills, California: Sage.
43. Neito, D.S., Raymond, T. & Horsley, D.L. (1989). Principles of therapeutic intervention with elders and their families. *Journal of Psychotherapy and the Family*, **5**, 13–27.
44. Antonucci, T. & Jackson, J. (1989). Successful ageing and life course reciprocity. In A. Warnes (Ed.), *Human ageing and later life*. London: Edward Gould.
45. Glidewell, J.C. (1972). A social psychology of mental health. In S.E. Golann & C. Eisdorfer (Eds.), *Handbook of community mental health*. New York: Appleton–Century–Crofts, pp. 211–246.
46. Viney, L.L., Benjamin, Y.N. & Preston, C.A. (1988). Mourning and reminiscence: Parallel psychotherapeutic processes for the elderly. *International Journal of Ageing and Human Development*, **28**, 237–249.

● *Some personal construct tools for better listening*

47. Kelly, G.A. (1955). *The psychology of personal constructs*. New York: Norton.
48. Viney, L.L. & Tych, A.M. (1985). Content analysis scales to measure psychosocial maturity in the elderly. *Journal of Personality Assessment*, **49**, 311–317.
49. Fransella, F. (1985). Individual psychotherapy. In E. Button (Ed.), *Personal construct theory and mental health*. Beckenham: Croom Helm, pp. 277–301.

50. Dalton, P. & Dunnett, G. (1992). *A psychology for living: Personal construct theory for professionals and clients.* Chichester: Wiley.
51. Epting, F.R. (1984). *Personal construct counseling and psychotherapy.* Chichester: Wiley.
52. Neimeyer, G.J. & Neimeyer, R.A. (1993). Intervening in meaning: Defining the boundaries of constructivist assessment. In G.J. Neimeyer (Ed.), *Casebook in constructivist assessment.* New York: Sage.
53. Neimeyer, R.A. (1987). An orientation to personal construct therapy. In R.A. Neimeyer & G.J. Neimeyer (Eds.), *Personal construct therapy casebook.* New York: Springer, pp. 3–19.
54. Neimeyer, G.J. (1987). Personal construct assessment, strategy and technique. In R.A. Neimeyer & G.J. Neimeyer (Eds.), *Personal construct therapy casebook.* New York: Springer.
55. Winter, D. (1992). *Personal construct psychology in clinical practice.* London: Routledge.
56. Leitner, L.M. (1985). Interview methodologies for construct definition: Searching for the core. In F. Epting & A.W. Landfield (Eds.), *Anticipating personal construct psychology.* Lincoln: University of Nebraska Press.
57. Viney, L.L. & Bousfield, L. (1991). Narrative analysis: A technique for psychosocial research in AIDS. *Social Science and Medicine.*
58. Nadelson, T. (1990). On purpose, successful ageing and the myth of innocence. *Journal of Geriatric Psychiatry,* **23**, 3–12.
59. Feinstein, D. (1990). Bringing a mythological perspective to clinical practice. *Psychotherapy,* **27**, 388–396.

4 Story retelling as therapy

In Chapter 3, I described how those who wish to work therapeutically with the elderly can learn to listen to their stories. Some criteria were also proposed for evaluating those stories in terms of the effects on their elderly tellers. When these stories are judged to be problematic, then psychotherapy or counselling is advisable. The aim of such work is, of course, to help the elderly tell and retell their stories. Many psychotherapists and counsellors have warned against working with the elderly, believing them to be rigid and inflexible.[1-3] Perhaps this is why there is still such a small range of therapies available for them. The reasons for this stance have much to do with the potential therapist's fears of becoming old, which will be dealt with later in this book. Freud, the founder of psychoanalytic psychotherapy, the first psychotherapy, uttered such a warning.[3] Yet he himself continued to change his own theories (or stories) and test them by self-analysis into his eighties. The ability to retell stories, which can be described as the capacity to learn, seems to be characteristic of everyone, wherever they are in their life span.

Other therapists who have worked intensively with the elderly, even psychoanalytic therapists, have reported them to have advantages over younger clients in therapeutic story retelling.[4] They see them as able to take a perspective from their lifetime of experience, and as having a learned flexibility and a sense of "it's now or never" that is very motivating.[5,6] They report that they can also be more single-minded than younger clients, because shame, or embarrassment at how others see them, is no longer an important issue.[3] They also have certain skills, acquired over a lifetime, that are helpful in therapy.[4] More of these later. If elderly clients have short-term memory problems, therapists can compensate by providing concrete cues and repetition. If they are physically fragile, then therapists can be flexible about the length of therapy sessions. Also, if they seem to be tuned into a wavelength of a bygone age, therapists can tune into that too, emotionally, imagining what it must have been like for them.

Those responsible for the well-being of the elderly have asked for more and better psychotherapies for them, especially from already existing theories of therapy.[7] This book provides one such approach, personal construct therapy, and this chapter deals with the story retelling that is basic to it. In its first section, the underlying reconstructive approach to therapy is described, together with later developments of it. One of the most exciting of these developments sees therapy as story retelling; so this idea is examined, together with how it can be applied to the elderly. Then some of the therapeutic processes that can be stimulated by the retelling of their stories by elderly clients are considered: age-appropriate processes, such as adjusting goals concerning work and relationships, working through grief and guilt from some earlier events, the development of strengths, both personal and interpersonal, the encouragement of creativity and enjoyment, and the attainment of that special quality reserved for the elderly, integrity.

Several types of techniques are available for encouraging story retelling in the elderly. Some of these are personal construct processes and can be summarised as a list of strategies for story retelling. Yet others come from different theoretical approaches to therapy such as the cognitive behaviour therapies. Others use special procedures, like group therapy. Then, there are some techniques which focus largely on having clients review and reflect, while others focus on having their clients express themselves. Story telling and retelling, which I consider last, have both reviewing and expressive aspects. Story retelling can also occur in the family, so one section of this chapter deals with this: how families construct stories, and retell them in the context of both marriage and family. I conclude this chapter with a brief overview of the outcomes of studies evaluating therapy with the elderly, because it is important to know what evidence there is that these techniques are of value, as well as a brief comparison of this with other therapies.

A personal construct framework for story retelling

This conceptual framework for a psychotherapy for the elderly examines first some traditional aspects of the personal construct therapy, and then some recent developments. I put forward the view that story retelling can be highly effective as therapy, and discuss some applications of it with elderly clients.

The personal construct approach

Meaning is the hub of this approach, meanings created and organised into construct systems.[8] People are seen as flexible and with several levels of awareness.

When their constructs are validated, they experience good feelings; when they are not, they do not. Clients and therapists come together to share meanings in a constructive dialogue, involving the interaction of two construct systems.[9] As they work in therapy, clients test the validity of their systems, making clearer their implications for emotions and action and extending the number of paths open to them.[10-12] Such is the therapeutic process of reconstruction. Therapists working with clients validate some parts of their construct systems and invalidate others, with some resulting changes of the clients' patterns of construing.

Much of this testing is carried out by loosening in some cases and tightening in others, or sometimes both are necessary.[13] Tightening enables clients to construe precisely enough to act on that construct. Loosening enables them to be open to a wider range of events, and may be necessary to prevent inappropriate and premature closure when making decisions. Elderly clients, with their access to a very wide range of events across their long life span, are often particularly good at this loose process of staying open to a wide range of eventualities.[14] Also as part of the reconstructive process, clients change the meaning of their constructs, apply new constructs to already experienced events and reorganise their construct systems.[15] Using enactment or role play and dream interpretation can be useful for therapists as they work with clients to avoid traps when their constructs are in conflict.

Other aspects of personal construct therapy

Since it has no specific techniques that are always used, this type of therapy can be said to be consistent over different contexts, whether it is applied to normal, neurotic or psychotic people.[16] This characteristic makes it particularly appropriate for the elderly, with whom making such a diagnosis may be difficult for a variety of reasons, such as physical fragility and the side-effects of prescription drugs. It is a therapy not so much for answering questions but for finding better questions to ask.[12] The process of reconstruction is also not as serious as it sounds, it often being quite playful, humorous and creative, as therapists and clients enjoy the new perspectives on the world which emerge.[13] For these reasons, the notion of psychotherapy as the retelling of stories fits very well within it.

Story retelling as therapy

In such therapy, then, clients and therapists tell their stories: therapists, about therapy, and clients, about themselves and their worlds. The reconstruction of those stories then begins. Both participants take part in these reconstructions, so that therapy becomes the shared retelling of stories.[17] Because the stories therapists tell in therapy are mostly about therapy, they may change less than those of the clients; but they do change.[18] Clients are often the first to tell their tales, which are marked by sad and frustrated content and by discontinuities, which therapists help them to reconstrue. Such reconstruction occurs, of course, only when a close, trusting relationship between client and therapist has developed. Often clients are reluctant to tell their stories or they are not aware of the full story they are telling; and they need help from the therapist to make that story explicit.[19] Therapists, however, are responsible for making their stories that are relevant to therapy sufficiently clear for their clients to understand them. They are also responsible for the stories clients carry away about clients and therapists.

Story retelling with the elderly

Story retelling is a highly appropriate form of therapy for the elderly. Their many life events have given them plenty of stories to draw from, and also a more distanced perspective on those stories than they would have had when younger. They can construe loosely and reflectively, and, at their age, are able to tell old tales without the shame that might have kept them hidden when they were younger. Reminiscence—telling stories from the past—comes naturally to people towards the end of their life span. In fact, it may be because they have lost so many sources of confirmation of their personal constructs as friends, neighbours and loved ones die, that they reminisce.[20] By telling their own stories themselves they can go some way to provide their own confirmation. This may be why story telling comes naturally to many of them. Stock-taking is also a common and age-appropriate activity, involving an element of evaluation. So that story retelling may also be said to be a natural process for the elderly.

Such story retelling can be based on very simple concrete cues so as to have lasting effects for the client. Widowed Mrs C, provides an example. At 72 years, she had had a mild stroke. As a result of it, however, she was withdrawing into her home and visiting only her son. She did not feel she could reach out to her male friend, because "I'm so thin and unattractive now". She also described herself as "dwelling in the past" and was very critical of herself for this. She had suffered considerable sleep loss and loss of appetite, and was depressed. It was therefore important to help her retell these sad stories.

Mrs C had also mentioned that she had had a very close and happy family, but that "life was hard; and you just had to keep going". This "having to keep going" sounded like the seed of another, more facilitating story for her. It proved to require a context of "being needed by other people". Her son was quite independent and provided no context for a current version of this story. Her therapist found, however, that she had a neighbour of long-standing, with whom she shopped and did many minor household chores. This friend was "getting a bit deaf", so Mrs C could see that she was needed by her. "I can keep going again, in fact, I can enjoy myself again" became the revised story that she could then tell. She was worried, however, that she would forget it. So she and her therapist designed a banner on which it was presented in large letters and hung it over her kitchen stove, "so that I can see it every time I put the kettle on".

The therapeutic processes in story retelling for the elderly

When stories are retold in the way described above, they can tap into so many therapeutic processes in the elderly. Some such processes involve the working through of age-appropriate issues which have not been effectively worked through before. Others deal with grief and guilt; yet others with strengths, personal and interpersonal. Creativity and enjoyment can also be released, and, perhaps most importantly, a sense of personal integrity can be experienced.

Age-appropriate issues

There are a number of issues with which the elderly need to deal, and which story retelling can be helpful in resolving. These include adjusting work and relationship goals, a process which continues over the entire life span. Continuing to make a contribution to society, even though no longer part of the paid work-force, can also be found by the elderly in story retelling. This contribution must still be seen to be made, even when they are confronted with their own physical limitations and, most difficult to contemplate, the proximity of their own death. A certain turning inward can be the product of ageing, and this is a shock to those who have been extraverted lovers of people. Reviewing and evaluating their own lives is also an issue which needs to be dealt with at this time.[21,22] This is, as I have indicated, central to this kind of therapy.

Guilt and grief

As the elderly review their lives they are often besieged by two types of remorse: guilt and grief.[23] Guilt arises as a result of reviews of life events which reveal that there were times that they did not behave in relation to other people quite as they felt they should. Their own expectations of "proper behaviour" from themselves had not been met. Some of their core constructs had been invalidated. Often, of course the people originally involved are long since dead or have left the neighbourhood, so such guilt needs to be faced in the imagination, perhaps by writing a letter of apology or by a role-played apology. Grief, however, involves mourning loss. Often this is loss of people who were very close, but it can also be loss of houses and pets. All of the natural mourning processes need to be worked through—the anxiety, anger and depression.[24-25] This can often best be done by having the bereaved tell their stories about the grieved one over and over again, until they, of themselves, come to retell those stories.

Personal strengths

Engaging in story telling and retelling can also give elderly clients greater access to many of their personal strengths. This happens in part through the reawakening of past abilities and interests which had for long lain dormant. In general terms, they can come to acknowledge that, when they were younger and coping with stress in their lives, they had been able to take a more distant perspective on what threatened to engulf them. Whether this distance was achieved through religion or humour, or in a range of other ways, these approaches are still available to them.[26] In more specific terms, they can remember activities that gave them pleasure and compensated for the stress, such as doing crossword puzzles. Regaining access to personal strengths also occurs for elderly clients when telling stories in which they mastered depression and demoralisation, which they may need to do again now.

Interpersonal strengths

Strengths in relating to others are as important to the elderly as their personal strengths. For example, they need to continue to take on meaningful roles in relation to others, that is, family and friends.[27] These relationships, then, are best for the elderly if they are reciprocal, so that they are giving as well as taking in life.[26-29] Stories told, or if necessary retold, in therapy provide opportunities to confirm how the elderly are construing these relationships. Interpersonal strengths are also important because, if elderly people do not continue to practice their interpersonal skills in relationships that are meaningful, they will be cut off from important sources of confirmation for their stories.[30] Just as young mothers can tap into a fund of ideas, ways of coping and feelings about child rearing at the baby health clinic and play group, elderly people can tap into a fund of ideas, ways of coping and feelings about the ageing process at the club and local shops. Here, they can hear stories like their own told, providing further confirmation for the telling and opportunities for retelling of their own.

Creativity and enjoyment

Being encouraged to tell their story in therapy, when they are so often ignored elsewhere, can often lead to a sense of creativity, of being able to be the source of things, which may have been missing in their lives for some time.[31] It can also tap into their sense of vitality, and release it for other activities, at a time when it is much needed.[31] There is a joy in this creativity too, a joy in relationships revisited, of loving and being loved.[32] There is also the joy of discovery and rediscovery, the joy of reinvestment in living and, perhaps most important, the joy of finding the self, with its sense of identity and belonging.[33] This description reminds me of that most important process of therapy with the elderly, developing integrity.

Integrity

The sense of integrity, available only to people later in life, can develop through story telling and retelling in therapy.[22] How the self is perceived is central to it. The elderly need, for example to maintain their sense of self-esteem in the face of repeated blows to it. They also need to retain a fairly stable picture of themselves, an identity in the face of often constant change. They need, too, to maintain a sense of belonging to family, age cohort and peers, in the face of constant alienation. All of this can be done, with the result that elderly clients experience a sense of integrity which brings together different aspects of the self. Those elderly people with integrity see others as very similar to and belonging together with themselves, even if they differ in time period or culture. They enjoy seeing patterns in human history, and their part in that history, which when they were younger they could not see. Elderly people who need therapy may tell stories that express the despair which is the opposite of this position: fractionated, alienated and resentful.

The processes of personal construct therapy with the elderly

The basic processes of personal construct therapy consist of loosening and/or tightening of the construing of clients. These processes are now considered, together with changes in the content of the stories of the elderly. I also describe some therapeutic movements initiated by elderly clients as well as those triggered by their therapists.

Loosening and tightening of the clients' stories are the basic techniques available to personal construct therapists. An elderly client, complaining about the fact that her husband did not help her in the kitchen, used construing which was too tight: "If I ask him to help he never will". When, with help from her therapist, she loosened this construing to "If I ask him to help when he has not started to watch TV, he may help", she found that her options opened up. She also found that, although no therapeutic work was done with him, her story change gave him room for change. "I asked him to do the washing up this morning, and he did!", she reported with pride. In another example, tightening was accomplished for an elderly client who, after a series of strokes, sometimes construed himself as "confused". He forgot his glasses, mislaid his toothbrush and so on. His therapist encouraged him to focus consistently on the other pole of his construct, "in control", and, while construing in this way, write down a routine which he could follow each morning. This procedure, after several weeks, led to him more consistently telling stories of himself as "in control". It tightened up his confusion not only about things physical, but about things psychological as well.

Changes in the content of the stories of elderly clients are also part of the psychotherapeutic process, for example from stories which are preoccupied with the body to those which are body transcendent. Stories of the former kind were told by another client who had had a stroke, this time resulting in considerable residual paralysis of her right leg. That leg was taking over her life: "I am my leg, disabled and disfigured". She became able to focus, at least for periods of time, on other aspects of her life which she could enjoy, such as her handicrafts. There is also the change from stories preoccupied with the self to those that are self-transcendent. Behavioural evidence of this change was apparent in a client who moved in therapy from turning in on his own confusions and memory losses, to turning out to the outside world. This change could be seen in the fact that he reordered his newspapers after a gap of 5 years. For him, this change was accompanied by change from socially isolated to interpersonally-related stories, from "I never see my family" to "I really enjoy my family these days". In this case, changes in behaviour led to changes in stories. Equally often, changes in stories lead to changes in behaviour. There is also the change from preoccupations with old roles to the integration of new ones. An elderly woman client, for example, moved from keeping her house "spotless" (and so having no energy left for other activities) to "letting it go a bit, now that I'm getting on" (and for the first time enjoying card games with friends).

The initiatives taken by clients will be considered now. Elderly clients can be eager to examine some of their stories for initiatives, especially when they were not receiving validation elsewhere for them. This validation was more than reinforcement or approval, consisting of confirmation of their expectations. The phrase "In my day . . ." was often on their lips, usually as a precursor to construing that which worked then but does not work now, in what they regard as not "their day". Our clients also tried to become aware of some of their non-verbalised stories. One very old client, for example, learned to connect her inappropriately high blood pressure with the frustration-laden stories associated with her declining physical abilities. With this new construing of her situation, she was able to learn to use relaxation techniques to gain some control of her blood pressure.

She had been quite unaware of this link. She showed insight, in the sense that she was more comprehensively construing her own thoughts and feelings.

Other initiatives can be taken by our therapists. For example, they can elaborate the alternatives which are available to their clients, for example, "You can work with your physiotherapist or not. It is your choice." They encourage their clients to seek validation for their stories outside the therapeutic relationship. "You say that the young people in your family don't agree with you (they don't validate your construct); why don't you try some people who might think like you do. Who could they be?" Therapists can encourage their clients to develop a meaningful relationship with other people, for example, "You are pretty good at bowls, aren't you? You could give some of the younger ones at the club a few pointers, couldn't you?" Such questions serve to bring to clients' attention alternative ways of construing themselves in relation to others.

Personal construct strategies for working therapeutically on stories

There are a number of personal construct strategies with which clients can be helped to work therapeutically on their stories. Some of these are:

1. Given the power of stories about the elderly, just telling their self-empowering stories to the therapist can be therapeutic for elderly clients, through the process of validation or confirmation.
2. Changing the ending of a story if it is self-defeating, can also be therapeutic. This is usually done by gentle and selective invalidation, in the context of validation for other more self-empowering stories of the client.
3. Applying the story in a different way after loosening or tightening it can also be effective. This can often provide a way of avoiding conflict with other stories.
4. Reducing the importance of the self-defeating story in relation to other self-promoting stories, again by gentle invalidation, can also be therapeutic.
5. Hearing that the story does not work for them, by therapeutic invalidation, may be necessary for some elderly clients.

Other techniques for story retelling with the elderly

A number of therapeutic techniques has been reported as being of use with elderly clients; and they can be used, when appropriate, in this personal construct therapy which is focused on story retelling. Using such techniques is possible with this approach because it considers therapy to consist of story telling, story testing and story retelling. Any techniques that help to test clients' stories can therefore be used by the personal construct therapist, regardless of their origins.

I shall first describe the techniques which have come from some major approaches to therapy with younger adults: the cognitive behavioural, rational emotive and client-centred therapies. I shall next deal with other techniques that have proved especially useful with the elderly. Then the reviewing therapies and the expressive therapies become my concern. All of these techniques can be employed to test clients' stories and to help them retell them. Finally, I examine already existing accounts of story telling and retelling, which of course combine both the therapeutic processes of review and expression.

Techniques from other approaches to therapy

Cognitive behavioural therapy   This is the therapy most commonly used today with adults.[34] It has been employed quite frequently with the elderly, especially with elderly clients who are depressed. This therapy shapes the depressive behaviours of clients by helping them to revise the depressive and often apparently illogical thoughts attached to them. Clients are, in fact, encouraged to revise the "short stories" they tell themselves as they move through the day, for example, "I'm not an attractive person" and "I don't deserve to succeed". Moving to more positive statements about self is then reinforced by being associated with some more enjoyable aspects of the person's life, such as going fishing or watching the soap operas on television, so that they learn to behave in less depressed ways.

Rational emotive therapy   A slightly different version of the cognitive-behavioural technique is provided by rational emotive therapy,[35] which focuses more on the illogicality of statements like: "If half the people with tickets got prizes, I still wouldn't get one", in order to diffuse the sad feelings. It also encourages the development of a new perspective, somewhat similar to that gained in personal construct therapy: "This may be the only life I ever have and I can live it confused and depressed, or I can get on top of it and enjoy it."

Client-centred therapy   There is also a version of client-centred therapy which is much in contrast to these approaches. In it, elderly clients are provided with a therapist who works hard to convince them that he or she is honest, can empathise or feel along with them and can accept them. These are the three essentials for change to take place in client-centred therapy. This technique is called "validation therapy";[36] and its aim is to support and confirm their stories. This is in contrast to the challenge to existing stories the client achieved by the cognitive behavioural techniques. When such validation had built trust, elderly clients were then seen to risk changing some of their more fragile stories.

It is hard to see each of these approaches being equally useful for elderly clients. Together they form a set of techniques for encouraging story retelling. Which one is chosen varies from client to client and occasion to occasion.

More useful techniques for the elderly

In this section I want to deal not with techniques of therapy but more with the way therapy is delivered. Two less expensive ways come to mind: telephone therapy and group therapy. These two techniques are useful for quite different reasons.

Telephone-based story retelling   This can be helpful for frail or disabled elderly clients for whom physical mobility is limited.[37] It is most effective once a relationship has been established face-to-face between client and therapist, and is ideal for supporting and confirming any changes clients may manage to make. It can still, however, maintain the intimacy of that relationship.

Group therapy   This breaks up this intimacy by including other people in the group, in the form of other elderly clients; but the gains from this can be great.[38-40] Elderly clients can share their experiences with people with similar experiences and values, often finding emotional release in this. They can also come to realise that they are not alone in the problems they face. They can share coping strategies with these people, and such strategies may be more appropriate than those suggested by a younger therapist. They can see them modelled by other elderly people; and they can work through some of their problems with them. They can even lead their own groups.[38] Such harnessing of the resources of the elderly can be a source of self-esteem and meaningful relationships, which have been seen to be so important.

Review therapies

That reviewing their past life could be therapeutic for the elderly was first suggested some 30 years ago,[41] and the techniques of life review have been refined over the intervening years.[42,43] The current procedure has three stages.[44] In the first, clients are encouraged to remember as much of their earlier life as they can. This might focus on a particular area of life, like family or work. This stage can be stimulated by physical momentos, like photograph albums. In the second stage, they are asked to take a somewhat critical approach to what they have recalled and evaluate it in the light of the values they hold now. In the third stage, clients are encouraged to see common patterns. They are also encouraged to make links between what they have remembered, to integrate what they have said before.[45] This is essentially a story telling therapy. It has also taken the form of structured reminiscence, in which memories have been reorganised in this way, as well as of an emotional connections' review.[42] In the latter form, clients focus especially on links between their feelings and what they remember. Yet another form of life review involves providing clients with evidence of the major historical events at the time of their personal histories, thereby giving an extra meaning to their lives.[43]

Expressive therapies

Essentially, the reviewing therapies provide a tightening process, after initially loose construing. The expressive therapies, on the other hand, are primarily loosening, encouraging non-verbal expression, as they do. They also encourage creativity. Art therapy and drama therapy provide the best examples. In art therapy,[39] the self expression can occur in any medium in which the elderly feel comfortable: felt-tip pens, oils, Plasticine or quilting. Of course rheumatism can limit the use of these techniques, so plain pencil may be fine. Art therapy actually combines verbal and non-verbal techniques to define problems, communicate about them and attempt solutions to them. Joint drawing between client and therapist can be revealing also, as can group drawings or sculptures, if the group setting is used. Drama therapy[46,47] involves the acting out of interactions between characters, which may grow from the clients' own problems or relate to some interests or values they have. This therapy is essentially a group process, so that the first result of this enactment is trust of the others involved. This often occurs, together with better physical awareness and improved short-term memory. In the longer term, it provides validation of life experiences and access to younger personalities now forgotten. These techniques both provide more tools for story telling and retelling.

Story telling

Story telling has recently been advocated as therapeutic for the elderly, together with its close cousin, poetry writing.[48,49] For centuries, elderly people have told stories to their families and friends, not only to entertain but also to pass cultural aspirations and values from generation to generation. In medieval Britain and Europe there was the tradition of bards; in the USA in the nineteenth century, the tradition of the respected raconteur and also reader of other people's stories; in Australia, there was a similar if younger tradition of yarn spinning or story telling. These Australian yarns often teased the listeners, but they still fulfilled the same functions. Also, in the USA and Australia, this tradition was maintained by their indigenous peoples. In this century, this role has been taken over by television and radio. It is no wonder, today, then, that elderly people have many stories, the telling of which may be therapeutic for them.

Story retelling in the family

All of the above techniques have focused on elderly clients as if they had no families. The stories of the elderly are often embedded in and supported by the stories of their families. These stories continually need changing because the roles of different family members keep changing. Story retelling, to be successful, may need to involve clients' families in that retelling process.[50-53] I shall therefore now look at how families construe events and tell stories about them, before dealing with how elderly couples and families with elderly members tell and retell their stories.

Families construe events and tell stories

The way families interact is structured by the ways in which they see the events which they share.[54] In fact, they cannot interact unless they share some common constructs, or accept some common stories. Families build systems of constructs just as individuals do, and sometimes the constructs of individual members are in conflict with those of their families.[55] These conflicts are often more evident in non-verbal than verbal behaviour, such as sighs or shrugs. This family construct system consists of shared meanings which govern how the family functions. These help families to operate as units, but can also make them resistant to change. The family that is not functioning well will have problems in negotiating changes in these common constructs and shared stories.

Marital therapy techniques are available in many forms and all can be used to help elderly married clients retell their shared stories of a lifetime together. Often this is necessary because one partner has changed from the person they were when they developed their pool of shared constructs.[56] Women grow in new directions when freed from the constraints of child-rearing earlier in their life spans. Men grow in new directions when freed from the constraints of being the financial provider and source of security for a family of children. Such couples will need to renegotiate their shared constructs and stories.

Retelling family stories

Retelling family stories becomes necessary as elderly family members change their roles in that family.[57,58] Families who can negotiate these changes function well. Those that do not can cause untold pain in family members. The family of Mr M, an elderly Scot who had migrated to Australia, was introduced in Chapter 2. At 80, he was living alone, but had begun to see that, with his increasing frailty, this might become more difficult. His three daughters and a son lived nearby, but had not invited him to live with them. In fact, the family was more like a series of armed camps in each house. Mr M was angry with his offspring, as he had been for decades. His short stories to himself were "I'll not forgive. I'm a Scot, and Scots do not forget." Of course with a father with such constructs, his children had grown up together drawing on this extremely intolerant family construct system. They had then each carried it on in their own lives: "He's an old bugger, and I'll not let him forget it". A therapist met, after many appointments, missed by family members, with all of the family but one, and described this process to them. She also gently suggested that they could change their shared story, but that, if such change was going to involve their father, it would need to be soon. The son eventually began the negotiation process which they found painful but ultimately worthwhile. Their father reluctantly joined in. They then arranged to keep their father in his own home as he wanted, taking it in turns to visit him regularly.

Outcomes of research evaluating therapy with the elderly

To undertake such story retelling therapy with the elderly would be invasive and unethical if some evidence were not available from research which indicates that it is of benefit to them. There is some such evidence which I shall review now; sufficient for me to feel justified in writing this book. However, as I have already noted, only a relatively small number of therapies specifically for the elderly have been developed, and many of these are quite recent. It follows, then, that the body of supporting research evidence is much smaller than it should be. I shall now look at evaluations of personal construct, reviewing and expressive therapies and then those from the cognitive behavioural and psycho-analytic therapies.

Outcomes for personal construct therapy

Personal construct therapy has been tested with elderly clients in only one research programme so far.[59] It used the therapy being described in this book. Evaluation was carried out in two areas for a group of elderly clients who were referred for a variety of problems, including anxiety and depression. The first of these areas was their emotional well-being, so that their anxiety, depression and anger, were evaluated three times: immediately before and immediately after therapy, as well as 4 months after therapy had finished. When these clients were compared with a group of similar elderly people who were referred and inter-viewed but not seen at that point in time, their anxiety, depression and their indi-rect expression of anger were considerably less. The second area of evaluation was their independence, a quality much valued in our societies.[60] Whether it should be so central to our work with the elderly I shall take up later in this book. The elderly clients expressed more competence, and less helplessness too. Not all of these gains remained over the 4 months' period of follow up.

Outcomes for the reviewing and expressing therapies

The main research to be reported under this heading is that evaluating the effects of life review therapy for the elderly. Its findings have been mixed, with some studies showing it no more effective than no therapy at all and a simple elapse of time, while others showed it to be effective.[61] One interesting study compared two types of reviews, one run conventionally and the other being more experiential and oriented towards personal feelings and thoughts, with no therapy.[62] Both client groups showed an increase in their satisfaction with life and increased self-esteem. Peer-led therapy has also been found to be successful.[63] Unfortunately, I could find no acceptable studies of the outcomes of art therapy. This may be because those who do it lack a tradition of evaluation by independent research. Such evaluations are to be encouraged.

Outcomes for cognitive behavioural and psychoanalytic therapies

The other therapies for the elderly which have been evaluated have mostly been the cognitive behavioural and psychoanalytic therapies. Their clients have been compared and also contrasted with a group of elderly people without therapy. Their focus has often been on severe depression.[64–67] In terms of that depression, both therapies have proved to be effective, in terms of better eating and sleeping and less sadness and anxiety. However, over a 1-year follow-up period, cognitive behavioural therapy proved more effective. Clients undergoing both therapies expressed more competence than the group without therapy; and the clients who had cognitive behavioural therapy expressed more satisfaction with life, but the clients with psychoanalytic therapy expressed more trust.

Is personal construct therapy like other therapies?

Personal construct therapy differs in a number of important and complex ways from, for example, the cognitive behavioural and psychoanalytic therapies. Its therapists assume that reality is available only through the personal meanings of client and therapist rather than through direct experience, as practitioners of the other approaches believe.[68] For personal construct therapists, thought, feeling and action are not separated, while the other therapists believe in the primacy of thought over the others.[69] For them, emotion is a powerful knowing process, while for the cognitive-behaviourists, at least, emotion is considered to be negative and in need of control.[70]

Because of these assumptions, counselling and psychotherapy are viewed by personal construct therapists as ahistorical. The stories of their clients about past events are important, but not in order to explore those past events. They are important because of their influence on how clients act now. This position is in contrast to that of psychoanalytic therapists, whose present interests are the history of their clients.[71] Personal construct therapy also is seen as providing opportunities for clients to grow, rather than to control their symptoms as is the case of cognitive behavioural therapy.[72] The relationship between client and therapist in personal construct therapy provides a safe and caring context for change by the risk-taking client, in contrast to the relationship in cognitive behavioural therapy which provides a context for instruction and guidance by therapists.[72] There are, however, some similarities to be noted. Personal construct therapy shares an ahistorical approach with the cognitive behavioural therapies, and provides opportunities for clients to grow, in agreement with the psychoanalytic therapies.

Story retelling as therapy

In this chapter, I have shown how psychotherapy with the elderly can consist of their telling and sometimes retelling of stories. This form of personal construct therapy is based on stories, in part because of the power they have over the elderly in our society and the extent to which the elderly are deprived of telling them and even hearing them told. This therapy is also based on stories because of their role in the psychological and interpersonal functioning of the elderly. It can be conducted, of course, only after the therapist has listened properly to the stories of their clients, to see whether their content was limiting or empowering. I have also suggested a set of criteria for the evaluation of such stories by therapists.

In this chapter on therapy as story retelling I focused initially on the meanings some therapists have given about elderly clients, and also on their special advantages in therapy. I then presented a personal construct framework for the reconstruction of personal construct therapy, dwelling on loosening and tightening of construing as important therapeutic processes, how personal construct therapy can be achieved by story retelling, and giving an example of the retelling of stories with an elderly woman. Then some of the important therapeutic processes that can be achieved for the elderly by their retelling of their stories were detailed: age-appropriate processes, such as coming to accept their physical fragility, working through grief and guilt, getting in touch with strengths, both personal and interpersonal, and unleashing creativity and enjoyment as well as that most fulfilling sense of integrity.

Then I described some of the processes of personal construct therapy that can be used with elderly clients, together with some strategies to encourage them to, where appropriate, retell their stories. Other therapeutic techniques described included cognitive behavioural and client-centred therapies, to name two well-known ones. They also included the range of reviewing therapies, such as life review and reminiscence, as well as the more expressive therapies, using drama and art. I also recognised that the use of tools such as these with elderly clients might well not be successful, if their family construct systems and shared family stories blocked these changes. I dealt briefly with marital therapy and family therapy, providing an example of the latter for an elderly man whose adult family were hanging onto the stories he originally taught them as children in order to exclude him from their lives. This chapter was necessarily concluded by an overview of the research which has been conducted to evaluate the outcomes of some of these therapies, and a comparison of personal construct therapy with other therapies.

In the next six chapters, I shall apply these ideas to particular stories that I, as a therapist, have found that elderly clients tell. The first three of these stories (in Chapters 5–7) are self-limiting and so, after their bad implications for the tellers have been examined, a range of ways of retelling them will be provided. The second three stories (in Chapters 8–10) are self-empowering stories; their good implications will be explored, together with ways of maintaining and encouraging these stories. In these six chapters my aim is to show something of the wide range of stories elderly clients can tell and to trace the complex implications of them. I shall then provide four chapters in each of which the actual personal construct therapy with an elderly client is described.

Suggested reading

● *Warnings and encouragements*

1. Colthart, N.E.C. (1991). The analysis of an elderly patient. *International Journal of Psychoanalysis*, **72**, 209–219.
2. Hanley, I. (1980). Psychological treatment of emotional disorders in the elderly. In F.N. Fraser Watts (Ed.), *New developments in clinical psychology*, Vol. 2. London: British Psychological Society.
3. Hildebrand, H.P. (1982). Psychotherapy with older patients. *British Journal of Medical Psychology*, **55**, 19–28.
4. Kastenbaum, R. (1983). Can the clinical milieu be therapeutic? In E.D. Bowles & R.J. Ohta (Eds.), *Ageing and milieu*. New York: Academic Press, pp. 3–16.
5. Baltes, P.B. & Danish, S.J. (1980). Intervention in life span development and ageing: Issues and concepts. In R.R. Turner & H.W. Reese (Eds.), *Life span developmental psychology: Intervention*. New York: Academic Press, pp. 49–78.
6. Sterns, H.L. & Sanders, R.E. (1980). Training and education of the elderly. In R.R. Turner & H.M. Reese (Eds.), *Life span developmental psychology: Intervention*. New York: Academic Press, pp. 307–330.
7. Myers, J.E. & Salmon, H.E. (1984). Counselling programs for older persons: Status, shortcomings and potentialities. *The Counselling Psychologist*, **12**, 39–53.

● *A personal construct framework for story retelling*

8. Kelly, G.A. (1967). A psychology of the optimal man. In A.H. Mahrer (Ed.), *The goals of psychotherapy*. New York: Appleton–Century–Crofts.
9. Guidano, J.F. (1991). *A redefinition of cognitive therapy: Using affect in the exploration of self*. New York: Guilford Press.

10. Epting, F.R. (1981). *Personal construct psychololgy: Recent advances in theory and practice.* London: Macmillan.
11. Kelly, G.A. (1969). Personal construct theory and the psychotherapeutic interview. In B. Maher (Ed.), *Clinical psychology and personality.* New York: Wiley, pp. 224–264.
12. Neimeyer, R.A. (1988). The origin of questions in the clinical context. *Questioning Exchange,* 2, 75–80.
13. Epting, F.R. (1984). *Personal construct counselling and psychotherapy.* New York: Wiley.
14. Powell, J. (1991). *"Motivational interviewing" with older hospital patients: A personal construct approach.* International Conference on Drug and Alcohol, Adelaide, Australia.
15. Fransella, F. & Dalton, P. (1990). *Personal construct counselling in action.* London: Sage.
16. Leitner, L.W. (1990). Terror, risk and reverence: Experiential personal construct psychotherapy. *International Journal of Personal Construct Psychology,* 3, 62–69.
17. Viney, L.L. (1989). Psychotherapy as shared reconstruction. *International Journal of Personal Construct Psychology,* 3, 423–442.
18. Bannister, D. (1987). A PCT view of novel writing and reading. In F. Fransella & L. Thomas (Eds.), *Experimenting with personal construct psychology.* London: Routledge and Kegan Paul.
19. Viney, L.L. & Bousfield, L. (1992). AIDS and the client "in the fast lane": Narrative construction and reconstruction. *The Psychotherapy Patient,* 32, 757–758.
20. Viney, L.L., Benjamin, Y.N. & Preston, C.A. (1988). Mourning and reminiscence: Parallel psychotherapeutic processes for the elderly. *International Journal of Ageing and Human Development,* 28, 237–249.

● *The therapeutic processes in story retelling for the elderly*

21. Agnew, D.P. (1986). Psychotherapy of the elderly: The life validation approach in psychotherapy with elderly patients. *Journal of Geriatric Psychiatry,* 16, 87–92.
22. Richter, R.L. (1986). Allowing ego integrity through life review. *Journal of Religion and Ageing,* 2, 1–11.
23. Sorensen, M.H. (1986). Narcissm and loss in the elderly: Strategies for inpatient older adult groups. *International Journal of Group Psychotherapy,* 36, 533–547.
24. Szapocznck, J., Kurtines, M.M., Santisban, D. & Perez-Vidaz, A. (1982). New directions in the treatment of depression in the elderly. *Journal of Geriatric Psychiatry,* 15, 257–281.
25. Landgarten, H. (1983). Art therapy for depressed elders. *Clinical Gerontologist,* 2, 45–53.
26. Griffen, M. & Waller, M. (1985). Group therapy for the elderly: One approach to coping. *Clinical Social Work Journal,* 13, 261–271.
27. Andersson, L. (1985). Intervention against loneliness in a group of elderly women. An impact evaluation. *Social Science and Medicine,* 20, 355–364.
28. Leszcz, M. (1990). Towards an integrated model of group psychotherapy with the elderly. *The International Journal of Group Psychotherapy,* 40, 379–490.
29. Natale, S.M. (1986). Loneliness and the ageing client: Psychotherapeutic considerations. *Psychotherapy Patient,* 2, 77–93.
30. Salvendy, J.T. (1989). Special populations in brief group psychotherapy: Experiences with the elderly. *European Journal of Psychology,* 3, 138–144.

31. Johnson, D.R. (1986). The developmental method in drama therapy: Group treatment with the elderly. *Arts in Psychotherapy*, **13**, 17–33.
32. Saul, S. & Saul, S.R. (1990). The application of joy in group therapy for the elderly. *The International Journal of Group Psychotherapy*, **40**, 353–355.
33. Johnson, D.R. (1985). Expressive group therapy with the elderly: A drama therapy approach. *The International Journal of Group Psychotherapy*, **35**, 109–127.

● *Other techniques for story retelling with the elderly*

34. Thompson, L.W., Davies, R., Gallagher, D. & Krantz, S. (1986). Cognitive therapy in older adults. *Clinical Gerontologist*, **5**, 245–279.
35. Keller, J.F., Croake, J.W. & Brooking, J.Y. (1975). Effects of a program in rational thinking on anxieties in older persons. *Journal of Counselling Psychology*, **22**, 54–57.
36. Babbins, L.H., Dillion, J. & Merovitz, S. (1988). The effects of validation therapy on disoriented elderly. *Activities, Adaptation and Ageing*, **12**, 73–86.
37. Evans, R.L. (1986). Cognitive telephone group therapy with physically disabled elderly persons. *Gerontologist*, **26**, 8–11.
38. Koenig, H.G. (1988). Shepherd's Centres: Helping elderly help themselves. *Journal of the American Geriatric Society*, **34**, 73.
39. Sherman, E. (1981). *Counselling the ageing: An integrative approach*. New York: Free Press.
40. White, D. & Ingersoll, D. (1989). Life review groups: Helping their members with an unhappy life. *Clinical Gerontologist*, **8**, 47–50.
41. Butler, R.N. (1963). The life review: An interpretation of reminiscence in the aged. *Psychiatry*, **26**, 19–29.
42. Butler, R.N. & Lewis, M.I. (1977). *Ageing and mental health*. Saint Louis: Mosby.
43. Lewis, M.I. & Butler, R.N. (1974). Life review therapy: Putting memories to work in individual and group psychotherapy. *Geriatrics*, **29**, 165–174.
44. Coleman, P. (1986). Issues in the therapeutic use of reminiscence in elderly people. In I. Hanley & M. Gilhooley (Eds.), *Psychological therapies for elderly people*. London: Croom Helm.
45. Webster, J. & Young, R.A. (1988). Process variables of the life review: Counselling implications. *International Journal of Ageing and Human Development*, **26**, 315–323.
46. Huddleston, R. (1989). Drama with elderly people. *British Journal of Occupational Therapy*, **52**, 290–300.
47. Mazor, R. (1982). Drama therapy for the elderly in a day care centre. *Hospital and Community Psychiatry*, **33**, 577–579.
48. Gutterer, S.M. (1989). Story-telling: A valuable supplement for poetry writing in the elderly. *Arts in Psychotherapy*, **16**, 127–131.
49. Keller, J.F. & Brownley, M. (1989). Psychotherapy with the elderly: A systemic model. *Journal of Psychotherapy and the Family*, **5**, 29–46.

● *Story retelling in the family*

50. Brody, E. (1966). The ageing family. *The Gerontologist*, **6**, 201–206.
51. Greenbaum, J. & Rader, L. (1989). Marital problems of the "old" elderly, as they present at a mental health clinic. *Journal of Gerontological Social Work*, **14**, 111–116.

52. Herr, J. & Weakland, J. (1979). *Counselling elders and their families*. New York: Springer.
53. Quinn, W.H. & Keller, J.F. (1981). A family therapy model for preserving independence in older persons: Utilization of the family of procreation. *American Journal of Family Therapy*, **9**, 79–84.
54. Reiss, D. (1981). *The family's construction of reality*. Cambridge: Harvard University Press.
55. Proctor, H. (1981). Family construct psychology: An approach to understanding and treating families. In S. Walrond-Skinner (Ed.), *Developments in family therapy*. London: Routledge and Kegan Paul, pp. 210–217.
56. Peterson, J.A. (1973). Marital and family therapy involving the aged. *The Gerontologist*, **46**, 27–31.
57. Combs, G. & Freedman, J. (1990). *Symbol, story and ceremony: Using metaphor in individual and family therapy*. London: Norton.
58. Proctor, H. (1985). A construct approach to family therapy. In E. Button (Ed.), *Personal construct theory and mental health*. Beckenham: Croom Helm, pp. 327–350.

● *Outcomes of research evaluating therapy with the elderly*

59. Viney, L.L., Benjamin, Y.N. & Preston, C.A. (1989). An evaluation of personal construct therapy for the elderly. *British Journal of Medical Psychology*, **62**, 35–41.
60. Viney, L.L., Benjamin, Y.N. & Preston, C.A. (1988). Promoting independence in the elderly: The role of psychological, social and physical constraints. *Clinical Gerontologist*, **8**, 3–17.
61. Sherman, E. (1987). Reminiscence groups for community elderly. *The Gerontologist*, **27**, 569–572.
62. Moran, J.A. & Gatz, M. (1987). Group therapies for nursing home adults: An evaluation of two treatment approaches. *The Gerontologist*, **27**, 588–591.
63. Lieberman, M. & Birdwise, N.G. (1985). Comparisons among peer and professionally-directed groups for the elderly: Implication for the development of self help groups. *International Journal of Group Psychotherapy*, **35**, 155–175.
64. Gallagher, D. & Thomson, L.W. (1982). Treatment of major depressive disorders in older adult outpatients with brief psychotherapies. *Psychotherapy*, **19**, 422–490.
65. Stever, J.L. (1984). Cognitive-behavioural psychodynamic group psychotherapy in treatment of geriatric depression. *Journal of Consulting and Clinical Psychology*, **52**, 180–189.
66. Thompson, L.W. & Gallagher, D. (1984). Efficacy of psychotherapy in the treatment of late life depression. *Advances in Behaviour Research and Therapy*, **6**, 127–139.
67. Thompson, L.W., Gallagher, D. & Breckenridge, S. (1987). Comparative effectiveness of psychotherapies for depressed elderly. *Journal of Consulting and Clinical Psychology*, **55**, 385–390.

● *Is personal construct therapy like other therapies?*

68. Mahoney, M.J. & Lyddon, W.J. (1988). Recent developments in cognitive approaches to counselling and psychotherapy. *The Counselling Psychologist*, **16**, 190–234.
69. Neimeyer, R.A. (1985). Personal constructs in clinical practice. In P.C. Kendall (Ed.), *Advances in cognitive-behavioural research and therapy*. New York: Academic Press, pp. 275–339.

70. Viney, L.L. (1992). Can we see ourselves changing? Toward a constructivist model of adult psychosocial development. *Human Development*, **36**, 65–75.
71. Mahoney, M.J. & Gabriel, T.J. (1987). Psychotherapy and the cognitive sciences: An evolving alliance. *Journal of Cognitive Psychotherapy*, **1**, 39–59.
72. Neimeyer, R.A. (1986). Personal construct therapy. In W. Dryden & W.L. Golden (Eds.), *Cognitive-behavioural approaches to psychotherapy*. London: Harper & Row.

SOME SELF-LIMITING STORIES FROM THE ELDERLY

5 "Sometimes I feel as if life isn't worthwhile"

Many stories that the elderly tell about themselves are self-limiting and distressing. This story, "Sometimes I feel as if life isn't worthwhile", is one such story. I shall now analyse it in some detail, using the plan of presentation to be followed with later stories. Initially, a number of different versions of it are introduced. Then two elderly people in different situations give their accounts of it. Then follows an analysis of the personal, social and cultural aspects of the narrative. The personal aspects of such story telling are seen to include their presentation of themselves and the age-related events they experience, the psychological functions the story fulfils for them, its implications for their emotions and actions, and the manner in which it links present, past and future for them. The social aspects of the story include its interpersonal context, who validates and supports it and to whom or what it allocates power. The cultural aspects of the story include the information which it shares with its audience and the values on which it is based. Then some research evidence about the physical effects of these tales on their tellers is reviewed. Finally, I suggest some strategies for the retelling of this story.

"Sometimes I feel as if life isn't worthwhile"

This story, when told by the elderly, says that what life brings for them can be both distressing and overpowering. Some versions of it show an emptiness: "There's no good things in my life, I've got no interest whatsoever in anything at all. I'm getting that way that I don't even want to wash myself." Others show depression: "When I wake up in the morning now, I start to cry. I don't want to wake up. That's the state of mind I've got myself into." Sometimes it is associated with blaming themselves, as in this version, and sometimes with blaming others, as in the one that follows. "There's not too much going for me. Lack of health, lack of company . . . I get that depressed; and no-one seems to care." Loneliness is often linked with this story too. "I don't feel wanted, you know; and you can destroy a person by getting them to feel that." "It's very hurtful to be left on your own."

Two clients tell the story

Two women who told different versions of this story provide examples of the different kinds of situations that can lead to it being told.

Mrs U, at 67 years, was a widow. She was very agitated, short of breath and overweight, with much excess fluid at her ankles and open sores on her arms. She was also very tired, reported hardly sleeping at all. A community nurse worked therapeutically with her, and, because of her physical condition, this work was done in her home. Her medical practitioner had recommended that Mrs U cut down her 30 cups of tea a day to three, and recommended herbal tea. "I am fat and sick and there's nothing I can do about it", she responded to this advice. "I'm not responsible for the way I am. The doctor should be able to cure me." She was angrily mourning the loss of many aspects of her previous life which she had enjoyed. "I can't be like I used to be, so my life now is finished." Her relationships with her son and daughter were an important source of tension. She fought a lot with her son who was living with her, "about everything", and with her daughter on Friday nights when she came to visit her. "My children don't care about me or love me any more, so I don't care about them."

At 69, Mrs Q was still looking after her "difficult" 90-year-old mother at home. She, also, was therefore seen at home initially by a psychologist from a university-based clinic, but later she was seen by her at the clinic. Her continued responsibility for her mother was probably because of the rejections she had experienced from her earlier, which had led to her continuing, throughout her life, to try to win approval from her mother. Having initially seen her sister favoured over her, she now saw her sister's daughter favoured over her own. "I have to try to make my mother love me, and so I have to hang onto her." She had a history of physical symptoms when under great stress: 6 months of blindness when her first husband died and 2 months of paralysis when her mother first came to live with her. Her first husband had never worked, so she had supported her family financially. The same was true of her second. As a consequence, she saw him as having no rights in their household and as merely an extension of herself. "If we weren't so tied down," she said, "it might be easier. How can it be easy when you've got all this going. I mean we haven't even got a life of our own. We don't go out anywhere and we haven't any friends."

Some personal aspects of the story

Self

This story, "Sometimes I feel as if life isn't worthwhile", presents its elderly tellers in a narrow range of ways. They are nearly always passive. Even when the heroes or heroines of this story make an effort, they do not succeed because they are prevented by events. They could be decision-makers but are not. They could take charge, but they do not. They see themselves as lacking the ability to deal with, as well as being overwhelmed and deprived by, age-related events. Their only active role is that of knower. They are aware of and can reflect, to some extent, on what is happening to them. They are reduced to being receivers of advice, with no real choice about whether to take it or not.

Age-related events

Age-related events, such as illness and disability seem, in this story, to make it not worth the effort to enjoy some of the better things of life. Of course, these constraints are not only physical, but psychological, social and financial as well. Becoming old can act on the feelings and thoughts of those who tell this story in ways beyond their control. It can affect their relationships with others. It can also affect them economically, undermining their ability to make an appropriate living and so increasing their dependence on others.

The psychological functions of the story

This story fulfils a number of functions for those who tell it. When the story teller uses his or her established personal style to narrate it, this can help to maintain his or her identity. Some versions of this story also provide information for the audience, for example, about the effects of traditional medical and welfare-related services for the elderly. Others provide expression of feelings for both the tellers of the tale and their audience, as when the story deals with some of the most feared results of ageing, such as cognitive impairment. Yet others enable the teller to avoid accepting personal responsibility for what happens as they age.

The implications of the story for the emotions and behaviour of the teller

Most stories have some implications for both the feelings and behaviour of the story tellers. This one, while leading to a variety of distressing emotions, all too frequently has no such implications for action. Some versions of this story imply that the tellers are confused, but no course of accompanying action is identified in them. Similarly, there is a version in which the dominant emotion is depression, but again no action is implied. This pattern of events also holds for versions of the story in which the tellers feel helpless. However, this story can have a version in which some action is implied, but it is of a limited kind. For example, the story tellers experience uncertainty or diffidence, and as a result their plans of action become rather half-hearted. There are even forms of the story which, so much are they abbreviated, have no implications for either emotions or actions.

Past, present and future

The past, present and future are not well linked in this story. "Sometimes I feel as if life isn't worthwhile" suggests that now and probably not in the past, the story tellers find it hard to cope. How they relate these aspects of their experience to their future depends largely on the pessimism they introduce into their stories. For a few it could mean that the goal of taking a grip on life is likely to be maintained as it has been in the past. For many more, it could mean that they could not achieve some of their goals. Often the relationships between the time elements in these stories were vague and confused. The most common version of the story related past and present age-related events to each other, but failed to link them to future or anticipated events.

Some social aspects of the story

Its interpersonal context

While many stories of the elderly have an interpersonal context, this was rarely the case for this one. They most often told it to themselves in private, although it might occasionally be shared with a therapist. On some occasions, other people were an essential part of the plot—family, friends and health professionals—and on such occasions they often provided an audience for it.

Sources of validation for the story

This story received its validation primarily from those who told it. They told it when depressed or helpless and provided their own confirmation of it. This reliance on internal confirmation left them with few opportunities to alter it. However, for some elderly, this story was provided, not only with internal support, but support from family members, some of whom, unfortunately, responded to it as if it were an appropriate account of events.

Power in the story

In this story, the power has not been allocated to the teller. It has most often been handed over to the ageing processes or to other people, such as the medical practitioners and community nurses as well as family. In the story, the only aspects of the story tellers said to have power were their bodies, but these were alienated and detached bodies with great power over the minds they accompanied.

Some cultural aspects of the story

Information

The information this story provides is largely self-knowledge for its tellers. This knowledge may involve, for example, acknowledgement that they have their own unique ways of coping, which are often not successful. Such self-knowledge is not of course of much use to their audience, unless they too happen to use these coping strategies. What information is communicated in this tale often is about age-related events, for example about the physical symptoms likely to be experienced by the elderly, although it can also involve the psychological results of ageing. Valuable information that may be communicated in this, to other members of the culture, concerns the recognition that life is not always overwhelming for the elderly. "*Sometimes* I feel as if life is not worthwhile." It is appropriate to feel depressed and helpless when facing the physical effects of ageing; but it is also possible to take some control of and use these reactions as it has been with illnesses they have experienced earlier in their lives.

Values

The cultural values which underlie this story also vary somewhat from teller to teller. Occasionally a chaos reflecting a lack of accepted values is apparent. These values, however, are the most common. Everyone should have shelter, rest and other resources. They should also have health and energy, as well as people to share their stories with. Unfortunately, ageing can put at risk these values. Also, each person should make an effort, taking responsibility for decisions and work. This, of course, involves work at home, but our culture clearly prefers it to be in the visible paid workforce. The last and perhaps most important of these values deals with the right of people to have as much information as they can make use of when responding to events which concern them. It follows that the elderly have a right to the latest information about ageing. Education about ageing in this culture is, in principle at least, judged to be important for them, as it is for their families and for the community as a whole. In practice, such information is not so available as it should be.

Some physical effects of telling the story

The helplessness that is central to this story has been shown by researchers to have unwanted consequences for their physical well-being. It can lead to illness. Often a sense of psychological impotence is involved, a feeling of being unable to cope with changes in one's world and a recognition that one's own means of coping no longer seem to work.[1] These constructs can lead the elderly to "give up", which in turn leads to increased vulnerability to disease and even to death. Researchers in the field are coming to accept that this is so; perhaps because of the evidence available that suggests that identifying people who feel helpless may be an effective aid in predicting the likelihood of cancer.[2] People telling helpless stories like this one may also be more vulnerable to the illness-provoking effects of stress.[3,4]

There is also evidence that helplessness is associated with poor rehabilitation and recovery.[5] For example, more passive coping with their disability and treatment by people with severe burns has been found in those who recover from those burns more slowly and less completely than those who are more active. People with cancer who tend to see the people and events of their physical world as determining their fate tend not to adjust so well to their illness as do those who view themselves as the most important influence in their lives, and their illness is more likely to have a poor outcome.[6] Similarly, elderly people with a range of chronic illnesses who tell this story may show little rehabilitation later, in comparison with those who do not.[7] Effective rehabilitation has been shown to include an increase in people's stories of control and competence, as well as a decline in their stories of helplessness. Ill and injured people who do not experience such helplessness are more likely to be involved in successful rehabilitation, including more gains from treatment for chronic pain.[8]

Retelling the story

In this story, "Sometimes I feel life isn't worthwhile", the elderly present themselves as passive, deprived, lacking ability and dependent. If they try to achieve something, they are likely to fail. It can enable them to maintain some sense of identity but also to avoid taking responsibility for themselves. It often links their present, past and future only poorly. It is told by the self, and validated by the self; but what power it allocates goes to the ageing processes or to other people, especially health and welfare professionals and friends. However, this story provides signs of breaking through this dependency to some optimism by its beginning, which qualifies it as relevant only "sometimes". Nevertheless, the feelings expressed in it involve being overwhelmed and distressed, apathetic and empty, angry at self and others, and alienated, as well as lonely and depressed. This type of story, when told by the elderly, may also be associated with increased illness as well as poorer recovery from it.

Helping the elderly to retell this story is, then, important. The description of personal construct therapy in Chapter 4, especially the section in which I deal with story retelling is, of course, useful in this task. However, there are a number of ways of retelling stories that are specifically for such helpless tales as this one. They include helplessness inoculation, independence training for the elderly in institutions, and practice in taking responsibility for monitoring and maintaining their own health. Ways of story retelling more directly involving younger people as well as the elderly include techniques to help them break down their isolation and build better ties with their families.

A form of stress inoculation has been developed with the aim of changing helpless elderly people into resourceful people.[9] This technique has much in common with rational emotive therapy.[10] It focuses on their appraisal of the events with which they have to deal and of their own capacity to cope with them, their learning and trying out of new skills.[11] That appraisal is, of course, carried out by telling short stories about self in relation to the relevant events. Different stories are useful at different stages of the coping process.[12-14] During preparation, these kinds of story work against the more helpless story: "I can develop a plan. I'll just think about it first. I feel anxious because I want to do well, and that's in my favour." During the actual event, these stories will be effective: "I'm in control. One step at a time. I can do it. My anxiety is a way of reminding me that I am making a big effort." There are stories, too, that can deal effectively with feelings of being overwhelmed: "I'll just deal with the here and now. It will be over soon." There are also self-congratulatory stories that underline successes: "I did it! It gets easier every time!" These views of themselves as competent can become available to the elderly who retell this story of helplessness if they choose to use them.

Mrs Q, still looking after her cantankerous 90-year-old mother, could have benefited from this approach. Her story appeared at the beginning of this chapter. The physical symptoms of blindness and paralysis that she had had in the face of earlier stress had supported well her telling of her helpless story at that time. It was important then to provide her with some concrete tools to deal with some of the helplessness she was feeling, in case such physical expressions of helplessness started to overtake her again.

Living in institutions, whether hostels or nursing homes, has been shown to promote this kind of story being told by the elderly.[15] A kind of independence training has been developed, therefore, which creates opportunities for the elderly to make more choices and take more responsibility.[16] For example, they can be offered a variable range of menu items from which to choose. They can also be encouraged to grow plants or even keep a small and non-threatening pet, for which they themselves take the responsibility of providing water and food. A change of surroundings can supply these opportunities but, because of their physical frailty, the elderly often resist moving. They can also be encouraged to test their own ways of being independent in a therapeutic relationship with a therapist. Often a professional therapist is needed, not so much to provide special techniques to overcome helplessness but to give permission to the elderly person to try out less dependent versions of this story.

Most of us feel helpless when we are ill. The elderly are more often ill than most of us, and so have many sources of validation for this type of story. In this situation they can become dependent on their care-givers. However, there are methods that they can use to deal with this.[17–19] Taking some control in the relationship between patient and health professional, be it with a nurse, social worker, occupational therapist, physiotherapist or even medical practitioner, is one such method. Elderly people who are ill can ask to be shown the treatment options open to them and to participate in their selection. They can also choose to work on keeping the parts of their bodies not affected by the illness or injury as healthy and functioning as well as possible, and retell their helpless stories by success in this area. Recognising that control, especially of illness, is not all-or-none but a matter of degree can be helpful for them, as can establishing control over other areas of their lives. Those experiences intrinsic to being seriously ill, such as waiting for appointments and transport, which are also fraught with helplessness, can be modified by effectively predicting them and planning strategies to deal with them.

Breaking down the social isolation that can accompany this story is also possible. It is often experienced by elderly people who feel estranged from, misunderstood by, or rejected by, others. They lack appropriate partners for the activities they want to pursue, particularly activities that provide them with a sense of sharing with others and developing an intimate relationship. Two methods to deal with such a version of this story, then, involve changing the elderly who tell it in some way, but the third involves changing their social context. Changing elderly clients includes developing their social skills and retelling some of their stories about other people,[19] as well as providing them with opportunities to mourn their losses.[20] Changing their social context involves restructuring their current interactions with others and increasing their support networks.[21] Mrs Q told her story of isolation even though she lives with many other people. Her social skills, not used for years, could have benefited from some retraining, as well as from the retelling of her deprived and resentful story about those close to her. She could also gain from changing her current ways of interacting with them and, from having permanent or, at least, respite professional care established for her mother. She needed, too, to mourn the loss of her old enthusiasm and energy. She could use the newly available time and strength to seek among local walking and card-playing groups, other sources of support for herself and her retold stories.

Building better ties with more flexibly functioning families is also possible for the elderly people who tell this story.[22,23] This was much needed by Mrs U, whose story was also told at the beginning of this chapter, with her continual arguments with her daughter and son. Her subplot for this story involved rejection by them. Personal construct therapy for the family would, of course, require all family members to meet with a therapist. This is not easy to arrange, especially when their interactions are marked by anger. Had Mrs U's children, and husband, been available, their stories about family life could also have been examined. It is very likely that they would have expressed parallel construing to that of their mother, that is, they would tell of her as rejecting them and consequently also feel deprived as well as angry. If all of the family members, including Mrs U, were then able to reflect on their construing, they could then conclude that it would interfere with their relationships with each other and could choose to resolve to provide no more validation for it.

Suggested reading

- *Some physical effects of telling the story*

1. Seligman, M.E.P. & Garber, J. (Eds.) (1980). *Human helplessness: Theory and applications*. New York: Academic Press.
2. Hutschnecker, A.A. (1981). *Hope*. New York: Putnam.
3. Matheny, K.B. & Cypp, P. (1983). Control, desirability, and anticipation as moderating variables between life change and illness. *Journal of Human Stress*, **2**, 14–23.
4. Lachman, M.E. (1986). Locus of control in ageing: A case for multi-dimensional and domain specific assessment. *Psychology and Ageing*, **1**, 12–18.
5. Wan, T.H., Odell, B.G. & Lewis, D.T. (1982). *Promoting the well-being of the elderly: A community diagnosis*. New York: Howarth Press.
6. Greer, S., Morris, T. & Pettingale, K.W. (1982). Psychological response to breast cancer: Effect on outcome. *Lancet*, **111**, 785–787.
7. Viney, L.L. & Westbrook, M.T. (1982). Psychological reactions to chronic illness: Do they predict rehabilitation? *Journal of Applied Rehabilitation Counselling*, **13**, 38–44.
8. Chapman, S.L. & Brena, S.I. (1982). Learned helplessness and responses to nerve blocks in chronic low back pain patients. *Pain*, **14**, 355–364.

- *Retelling the story*

9. Meichenbaum, D. (1977). *Cognitive-behaviour modification: An integrative approach*. New York: Plenum Press.

10. Ellis, A. (1984). The essence of R.E.T.—1984. *Journal of Rational-Emotive Therapy*, **2**, 19–26.
11. Dush, D.M., Hirt, M.L. & Schroeder, H. (1983). Self statement modification with adults: A meta analysis. *Psychological Bulletin*, **94**, 408–422.
12. Gallagher, D.E. & Thompson, L.W. (1983). Effectiveness of psychotherapy for both indigenous and nonindigenous depression in older adult outpatients. *Journal of Gerontology*, **38**, 707–712.
13. Marmar, G.R., Easton, L. & Gallagher, D. (1989). Absence and outcome in late life depression. *Journal of Nervous & Mental Disease*, **177**, 464–472.
14. Moorey, S. & Greer, S. (1987). *Adjuvant psychological therapy: A manual for the treatment of patients with cancer*. London: Cancer Research Campaign Psychological Medicine Group.
15. Oberleder, M. (1966). Psychotherapy with the ageing: An art of the possible. *Psychotherapy*, **3**, 139–142.
16. Rodin, J. (1980). Managing the stress of ageing: The role of control and coping. In S. Levine & H. Ursin (Eds.), *Coping and health*. New York: Plenum.
17. Bannister, D. (1975). Personal construct psychotherapy. In D. Bannister (Ed.), *Issues and approaches in psychological therapies*. Chichester: Wiley.
18. Fransella, F. (1972). *Personal change and reconstruction: Research and treatment of stuttering*. London: Academic Press.
19. Kelly, G.A. (1955). *The psychology of personal constructs*. New York: Norton.
20. Sholomska, S.A.J., Chevron, E.S., Prusoff, D. & Berry, C. (1983). Short-term interpersonal therapy (IPT) with the depressed elderly: Case reports and discussion. *American Journal of Psychotherapy*, **37**, 552–566.
21. Rook, K.S. (1984). Promoting social bonding: Strategies for helping the lonely and socially isolated. *American Psychologist*, **39**, 1389–1407.
22. Proctor, H. (1985). A construct approach to family therapy. In E. Button (Ed.), *Personal construct theory and mental illness*. Beckenham: Croom Helm.
23. Viney, L.L., Benjamin, Y.N. & Preston, C. (1988). Constructivist family therapy with the elderly. *Journal of Family Psychology*, **2**, 241–258.

6 "I worry about the future"

In this chapter I deal with another self-limiting and distressing story that elderly people tell: "I worry about the future." This story, too, I shall analyse in some detail, beginning with a number of different versions of it. Then two elderly people, in somewhat different situations, show something of its meaning for each of them. Analysis of the personal aspects of such story telling follow: their presentation of themselves and age-related events, the psychological needs the story meets for them, its implications for their emotions and actions, and the way it links their present, past and future. The social aspects of the story to be considered are its interpersonal context, who supports it and to whom it allocates power. The cultural aspects of the story include the information it provides for people who hear it, and the values on which it rests. After such detailed analysis, the research literature on the physical effects of such a story on its tellers is reviewed. Finally, some ways in which this story can be retold are provided.

"I worry about the future"

This story can be about niggling, specific concerns, or anxiety about larger, more diffuse issues. Some examples of specific concerns follow. "I think a lot about what might happen." "I worry that things won't work out." "It's a horrible thing I'm faced with." "We could have moved into a new unit, but when I thought about it, well, we'd be further from the family and they mightn't visit us so much; and we'd be further from the shops . . . And the stairs might be too much for Norm and we might loose our spot of sun in the mornings . . . And then there's the neighbours, we'd miss them . . . " This last example came from an elderly woman who, in her concern about the effect of a move to more physically suitable accommodation, was almost obsessive in her hanging on to legitimate worries that might protect her from testing out a new way of life. Such concerns can also be linked with suspiciousness: "I couldn't use a house cleaning service. It would mean having strangers in; and I'd have to worry all the time about my valuables."

This story can also express anxiety of a more diffuse kind. "I don't know what's going to happen to me." "I get so tense at times. I don't know why." "We can't know what's going to happen in the end." In personal construct terms, people feel anxious when they realise that their system of constructs cannot make current events meaningful or anticipate future ones. For the elderly, then, with complex systems of constructs developed over a lifetime of experiences, this feeling is probably rarer than it is for younger people. However, there are a number of losses which most elderly people anticipate, that are so unique as to make meaningful interpretation difficult, even for them.

Loss of close family members will probably have been dealt with by them before, but loss of parents they have grown away from is very different from loss of spouse whom they have grown with. So is losing contemporary friends different from losing friends of parents. "I think a lot about losing Bill (her husband), and it shakes me up completely." Loss of physical ability and strength also is relatively unlikely to have been experienced before, except for very short periods as a result of illness. "I wonder what life will be like if I decline physically; and it really scares me." These losses may not actually occur, but it is anticipating them that is so frightening. The most anxiety-arousing, however, which is inevitable for us all, is death. This is partly because, not having experienced it yet, none of us can be sure what happens at death. "There are days when I can feel an awful shadow of death on me."

There is another potential loss which some elderly can face. They are people who have achieved some balance of integrity against despair, but are much threatened by the possible return of despair. They have been able to maintain their wisdom, accept themselves and others and perceive some meaning in their lives. However, they acknowledge that their wisdom can deteriorate to disdain, they can become very self-critical and critical of others; and they can lose the meaningfulness of their lives. "I know I do have times when I have nothing to live for." They may, alternatively, be aware of their tendencies to assume a compulsive pseudo-integrity or a dogmatism in the face of despair. They also know that caring can become rejecting, being faithful can become undermining, feeling competent can become inertia, and, perhaps most of all, hope can become passive withdrawal. "I am very fond of the grandchildren; but, sometimes, when they run in all excited, I just want to say: Go away! I'm not up to it. I just don't have anything left for anybody today."

Two clients tell the story

The accounts of a woman and a man who told different versions of this story—"I worry about the future"—will help in understanding it. Mrs O, 72-years-old, had recently had one leg amputated above the knee, and was returning from the rehabilitation hospital to live at home. She was referred for therapy because of lack of confidence since the operation. It was apparent that little family support was available to her during this difficult time, because her husband and both of her sisters had died within the past 2 years, and her two children were living hundreds of kilometres away in other states. Her main source of support appeared to be her church group. In her first sessions with her therapist she was very much preoccupied with the physical aspects of her experience: the apparently poor fit of her prosthesis, headaches, pains in her hands and her need for a new prescription for her glasses. "I've always been a worrier," she said, "I've always been like this; and I'm too old to change." She also described how, now, when she goes outside her home, she feels "churned up" and worries that she is so slow, that she might fall, and about the cost of the surgery and subsequent rehabilitation services. For these reasons, her therapeutic work was carried out in her home, by a visiting social worker.

Mr N, at 86, was considerably older. He was a pensioner living in a pleasant hostel unit, with his family readily available. He was referred to us because of his anxiety and depression. His wife had died only 12 months before. Only 3 years before she had, after brain surgery, suffered from dementia, and he had been successful in finding good nursing home accommodation for her and hostel accommodation for himself in the same retirement village. When he first came to the village he sang in its choir and played indoor bowls, making several friends of his own age. Recently however, he had withdrawn both physically and psychologically. When his therapist, a community nurse, first saw him, which was in his unit, he was in pyjamas and in bed. He felt cold; his eyes were expressionless, and his face seemed to have fallen in. "I don't want to live. I don't care what happens to me. They can do what they want." He was in the grip of despair, severe anxiety and lack of faith in self and others. He was withdrawn and inert in response to his serious concerns about the future.

Some personal aspects of the story

Self

This story, "I worry about the future", presents its tellers in a less narrow range of ways than the story, "Sometimes I feel as if life isn't worthwhile", of the previous chapter. They are not necessarily so passive, since they do "worry". "Worrying about" things is not far removed from "worrying at" them, which can be quite active and even fruitful. The quality of the experiences of the tellers becomes of concern as the "worrying" becomes more repetitive and circular. "Worrying" that is driven or compulsive also brings back the concept of the essentially passive teller, acted on by circumstances or largely uncontrollable internal mechanisms. There is, in this story, also an anticipation of the future, which suggest that its tellers are active in reaching out in that way.

Age-related events

It is the age-related events of disability, lack of financial viability, bereavement, death and loss of integrity in their future, that the tellers of this story view with such concern. Many elderly people can accept that they will experience such events; and I shall present some of the more self-fulfilling and enjoyable stories they tell in the face of them in the next section of this book. Others, however, become fixated on what evils might befall them and feel they have no ability to change this fixation. The focus of their experiences becomes the more unpleasant events of their age, and their stories centre on them.

The psychological functions of the story

This story fulfils certain psychological functions for the elderly who tell it. Like the story of the previous chapter, when this one is told in the personal style of the teller, it can help to maintain his or her identity. This is the case, in fact, for all of the stories told by the elderly. It also enables its tellers to acknowledge their own concerns, an improvement on being affected by them without being able to identify or articulate them. A further version of the story can even involve some helpful expression of emotions, such as anxiety, or catharsis, which often aids in the process of retelling stories, like this one, that need to be retold. The story also enables its tellers to take some personal responsibility for the events that occur as they age. This sense of responsibility can help people to make changes in their lives when they feel they are necessary.

The implications of the story for the emotions and behaviour of the teller

Most stories have implications for the emotions experienced by and the actions taken by the elderly people who tell them. This story is told by people who have many everyday, specific worries, as well as by those with more general and pervasive anxiety. The worrying can be associated with repeated thoughts and compulsion to check and recheck or with suspicion and anger. The anxiety, while sometimes intense and overwhelming, is linked with those future losses and subsequent depression which the elderly tellers fear. This story, then, involves some powerful emotions, as well as some important implications for behaviour. Its tellers are already active in their "worrying", which involves many physiological responses that prepare them for coping with events. These responses can be experienced as muscle tension, sweating and "butterflies in the tummy", amongst other things. The question of interest to the therapist is whether the physical preparation involved in "worrying" is used to act decisively, or whether the elderly tellers get side-tracked on to a version of this story in which they keep worrying without using this state to help them to act effectively.

Past, present and future

Because this story is based almost entirely in the future, it provides for its tellers very few links of the past and present with that future. If their focus is on the future alone, they deprive themselves, in a sense, of the benefits of their past learnings. People whose main story is "I worry about the future" have little access to past occasions when they dealt effectively with disruptive and distressing events. They also lack any sense of oneness, or the integrity, of their own present, past and future. This is in contrast to the previous story, "Sometimes I feel as if life isn't worthwhile", in which the past and present were related closely to each other, but the future was unconnected and so unpredictable.

Some social aspects of the story

Its interpersonal context

This story was told quite often to other people. Sometimes this was to family members and friends; sometimes to health professionals, such as visiting nurses and general practitioners; sometimes it was to husband or wife or very close friend. In each of these contexts the effects of telling this story varied somewhat. To family and professionals, it often communicated about the necessarily different needs that each of these groups could fulfil. When told to someone very close, however, it was received less as a statement of need and more as a confirmation of the closeness of that relationship. In that last context no further action was seen as necessary.

Sources of validation for the story

The main sources for validation of this story did not lie with the tellers, as for the previous story, but with the three groups of listeners to it that I have just described. This meant that invalidation of this story was possible, even though it was not so for the earlier one. If the "worries" of which the elderly tell are unlikely, can be avoided or can be handled effectively, then family members, professionals and those close to them have the opportunity to provide relevant feedback about this to the story teller.

Power in the story

In the self-limiting story examined in the last chapter, no power was allocated to the tellers, only to their ageing bodies, families and health professionals. In the present story, "I worry about the future", some power to reflect, to think, to feel and to agitate has been assigned. However, this story can become empowering to its tellers only if they move on from this initial reflection and agitation to act on their sources of worry. Without this step, they are as helpless as the tellers of the first story.

Some cultural aspects of the story

Information

The information this story provides is partially, as for the earlier story, self-knowledge for the tellers. They learn or confirm that they have concerns, of either a specific or vague kind. However, this story, like many we tell, also provides information for others. It enables the elderly to share with others what is troubling them. This is a necessary preamble to having others do something about these problems. It also specifically points to the future rather than focusing on the present alone, which also may be effective in having something done. A range of knowledge for self and others is provided, then, by this story.

Values

This story is squarely based on a central Western value: to anticipate is to be human. This is also a fundamental assumption of personal construct therapy. Any person who is alive will be trying to interpret what is happening to them now and predict what will happen in the future. However, anticipation for the elderly reaches out into some pretty unknown and forbidding frontiers, such as physical disability and the processes of dying. So much of this is unknown territory that it becomes far too threatening to many younger potential listeners to this story. In some circumstances, elderly people telling this story can be so threatening to younger people that they are no longer heard. The result is the alienation of the elderly that can be seen in many Western societies. It is important that therapists working with elderly clients can recognise and handle this threat. In the last chapter of this book I shall deal with this issue in more detail.

Some physical effects of telling the story

The worry and anxiety that are the focus of this story have been associated in the literature for some 30 years with increased vulnerability to illness and with the onset of certain diseases.[1] People telling the story have been more open to infection, more liable to develop gastrointestinal problems, such as ulcers, and more likely to suffer from hypertension and heart disease.[2] Heart disease has been studied in more detail than other illnesses, and it seems that it may be stimulated by the way people manage their anxiety.[3] If they ignore and deny it, they may experience no anxiety, but their bodies will react as if they are ready to cope with threat.[4] It is probably this constant readiness to deal with stress without a controlling awareness of it which imposes too much strain on the cardiovascular system.

The evidence for the links between anxiety and vulnerability to illness are convincing and point to ways of retelling anxiety-based stories like this one. Somewhat surprisingly, because anxiety is so distressing, it seems that for people who are already ill the effects of telling some parts of this story are to encourage quicker recovery and more successful rehabilitation. It seems in dealing with the stresses of illness and injury, as with other sources of stress, too little or too much can make for difficulties. A moderate amount of manageable anxiety can be helpful. People who tell anxiety-acknowledging stories have been found to have recovered more quickly from surgery[5] and to have survived cancer longer than those who do not.[6] A similar effect on rehabilitation has been found for heart conditions, as well as for a range of chronic illnesses.[7] The only research disputing these claims has been for people with heart problems who told this story and subsequently had a more complicated recovery in hospital than those who did not.[8]

Retelling the story

In this story, "I worry about the future", the elderly present themselves as not so passive as in the self-limiting story of Chapter 5. They are people who can feel but also, potentially at least, can act as a result of that feeling, even if it is one of distress. They are concerned about age-related losses of friends, lovers, homes, physical agility and financial viability. Fixation on these distressing events is possible when this story is told. However, in terms of personal gains from this story, it does permit acknowledgement of distressing feelings, which is necessary to any attempt to cope. This story involves both specific worries and vague anxiety, if these states lead to effective behaviour, much can be achieved; yet they can involve an almost circular and debilitating cycle as the "worrying" goes on and on and on. Because this story is based in the future, it provides for its tellers few links with their past and present, usually an important function of people's stories.

Socially, this story, unlike the first, was often told to others, thereby opening up opportunities for validation or invalidation by family, health professionals and those very close. It allocates some power to its tellers. Culturally, it provides useful information on which others can act and is based on that important human quality of anticipation. Unfortunately, however, by asking others to anticipate dealing with disability and dying, it can result in the alienation of its elderly tellers from their hearers. In terms of the physical effects of this story, it seems that some worry and anxiety can be helpful in avoiding illness and aiding recovery, but only if the anxiety acknowledged is not overwhelming.

Some of the most useful ways of retelling this story, when the anxiety it contains is overwhelming, involve dealing with clinical denial and avoidance of the worries and anxiety integral to it and encouraging their identification and acceptance. However, anxiety that is threatening to overwhelm elderly clients is best modified by the strategy shared with most clients who are anxious, differential muscle relaxation. Deep breathing is also helpful. The use of these techniques to retell the story, "I am anxious about the future", is described here for Mrs O, who was introduced earlier in this chapter. The retelling of her short stories, a technique used with the helpless story of the last chapter, also proved useful. Mr N, the other client introduced in this chapter, shows that the use of reminiscence leads to his retelling of his withdrawn version of this story.

Avoidance of anxiety and denial of its cause can be acceptable for elderly people coping with stressful events, so long as there is no useful way to deal with those threats.[9] However, if these people can act to help themselves, avoidance and denial take this opportunity away from them. The split that exists between their stories and actual events becomes too wide. They can no longer cope realistically; and more anxiety arises from this failure.[10] The way to help such elderly clients out of such a vicious circle is to help them focus on their strengths. Often when people are able to remember how well they coped with other events, it gives them strength to cope with the current one. Sometimes, too, they find that some coping strategy that worked for them before will work with current events.

There is another form of avoidance and denial that elderly people sometimes use when faced with, for example, severe illness. It is not the anxiety that they do not acknowledge, but rather the part of their body that is causing them anxiety. For example, an elderly man in hospital with a diseased tibia said: "I'd rather go to the bathroom than have a bed pan; but the leg won't let me." The offending leg was not being recognised by him as his own leg, connected to his body, but an alien object over which he had no control. This psychological lack of body integrity seems unlikely to promote healing. A therapist working with such a client would take care to provide such integrity in his stories about the client; for example, "Is that because your leg is painful?" Drawing a picture of themselves to include the body part can lead to better bodily integrity, since, while telling a non-verbal story of this kind, they often amplify it verbally with accounts of their construing of that body part, their treatment and their chances of recovery.[9]

Differential muscle relaxation proved to be an extremely useful tool with Mrs O, a recent leg amputee now trying to learn to live at home alone. It involves learning to relax specific muscle groups at will, until a general relaxation has been achieved.[11] Mrs O was provided with a tape of relaxation instructions with which she was asked to practice every day initially, and later twice a week. She found this relaxation effective from the first, which helped her get enough practice with the tape for her muscle groups to learn the progressive relaxation responses. She was also shown how taking slow, regular and deep breaths could calm her; but she found this less helpful, unless she was lying down. With other elderly clients telling this anxiety-based story, this breathing technique can be a very effective way of becoming able to retell that story.

Yet another tool for this purpose is the retelling of the much shorter anxiety-based stories which everyone tells themselves as they deal with events.[12-15] Mrs. O also provides an example of the use of this technique. As she told her therapist of her efforts to make use of the physical support of other people when she moved out beyond her home, many of them ended disastrously in falls or misunderstandings. Some of her short stories told only to herself during these events included "You're a cripple" and "You should hurry up." They were clearly engendering psychological tension that then led to physical tension as well, hence the falls and misunderstandings. Here was another self-defeating cycle. She was therefore encouraged to tell herself instead "You're going really well" and "There's no hurry." Within weeks of using these techniques she seemed more relaxed and positive, and was able to risk testing her new stories, firstly, at the supermarket and then at the hairdresser. While initially with her success she tended to thank her therapist profusely, Mrs. O was later able to see that she was the only person who could retell her own stories. This acknowledgement of self as construer and reconstruer by clients is crucial, of course, for the gains of therapy to be maintained.

Reminiscence can also provide opportunities to retell this anxiety-based story.[16-18] This was effective with Mr N, whose withdrawal in the face of his anxieties about the future made more client-dependent techniques like relaxation inappropriate, at least at first. The first invitations by his therapist to: "Tell me about the old days" were ignored. However, when he eventually did begin to talk, it was about an early job he had at the mines, looking after the pit ponies. He talked a little about how hard the conditions were for workers, but, on the positive side, about how that job had actually kept him from having to go underground. In subsequent therapy sessions, at which he appeared dressed, he explored many events in his early family life, often repeating himself. The common theme that emerged from these reminiscences was one of rejection, not necessarily of himself, but of other family members. He dwelt many times, for example, on how his mother had been refused communion by the Church of England because she was not a communicating member. He later related this to his relationship with his two estranged sons. He was becoming able to move easily between these events, seeing their loose links and the choices they represented for him.

One day, however, when his therapist arrived he had withdrawn back to his bed where he was lying passively again. His therapist discussed with him the choices he now had available to him: essentially between "lying down" (or dying) and "standing up being counted" (or living). She left his room for him to make a decision; and an hour later he emerged, showered and shaved and ready for lunch in the dining room. On her next visit she found him up, talkative and cheerful about his son who had come to see him. "I did some painting yesterday. It was alright. I painted mountains and a sun. It was supposed to be our states of mind. Come and I'll show you . . . " How Mr N used reminiscence to explore loosely the issues that were important to him was not entirely clear then to his therapist. Nor are they to me; but use them he did.

Suggested reading

● *Some physical effects of telling the story*

1. Viney, L.L. (1989). *Images of illness*. Florida: Krieger, Second edition.
2. Shapiro, A.P. (1978). Behavioural and environmental aspects of hypertension. *Journal of Human Stress*, 4, 9–17.
3. Siegrist, J.S. & Halhuber, M.J. (Eds.) (1981). *Myocardial infarction and psychosocial risks*. New York: Springer.
4. Radley, A.R. & Green, R. (1985). Styles of adjustment to coronary graft surgery. *Social Science and Medicine*, 20, 461–472.
5. Johnson, M. & Carpenter, L. (1980). Pre-operative anxiety. *Psychological Medicine*, 10, 361–367.
6. Derogatis, L.R., Abeloff, M.D. & Melisaratos, N. (1979). Psychological coping mechanisms and survival time in metastatic breast cancer. *Journal of the American Medical Association*, 242, 1504–1508.
7. Viney, L.L. & Westbrook, M.T. (1982). Psychological reactions to chronic illness: Do they predict rehabilitation? *Journal of Applied Rehabilitation Counselling*, 13, 38–44.

8. Blumenthal, J.A., Thompson, L.W., Williams, R.B. & Kong, Y. (1979). Anxiety-proneness and coronary heart disease. *Journal of Psychosomatic Research*, **23**, 17–21.

● *Retelling the story*

9. Viney, L.L. (1989). *Images of illness*. Florida: Krieger, Second edition.
10. Viney, L.L. (1986). Physical illness: A guidebook for the kingdom of the sick. In E. Button (Ed.), *Personal construct theory and mental health*. Beckenham: Croom Helm.
11. Rimm, D.C. & Masters, J.C. (1979). *Behaviour therapy*. New York: Academic Press.
12. Ellis, A. (1984). The essence of R.E.T.—1984. *Journal of Rational-Emotive Therapy*, **2**, 19–26.
13. Forester, B., Kornfeld, D.S. & Fleiss, J. (1982). Effects of psychotherapy on patient distress during radiotherapy for cancer. *Psychosomatic Medicine*, **44**, 118–126.
14. Greer, S. & Moorey, S. (1987). Advanced psychological therapy for patients with cancer. *European Journal of Surgical Oncology*, **13**, 511–516.
15. Keller, J.F., Croake, J.W. & Brooking, J.Y. (1975). Effects of a programme in rational thinking on anxieties in older persons. *Journal of Counselling Psychology*, **22**, 54–57.
16. Leitner, L.M. (1982). Literalism, perspectivism, chaotic fragmentalism and psychotherapy techniques. *British Journal of Medical Psychology*, **55**, 307–317.
17. Rowe, D. (1987). *Beyond fear*. London: Fontana.
18. Viney, L.L., Benjamin, Y.N. & Preston, C. (1988). Mourning and reminiscence: Parallel therapeutic experiences for the elderly. *International Journal of Ageing and Human Development*, **28**, 237–249.

7 "I don't want to be a burden to anyone"

The story examined in the last chapter, "I worry about the future", expresses the distress of the elderly who tell it, yet it also provides some basis for action. While it can be associated with their dwelling on age-related losses, it permits the tellers to acknowledge their own anxiety and worries. The story of this chapter, "I don't want to be a burden to anyone", is the last of these self-limiting stories that I shall examine in detail. As with the two earlier stories, a number of different versions of it are provided first. Then I tell the stories of two elderly clients, making clear the different situations which gave rise to this tale. The personal aspects of the story are examined, including how the elderly clients present themselves and age-related events, which psychological needs the story meets, its implications for their emotions and actions, and the links it provides for them between present, past and future. The social aspects of the story include its interpersonal context, who supports it and to whom it allocates power; while its cultural aspects involve the information it provides and the values it represents. As in earlier chapters, I examine the literature about the effects of the story on its tellers , as well as describe some strategies for its retelling.

"I don't want to be a burden to anyone"

The main different versions of this story focus on the social isolation of its tellers, their detachment, their underlying anxiety and their attempts to deal with major losses, such as disability and death. "I'm all alone, and I wouldn't like to have to rely on anyone now." "I hardly ever see anyone these days. Perhaps it's just as well, I wouldn't have much to offer them." "The family doesn't come to see me any more. They're busy with their own lives." "I used to go to the club each week; but I don't get out much any more." "No-one wants to spend time with an old person." "I had a really lovely woman to come in and help with the house, but she was killed in a car accident and I wouldn't like to ask anyone else to do it all."

The versions of this story based on detachment provides a contrast with these isolation versions just listed. While for the former stories the isolation is often imposed by others, in the detached stories it is more likely to be caused by the elderly clients themselves: "I used to have a lot of friends and a very busy social life. Now it just doesn't seem worth the effort." "I don't see many people these days apart from the family." "I'd rather read or watch the telly." "People aren't as important to me as they used to be. I have my interests, like the horses. And as long as I can get a few bets on each week, I'm O.K." "My daughter and I have never seen eye to eye, right from when she was a tiny child. I don't worry about her nonsense these days."

There is also a version of this story that is laden with anxiety, in contrast to the final version of the story above which was laden with anger. Relationships may now have become, or always have been, primarily sources of risk rather than of support and confirmation for the elderly person. This feeling is often expressed by denial that there is loneliness. "I don't need people. I can manage very well without them." "I'm fine on my own." Then there are versions that admit more directly to this fear. "I have never been much good with people; and now I find it easier just to avoid them." "I'd rather not have the hassles seeing more of my family might bring." "Close relationships have always taken a lot out of me, and I just don't have the energy for them now."

Disability resulting from illness is one of the chief causes of isolation in the elderly. It is central to many versions of this story. "Healthy people don't understand what its like to be ill; so they can't really help you." "I can't tell my husband about my diabetes." "Don't depend on your family. I've learned that from my heart attack." "Nobody wants you if you're going to be grizzling all the time." "People stare at you when you're in a wheelchair. I don't like that, so I don't go out." "There was no-one I could talk to about what was happening to me." Elderly people who are dealing with illness, then, can be especially concerned to see that they do not become a burden to others—family and friends as well as health professionals. "I don't tell the doctor about all of my little problems. I mean, I don't want to worry him."

Just as people who grow older worry about being "a burden" to others in the event of disability, they also worry that they might be a burden when they die. "I just hope when I die I don't have to lie on the floor for days before someone finds me. I don't want that." "I've thought of all the preparation I can make—the will, the burial service, the money for my coffin—and I think I've got it pretty well organised. I wouldn't want the wife to have to worry about it all when I go." "I don't want to cause any trouble when I die—just in my sleep would be best, I think." If life is a story that we can each choose to live in our own individual way, then death provides the final challenge to be integrated into that story we have created. Some people will want that phase of the story to fit with those that come earlier, for example, continuing a tale of independence and self-reliance.

Two clients tell the story

I have chosen two women clients to show how quite different situations can lead to this story being told. The first, Mrs M, at 65 years of age, had recently had surgery for cancer in one of her legs and had become somewhat disabled. As a result of "the leg" she felt handicapped and mutilated. She was a widow and socially isolated, her only contacts with people having been through her part-time job which she had just given up. She was critical of her daughter, whom she described as "bombastic", and reported shoulder, neck and head pain after talking to her, even on the telephone. It became apparent to her therapist, a welfare worker, that Mrs M was not asking people for what she wanted—neither family nor friends—and so she was not getting it. Even the visits to the family physician she had for decades were a trial for her. "I don't tell him about my problems. I don't want to be a burden to anyone." She and her therapist worked together in Mrs M's home.

Mrs B, at 86 years, was older and more frail. She was, however, also a widow, and similarly isolated. She wanted to stay in her own house, but her son's family wanted her to move in with them. She had grounds for doubting whether they would provide what she wanted, since they rarely visited her. Also, in spite of having left their goats in her backyard for her to look after, they had provided no help with yard chores or even repairs to her house. She revealed considerable guilt over her role in the deaths of her daughter, husband and father and a perhaps consequent fear of dying alone. The reasons for her guilt will become apparent during therapy. This was the only factor which prompted her to consider moving in with them; but she wanted very much to make it alone. Yet, as she said: "I'm proud. I want people to remember me as strong." Such stories are very difficult to change and also set very demanding standards to meet. Because keeping her house running was getting beyond Mrs B physically, she had tried state-provided home-help. However, when this did not work well, she did nothing to ensure that she continued to have help. One of her versions of this story she told in relation to that home help: "I didn't want to complain . . ." She and her therapist, also a welfare worker, worked in her home. Helping her in this context proved to involve putting up again, on a precarious ladder, her bedroom curtains that had fallen off their tracking, and cutting the beak of her budgerigar which had grown dangerously long.

Some personal aspects of the story

Self

The first self-defeating story of this section of the book, "Sometimes I feel as if life isn't worthwhile", has been seen to present its elderly tellers as passive, unsuccessful, disabled victims of fate. The second, "I worry about the future", has provided a role for them which, while equally distressing, can involve some action. This one, "I don't want to be a burden to anyone", also allows for some action. In fact, it can provide a powerful motive for actively coping with age-related events. There are three aspects of this story that do, however, make it self-defeating. The first self-defeating aspect is the isolation which can be an important part of it: "I must not" or "I cannot rely on anyone else." It is easy, given the unflattering stories told about the elderly that I identified in the first chapter of this book, to imagine the gradual alienation from community, professional support and even family that could lead to this story of isolation. Its second self-defeating aspect is the lack of self-respect it can reflect. "I am not worth the time and concern of others." The third self-defeating aspect can be guilt. "I do not deserve their consideration." "I couldn't meet the families' needs at times, so why should they meet mine."

Age-related events

In this story the focus on age-related events, to the exclusion of others, as in the earlier two self-defeating stories is overly selective and limiting. Many of these events, such as having grandchildren and great grandchildren, can be sources of enjoyment and pride for the elderly, and also for those who share their lives with them. However, the elderly whose main story is, "I don't want to be a burden to anyone", are not focusing on these happy events but on those, such as disability and death, that are traumatic and troubling. It is in this way that the isolation, noted earlier, arises.

The psychological functions of the story

Like the earlier stories examined in this section, the telling of this story helps to confirm the identity of those who tell it. This is partly because, in it, they can use their personal style but it is also because this story defines its teller as a particular type of person, an independent person. Here the tellers take responsibility for what is happening to them. However, this responsibility can be hazardous to them if the physical, psychological, social or financial constraints on them make it difficult for them to act on that sense of responsibility. It can also protect them from having to put their ability to trust others to the test.

Implications of the story for the emotions and behaviour of the teller

While the earlier self-defeating stories reviewed have clearly had strong emotional components, this one seems to be, at one level at least, an attempt to avoid distressing emotions. At another level, however, two sets of emotions seem to pervade it. The first consists of loneliness and isolation, as a result of the alienation that many elderly tellers of this story experience. The second consists of depression and guilt, associated with lack of self-respect and of feelings of worth. Action can then result, but whether this action is effective or necessary seems unlikely in the face of these emotional clouds.

Past, present and future

This story, of the three self-defeating tales considered here, best links their present, past and futures together for its tellers. There is a sense in which this story shows its tellers to be currently strivers for their own independence. This striving, the story implies, has marked their past actions and will, if they have any say about it, go on to mark their future actions. Its tellers then have a powerful means to help them maintain their identities. However, if change in this construing of themselves is needed, and with many events of old age it is, then such a story could make change, especially in the form of story retelling, difficult.

Some social aspects of the story

Its interpersonal context

For this story, unlike the other self-defeating stories, an interpersonal context was essential. Without an audience this story was almost meaningless. Its chief function was to inform others about the strivings for independence of the tellers. It helped to make others dealing with elderly clients telling it examine carefully any actions of theirs which might invalidate such independence.

Sources of validation for the story

When an audience is crucial to a story such as this, it might be expected that support or invalidation of it should come from that audience. For some tellers this was true. They wanted, as for the anxiety-based story, opportunities for story retelling as a result of feedback from the audience of family members and health professionals. Other tellers of it, however, let avoiding being "a burden to anyone" rule out even feedback from others about their capabilities and opportunities. They were stuck, as a result, with a story that was very difficult to change.

Power in the story

For tellers of the earlier self-defeating stories there was considerable risk of powerlessness, although the anxiety-based story suggested some potential for empowerment. For this story, whether it allocated power to the teller or to age-related events depended on two different implicit meanings which now need to be identified. Some elderly clients told this story with an underlying sense that they could choose how independent they were going to be, or choose to be "a burden" if they judged it to be appropriate. More of its tellers, sadly, told it with the implicit meaning of feeling forced to avoid being "a burden". Theirs was, of course, an essentially powerless position.

Some cultural aspects of the story

Information

This story, like the earlier stories, provides self-knowledge for the tellers. It confirms at least at one level their view of themselves as independent and non-demanding. Whether it actually does so at a deeper level needs to be assessed by each therapist working with a client telling this story, as well as by the clients themselves. This tale also provides information for others, in its sign posts labelled "Keep off" and "I'd rather do it alone." Knowledge for both self and others is provided by this story too.

Values

Independence, the central value of this story, is much prized in our individualistic, free-enterprise Western societies. It is much less advanced in more communal-sharing Eastern societies. It is not, therefore, a universal human value. For us in recent decades it has taken on increasing importance in health and welfare work with the elderly, where it has become a crime to infringe their "independence". What does this word mean? For Western governments it tends to imply "financial viability", with a drive to maintain more to do with saving money than preserving the "independence" of the elderly. And what does "independence" mean to the elderly themselves? These meanings will be explored repeatedly in this book, as different clients struggle with it. The appropriateness of independence as a value on which to base work with the elderly, I shall deal with again when I consider the stories of therapists, rather than clients, in my last chapter.

Some physical effects of telling the story

The loneliness and isolation that are central to this story of not wanting to be "a burden" have been linked, in the research literature, with increased illness. Its tellers report more psychosomatic disorders.[1-5] They may also be more prone to heart disease then those who do not tell it.[6] They can also be more likely to have accidents producing injuries.[7] Reactions to stress which are not modified by good relationships with others seem to be important here.

Unfortunately the illnesses elderly people suffer seem likely to generate greater isolation for them.[8] People experience illness and injury alone. This is especially true if the illness changes their experiences or their ways of relating to others, as cancer can.[9] Hospitalisation of itself means isolation, especially for elderly patients who may find the routines and technologies of the hospital confusing. It can also disrupt family relationships. If their illness is short-lived, then elderly people can probably cope with such isolation; but if their illness is chronic, as that of many elderly clients is, then opportunities for retelling their stories in less isolated ways is much needed.[10]

Additional isolation as a result of illness is also bad for elderly clients in that it interferes with their recovery and rehabilitation.[2] Tellers of this story of isolation both develop more severe symptoms than elderly clients who do not tell them[4], and cope less well with the acute illness itself.[11] When it comes to the chronic illness common among the elderly, they benefit less from rehabilitation.

Retelling the story

In this story, "I don't want to be a burden to anyone", the elderly present themselves as isolated and lacking self worth. Its self-defeating aspects are, however, somewhat balanced by the way it pushes its tellers into action. The self-defeating character of this story comes in part from its focus on negative events to the exclusion of positive ones. It defines its tellers as independent people, but, in doing so, it may take on more responsibility for them than is appropriate. Further, any action that is taken as a result of this story seems unlikely to succeed, given the loneliness and depressive feelings underlying it. This story was told for the message of independence it conveyed to its audience. For some of its tellers, feedback from the audience of family and health professionals could be received and could provide opportunities for story retelling, but others were not really open to this feedback. This type of story has been linked with increased illness in its elderly tellers, as well as with poor recovery from illnesses. Unfortunately illness can lead to isolation for elderly clients, so that telling this story could lead to a never-ending cycle of illness and isolation.

Helping elderly clients learn to retell this story is, then, likely to be useful to them. A range of strategies for doing so follows. Firstly, I shall focus on individual therapy strategies using Mrs M and Mrs B as examples. Talking to the therapist in the role of confidante is one such strategy, and testing constructs of isolation with a therapist is another. How they were used with Mrs M will become apparent. Secondly, I shall describe how both help with coping with loss and subsequent guilt through sad reminiscence, and the use of creative, positive reminiscence were effective with Mrs B. Both of these forms of reminiscence can be useful with other elderly clients. I then conclude this section by considering self-help groups, both those which are professionally led and those led by peers.

Elderly clients who feel lonely are going to have difficulty trusting others to let them into their worlds. For therapists to provide merely a confidential and empathic ear, can go far to break down this story of not wanting to be "a burden" to anyone.[12] Mrs M, with her post-operative leg condition, was one who told this isolated story. Her welfare worker, in taking this listening role, was soon able to identify other stories of Mrs M's about her acting with purpose, and even making difficult requests of others. It required little more than the validation of her constructs of herself as capable from these older stories, to have Mrs M able to ask her landlord to provide a handrail for her back steps.

Getting clients to test their stories for their ability to predict effectively is another technique that has been used to break down this story.[13] Mrs M had been using her disabled leg to protect her from social interaction. Her testing of her constructs about this can be heard in this interchange with her welfare worker (WW) in the last of their six sessions.

WW.   What would you like the future to be like?
Mrs M.   A little bit busier.
WW.   And how can you make it that way?
Mrs M.   Well, it depends, when you are handicapped to the extent that I am, it's difficult to find the opportunities.
WW.   Do you have to find the opportunities? Couldn't you make the opportunities yourself?
Mrs M.   Well, yes, I suppose I could.
WW.   How could you do that?
Mrs M.   Oh, by ringing a nursing home, I suppose. I could offer to help out . . .

WW.   You don't sound very keen.

Mrs M. Oh, I suppose it's just with this leg, people would see me coming. And oh, I don't know. They'd think it's the blind leading the blind.

WW.   Well, if you were going to teach fitness or Olympic sprints, that might hold; but if you want to help out at a nursing home by playing the piano or reading to them, your "leg" is not really a good excuse, is it?

Mrs M. Well . . .

Her welfare worker then went on to talk of Mrs M's many talents, such as her lively mind and sense of humour, and how much she could, because of these, add to the lives of others. Mrs M did explore this venue of social contact and found it enjoyable and supportive of some of her most central constructs. By using some tapes with instructions for differential muscle relaxation, she became able sometimes to relax with her daughter. She also started to work on some other possible improvements to her life, getting her car repaired and starting a short language course.

Lonely stories like this one can be retold in three main ways. This can involve changing clients, for example, by providing them with relaxation training, as Mrs M's welfare worker did.[14] It can involve providing them with new opportunities for social contact,[15–17] as Mrs M's therapist also achieved with her. It involves too, helping clients to deal better with the interpersonal losses which have alienated them from others.[18,19] Mrs B, badgered to leave her home by the family from which she was quite alienated, needed further work on her losses. She was experiencing much guilt associated with these losses of daughter, husband and even father. Her welfare worker first used with her the life review[20] approach to sad reminiscence, as they sipped the tea that Mrs B had made together, but was later able to use those reminiscences more creatively.

Mrs B.   This is the day, the exact day, my husband died. Thirty years ago now. He used to work at the foundry up at ____ and he drove a car that wasn't much good. And one day they just rang me from his work and said: "Ella, he's had an accident." And I thought: "No, please God he's still with us . . ." But he wasn't . . .

I feel so sad that they wouldn't let me see my husband when he died. He had a heart attack at the car wheel; the car rolled forward into a wall and very badly injured his face! I never saw him again . . .

And my daughter, she's gone too now, with the cancer. And I just don't know whether she ever forgave me. You, see, when her father died that night, I didn't wake her up. I let her sleep. I just thought what good would it do. It can't bring him back. And now she's gone too and I have this terrible fear that she's never forgiven me . . .

And then I wasn't there when she died. I wasn't there for her. I looked after the grandchildren. I had been with her everyday for months but that day. I feel I've failed her somehow . . .

My father, too, I feel bad about what happened when he died too. It seems as if I can't be there for anyone else at that time, why should anyone else be there for me?

Mrs B needed to repeat these guilty themes of failing to live up to her own most central, core constructs. Her reminiscences, many times in the 10 therapy sessions, were accompanied by tears. However, eventually considerable relief from expressing and sharing these feelings became apparent.

A more positive and creative form of reminiscence was also used with Mrs B to encourage her to be more assertive with her family.

WW.   Sounds like the driving skills you had were quite amazing!

Mrs B.   Yes, I learned to drive early, and I drove for quite a while. I was on the payroll for a large mining company. Done all their work. I used to come in and meet the paper train of a morning, to pick up the Mine Inspector, and one thing and another, to take out to work.

And then I'd drive up that mountain sometimes three times a day. Take them up there, then come back down, then go back up and pick them up again and take them in to the train.

And then I'd run hire of a Saturday morning, and take the footballers to wherever they had to play on Saturday afternoons. I'd race the children from there for a free ride into the matinee.

And I could look after the maintenance too. In those days, not too many women changed a tyre; and I did that often. And the number of times I've dealt with overheating as you go up the mountain . . .

Those were good days; and I felt like I was doing something worthwhile. And I took on the local Council a few times and won, over one thing or another.

As Mrs B listened to her own stories of independence and competence in handling others, she began to realise that she continued to have these abilities and could use them in dealing with her own family. She was able to negotiate, mainly through her son, a new arrangement whereby she had more help from her family in and outside her home.

Self-help groups can also be effective for elderly clients telling this story of isolation.[21,22] Invalidation of isolation-laden constructs can occur because, "there are other people like me." A sense of solidarity should develop as the group pursues common goals. Support is also available and valuable feedback about their stories can be had by elderly clients. A variety of potential solutions to common problems can also be explored.[16] In this atmosphere, there are opportunities, too, for empathic listening to others and increased self-esteem through what the clients themselves offer the group.[19] Health professionals often take the role of leader in these groups.

Self-help groups which are not led by professionals but by peers can also provide opportunities for retelling stories of isolation like this one.[22] They are often more informal and less judgemental, and so give more opportunity for spontaneous self-expression. A supportive atmosphere is quickly achieved. Nor is there the mystification of the peer-led group processes which professionals, unintentionally can introduce. Whatever is accomplished by the group, the group members come to recognise that they are doing this for themselves. Their self-respect can be considerably increased by this knowledge. Also, tests of stories about isolation are made without the rather special ingredient of the professional leader, and so can be viewed as providing feedback closer to that of the ordinary world.

From self-limiting stories to self-empowering stories

In the three chapters which have formed this section of my book on personal construct therapy for the elderly, I have dealt with three stories that are predominantly self-limiting: "Sometimes I feel life isn't worthwhile", "I worry about the future" and, in this chapter, "I don't want to be a burden to anyone." I have provided different versions of these stories, shown how they have been told by elderly clients, analysed their personal, social, cultural and physical implications for their tellers, and suggested strategies by which they can, when appropriate, be retold.

I shall now move on to perform a similar analysis of three more stories, each of which is, potentially at least, self-empowering. With these stories, I shall provide some therapeutic strategies for confirming them and for retelling other, self-defeating stories to follow more closely their plots. Why are such stories included in a book about therapy for the elderly? Because, firstly, they show the quality of life that can be achieved by these clients, and secondly, even those who tell such stories about some areas of their lives can still work therapeutically on others. Two of the happier self-empowering stories I shall consider are: "It is marvellous, being able to do what I want to do when I want to do it" (Chapter 9) and "I have a wonderful relationship with my grandchildren" (Chapter 10). However, the story of the next chapter (Chapter 8) is, simply: "I enjoy myself these days."

Suggested reading

● *The physical effects of telling the story*

1. Vandenberg, J.H. (1980). *The psychology of the sick bed.* New York: Humanities Press.
2. Bloom, J.R. & Spiegel, D. (1984). The relationship of two dimensions of social support to the psychological well-being and social functioning of women with advanced breast cancer. *Social Science and Medicine*, 24, 831–837.
3. Hartsfield, J. & Clopton, J.R. (1985). Reducing presurgical anxiety: A possible visitor effect. *Social Science and Medicine*, 25, 529–533.
4. Kaplan, B.H., Cassel, J.C. & Gore, S. (1977). Social support and health. *Medical Care*, 15, 47–58.
5. Rolland, J.S. (1987). Chronic illness and the life cycle: A conceptual framework. *Family Process*, 26, 203–221.
6. Lynch, J.J. (1977). *The broken heart.* New York: Harper and Row.
7. Linn, J.G. & Husaini, B.A. (1985). Chronic medical problems, coping resources, and depression: A longitudinal study of rural Tennesseans. *American Journal of Community Psychology*, 6, 733–42.
8. Unruh, D.R. (1983). *Invisible lives: Social worlds of the aged.* New York: Sage.
9. Alonzo, A.A. (1984). An illness behaviour paradigm: A conceptual exploration of a situational-adaptation perspective. *Social Science and Medicine*, 24, 499–510.
10. Viney, L.L. & Westbrook, M.T. (1984). Coping with chronic illness: Strategy preferences, changes over time and related psychological reactions. *Journal of Chronic Diseases*, 106, 1–14.
11. Viney, L.L. (1989). *Images of illness.* Florida: Krieger.

● *Retelling the story*

12. Fransella, F. & Dalton, P. (1990). *Personal construct counselling in action.* London: Sage.
13. Epting, F.R. (1984). *Personal construct counselling and psychotherapy.* New York: Wiley.
14. Viney, L.L. (1989). *Images of illness.* Florida: Krieger, Second edition.
15. Andersson, L. (1985). Intervention against loneliness in a group of elderly women. An impact evaluation. *Social Science and Medicine*, 25, 355–364.
16. Rook, K.S. (1984). Promoting social bonding: Strategies for helping the lonely and socially isolated. *American Psychologist*, 39, 1389–1407.
17. Vachon, M.L.S., Lyall, W.A.L., Rogers, J. *et al.* (1982). The effectiveness of psychosocial support during post-surgical treatment of breast cancer. *International Journal of Psychiatric Medicine*, 11, 365–372.
18. Natale, S.M. (1986). Loneliness and the ageing client: Psychotherapeutic considerations. *Psychotherapy Patient*, 2, 77–75.
19. Weinberger, M., Hiner, S.L. & Tierney, W.M. (1986). Improving functional status in arthritis: The effect of social support. *Social Science and Medicine*, 23, 899–904.
20. Coleman, P. (1986). Issues in the therapeutic use of reminiscence in elderly people. In I. Hansey & M. Gilhooley (Eds.), *Psychological therapies for elderly people.* London: Croom Helm.

21. Blumberg, B., Flaherty, M. & Lewis, J. (Eds.) (1980). *Coping with cancer*. Washington, DC: US Department of Health and Human Services.
22. Dean, K. (1986). Lay care in illness. *Social Science and Medicine*, 23, 275–284.

SOME SELF-EMPOWERING STORIES FROM THE ELDERLY

8 "I enjoy myself these days"

In this chapter I deal with the first of three self-empowering stories of the elderly: "I enjoy myself these days." I shall analyse it exactly as I did the self-limiting stories that have been described. A number of versions of the story are provided; and then two elderly people give their accounts of what personal and situational factors led them to tell it. I use their own words wherever possible. Then follows an examination of the personal, social and cultural aspects of the story. Some research on the beneficial physical effects that this story can have for the elderly is briefly described. Then I suggest some ways to, in this case, support and maintain this story for elderly clients, together with ways to encourage elderly clients who do not tell it to do so.

"I enjoy myself these days"

When I searched for some ways in which elderly people were telling this story, I found that some of them differed because they dwelt on different activities, while others differed in the underlying reasons for such enjoyment. Yet all had sources of validation for their own stories and confirmation for their constructs. Of the activities, mobility was a particularly common one. Elderly clients who watch some of their contemporaries become disabled and handicapped can glory in their own ability to move. For some of them, such mobility involves being able to drive a car. "I love taking the wife shopping in the mornings. We make quite an outing of it and take the car." Others enjoy their bodily independence and the way they can walk quite long distances. "I enjoy my walk up to the paper shop every morning." "I really value being able to walk on the beach, because then I feel at one with nature." Yet others refer to the hand–eye mobility coordination they have continued to enjoy: "I've been working on some wooden toys for poor children at Christmas."

This last example of a story about mobility also focuses on creativity. Many elderly derive great satisfaction from a wider range of activities in which something new is generated. "These handrails in the shower, I did a lot to improve them before I installed them." "My knitting keeps me contented. It both gives me something I love to do and a way of being useful." "If it weren't for the garden, I don't know that I'd be so happy. There are always things that need doing but new things too. And that magical cycle of planting a seedling, watering it and watching over it, and the wonderful plant that comes. That's such an important part of my life now."

Many elderly people also greatly enjoy humour, both that of other people and their own. "If I couldn't have a laugh each day, I'd find it hard to go on!" Of course they do not talk much about humour; but they do tell funny stories of various kinds. One example, is the story with the unexpected but neat twist, as in this elderly man's account of the whistle he kept beside his wheelchair. "My method of communicating is a damn big whistle; and I get both my dog and daughter with it." Irony is another form of humour which is often used. This elderly man who had had medical advice to cut out alcohol from his diet said; "I drink soda water instead of beer. And I don't have to worry about the breathalyser on the way home." A story based on a metaphor can provide another form of humour, as this gently humorous story of physical deterioration by a 90-year-old man who was at last experiencing failure in several of his bodily organs. "They ought to have a scrap-yard for bodies, like they have for old cars. You could do away with the old junk and keep the spare parts. They might be good for someone else." He had recently signed a donor form for his still functioning kidneys.

The versions of this story based on different reasons for enjoyment included safety, self-esteem, personal integrity, accepting life and seeing meaning in it. The most important type of safety for the elderly seems to be personal safety. "It feels good to know the house has good locks on it." "It's great to be free of those fainting spells now." Safety can also be seen as security. "I feel confident that I've organised our money as well as I can and that we'll have financial security until the ends of our days." "I've just been altering my will again, but I feel sure now that it does the right thing by the family."

The versions of this story about self-esteem and personal integrity have much in common. Those about self-esteem expressed self-confidence. "I know I can do what needs to be done." "I feel good about the way I brought up my family, and how they turned out." The version of this story based on integrity deals with inner certainty and self-actualisation. "I really enjoy being by myself these days, you know. I didn't think I would when Ken died, but I have such happy memories of myself with him." "Not having to work has given me such great opportunities to do the things I've been putting aside for so long." Also, elderly people who experience this integrity tell more stories that indicate that they are satisfied with their lives. "I look forward to waking up in the morning." "I am so contented each day, a bit like a contented cat, I often think, basking in the sun."

The last two versions of the tale focus on accepting life and finding meaning for it. This acceptance goes beyond the present moment to a review of the whole life, its choice and paths, and an understanding that there is no need to pursue any other paths now. "I often muse on whether it was all worth anything, and, you know, I know now it was." "I can't imagine it any other way." "When I first left school, there was no work because of the Depression, but I've never looked back since I met my wife and got started at the Railways." "Life's been good to me, and I wouldn't have had it any other way." Finding meaning for their lives also provided some versions of this story. "When I wonder what it's all been about, I know that it's been worth while." "The children have grown up and have their own families; and I'm so proud of them. I feel that's my path and I followed it."

Two clients tell the story

This story, "I enjoy myself these days", was told by an 81-year-old widower and a 76-year-old widow whose family situations were quite different. Mr D had recently returned home from hospital. He had a range of health problems related to his tuberculosis, yet he was in very good spirits when his therapist, a community nurse, visited his home. Even though he had been referred for therapy for help with mourning his wife's death from cancer 10 years earlier, he considered: "I'm managing well." He had good support from his son and daughter-in-law, although they were living in another city. Meals were provided for him and there was a telephone beside his bed. He also happily described his "girlfriend", and how "in the years since we've met I've been the happiest I've ever been in my whole life." He was satisfied with his long, successful life. "I put it down to long-lived parents and healthy living" (not smoking and drinking little alcohol). He still enjoyed the beach, travelling and entertaining and had a wicked sense of humour. His religion was also important to him: "I feel as if I am being watched over, so I live in gratefulness and expectation."

There were other areas of Mr D's life too, that led to him telling different versions of this story. He was contented with his life in general and reflected with pride on his working days. Two of his constructs about dealing with age-related events in his life, such as increasing fragility and weakness, were "accepting what comes along" and "making the most of things." In fact by finding smaller goals to achieve he had been able to finish making a book holder for a disabled reader, by working at it in small, 20-minute bursts. He found himself able to stick to the diabetic diet and his exercise programme, although he allowed himself occasional treats. He has continued to read poetry from his earlier years, of which he said: "it gives my life meaning. Poems are mysteries; but all of life is a mystery. So I can accept my own life as a mystery." And, about his future, he concluded: "Life is a journey; and in it you have some good and a little bad. Well, I'm having an awful lot of the good." His only areas of concern were his losses, of his wife from cancer, as already mentioned, but also more recently of his driver's licence.

Mrs T was similarly happy and contented, except for occasional bouts of sad feelings, for which she was referred to a university-based clinic. She was surrounded by sons and daughters and their families in suburbs near to her home. She was a little overweight, with some angina, the counsellor who met with her noted. She had worked very hard during her years as a wife and mother. Her main philosophy of life was: "No matter what comes up in life, you can get over it." She described the happiness of her whole extended family and then, especially, her own: "I'm happy that I'm alive. I thank God when I can get up in the morning and see the sun rise." She could still be critical of some of her children's spouses, but she didn't let that spoil her enjoyment of living. "I might be a funny old woman, but nothing ever worries me for long."

Her telling of this self-promoting story focused on both the past and the present. "I've had a really good life. It's been a rewarding life and I've enjoyed it." And even though she had lost her husband within the last 4 years, she was already able to enjoy current experiences that flowed from losing him. Her children had helped her to buy a ground floor apartment with only two bedrooms and no garden. She was glorying in that: "I love the unit, in fact, I particularly love my new kitchen and the special treats I can work on in there." She was enjoying it for what she was able to do, but also for what she no longer needed to do: "Living in a unit is very good, because you just wake up in the morning and you have no outside responsibilities."

Some personal aspects of the story

Self

This story, "I enjoy myself these days", presents its elderly tellers as at its centre. This egocentricity is not selfish in any way but an acknowledgement that, however life has been for them before, now is the time to enjoy themselves. They may be conscious of the limited time they have left, in contrast with earlier in their lives, but they are also aware of having a right to have that contentment. While they may be reflecting on those earlier times, their emphasis is on "these days" and their current situation. It is as if they have learned, even after a life time of worry, that it is only now with which people ever really need to deal. Their happiness and contentment is apparently effortless, too, so that they only need to attend to it to experience it. This is one important expression of personal integrity that the elderly can make.

Age-related events

The age-related events on which this story focuses are quite different from those on which the self-limiting stories focused. The creativity, retained mobility and reflective humour of the elderly are at the centre of their attention, together with having a sense of safety and self-esteem and acceptance of life. Illness, disability and loss are not ignored, but seen as a challenge to be coped with, with enough psychological and physical energy to leave sufficient for enjoying the current good times. This story also deals with age-related events so that they are easier for others to cope with, making alienation from their children and grandchildren less likely.

The psychological functions of this story

When elderly people tell this story, or even hear it told, it helps them maintain their own identity as a person with a capacity to enjoy life. It enables them to express their own contentment; and for some elderly tellers this may not have been possible earlier in their lives. This story also provides information to family members, friends and health professionals alike, that the quality of their life is often still very good, and that they prize the living they still have to do. Finally, it provides its tellers with opportunities to take responsibility for what happens as they age, in that it implies that they can choose to enjoy themselves if they want.

The implications of the story for the emotions and behaviour of the teller

While the implications of the earlier self-defeating stories I considered were distressed emotions and problematic behaviours, this story is associated with positive emotions and productive behaviour. The feelings on which it is based are safety, contentment, acceptance, self-confidence and happiness, as well as enjoyment. The actions linked with it are active, responsible and purposeful ones. While no specific course of action is implied, this story shows that the elderly have both the rights and responsibilities of choice. Purposeful actions can only occur if the actor is feeling safe and confident. So what this story provides is a platform for effective behaviour.

Past, present and future

In a sense the present, past and future are not well linked for the tellers of this story. "I enjoy myself these days" is focused in the here and now, so it cannot provide such integration. However, it is important to consider again the criteria by which the stories of elderly clients can be assessed. I included integration as one such criterion, but also observed that such complete integration is not always necessary. Other criteria, such as whether or not the story provides viable paths of action, as well as hope that they will be successful, need to be considered. For this particular story, the platform for action and hope about the effects of that action it provides seem more important. It may even be that, when this story focuses on "these days", many of its tellers are implying that feeling contentment now indicates a similar contentment about the past as it is reviewed and about the future as it is anticipated.

Some social aspects of the story

Its interpersonal context

Elderly clients told this story both when alone and with others, and they also relished hearing similar stories from their contemporaries on radio, or seeing them in newspapers or on television. When the story was privately told, they were confirming that identity as one capable of enjoyment. When they shared it, it often provided messages for family, friends and health professionals that they had a lot of living yet to do. This story can contain acknowledgement of the contribution of the members of their audience to that happy state.

Sources of validation for the story

The plot of this story was validated by both the elderly tellers themselves and the members of their audience. This combination provided them with the best possible opportunities to test their story and alter it, if necessary, in the face of feedback. They reflected on it in their quieter moments alone, drawing on the wealth of experiences available to them over such long lives to make such tests. They also tested it with close friends and family, the actual sharing with them often providing more validation. The telling of this story to health professionals, where appropriate, would also hopefully provide the same validation. I am concerned, however, that some professionals, because of their own competing stories about the terrors of old age, may respond in ways that might validate their own stories but invalidate those of their clients.

Power in the story

Power has been a central issue in the three self-defeating stories that elderly clients tell that I have dealt with. It will be, also, in the story I deal with in the next chapter, "It is marvellous, being able to do what I want to do when I want to do it." Yet power is not a central issue for this story. As I have noted, however, the power to choose to be happy may be implicit in it.

Some cultural aspects of the story

Information

This story provides both self-knowledge for its tellers and information about some of the advantages of ageing to its audience. The self-knowledge involves acknowledgement of that capacity to be happy and to choose to enjoy themselves. The knowledge it provides for its audience focuses on the same capacities. It says that, in spite of the often debilitating age-related events they experience, such as disability and frailty, the elderly have opportunities for happiness that seem not available to those who are younger. It is important to ask, then, given the ease with which the Western cultures have incorporated the self-defeating and distressed stories of the elderly into its socially constructed accounts of what it is to age, why it is so resistant to accepting positive stories like this one.

Values

The main culturally shared value on which this story is based is that people should be able to enjoy themselves. Perhaps the clearest statement in the English language of this value is in the American Bill of Rights, in the form of the right "to pursue happiness". It is also worth noting that the central value underlying the self-empowering story of the elderly that I shall deal with next has been identified in another part of that Bill, liberty.

Some physical effects of telling the story

It may even be that to tell a happy story is to be less vulnerable to illness. If this is so, how does this link between physical and psychological events occur? At this time the answer appears to be that stress leads to illness through at least two physiological mechanisms: our physiological homoeostasis and our immune systems.[1] The functioning of our immune systems, knowledge of which has only recently become accessible through research, appears to be adversely affected by the negative psychological states brought about by stress.[2] Bereavement, with its anxiety, depression and anger, has also been linked with abnormal immune function.[3] Positive states such as happiness[4] and hope[5], then, may be associated with more effective functioning of our immune systems.

The relationship between stories containing these positive feelings and recovery from illness has been found to be an intriguing one. People recovering from surgery do so more quickly if their morale is high.[7] Raising of morale is seen as important to elderly cancer patients, indeed they have been encouraged to create positive images of their body overcoming their illness.[8] The ability to balance some of their self-limiting stories by self-empowering ones has also been linked with good coping with illness for the elderly.[9,10]

Supporting the story

In this story, "I enjoy myself these days", the elderly present themselves as at its centre, contented and happy. The current situation is their focus; and they are primarily concerned with the gratifying aspects of it. They are reflecting on their own mobility, creativity and humour, as well as showing a sense of safety, self-esteem and acceptance of life. This story confirms their identity as someone who can choose to enjoy life; and it is associated with positive emotions and productive behaviour. It does not integrate present, past and future well for its tellers; but it does provide viable if non-specific paths of action, and hope about the effects of that action. This story is told both privately and publicly, so that there are maximum opportunities for it to be tested. The issue of power, though central to many other stories of the elderly, was not to this one. It provides self-knowledge and cultural knowledge about the elderly. Its chief cultural value is that people should be able to enjoy themselves. This type of story, when told by the elderly, can be linked with less illness as well as better recovery from it.

Elderly clients, if they are telling this story, may need support from therapists to sustain it; and elderly clients who are not telling it need help to begin to tell it. Humour is one of the chief tools for developing positive feelings in any clients, but particularly for the elderly. This is because, however physically frail they are, they are still likely to be able to respond to it. To be successful, humour must be based on a sensitive and extensive understanding of the clients' stories and the construct systems on which they are based.[11] I explore this use of humour. I also deal with other individual reflective therapies to promote enjoyment: meaningfulness therapy and the playfulness and validation of personal construct therapy. I finally consider some group therapies for the elderly. These are based on self-psychology, role play and the experience of joy.

Humour is a creative act, very much like the telling of a story. It involves juggling with multiple meanings and reversals of these meanings.[12] Using humour to deal with a problem consists of using two sets of constructs about it at once, as in a metaphor. Humour accepts constructs which are common or shared by people but deals with others in fantasy. The effect of this occurring unexpectedly is to shake up both stories about the problem and so make them more flexible and open to change.[13] This provides the opportunity for a temporary side-step away from what is assumed to be "reality" to other interpretations of events, these interpretations also being shared with others. Laughter results. These aspects of humour can be seen in the humour of the elderly man who proposed that hospitals have a junk-yard for human parts. He built up two sets of images, one of human bodies which are no longer useful, the other of no longer useful machines. Both sets of constructs were shared by him with others. This examination of illness-related events freed up his stories enough so that he came to see that there were some parts of his old body which might be useful to others, and maybe even some parts of himself. With this personal construct account of humour, a sense of humour can be considered to be the capacity to accept and deal with other people's stories without invalidating or putting at risk one's own.

What purposes can elderly people's use of humour serve? Defining humour in this way makes clear how it can cut into the inflexibility that can be built into the stories of the elderly through their anxiety and depression.[14] It leads to a wider range of choices among the stories people use to make sense of events. It also lends a distance from and so a perspective on those events.[12,14] Often this new perspective leads to new stories, giving elderly people a kind of power over events.[15] Humour is particularly effective in breaking up some of the self-defeating stories with which I have dealt. It can reduce the power of anxiety-laden stories, especially those which are ridden with embarrassment. It permits expression of anger-laden stories, but in a socially acceptable way. Perhaps the most important function of humour is to maintain positive images of people as they interact with others.[16] It involves a sharing of stories and laughter which create bonds between people.

While humourous stories can be told by the elderly when alone, they can also be used effectively by therapists who want their clients to learn their own self-worth, to assert themselves appropriately and to take risks when necessary.[17] Mr D was an ideal client for their purpose, given his marked sense of humour. Humour can be used a little by family and friends, too, so long as it is with care and concern. One way therapists can use it is to "provoke" clients.[14] This is done gently, using images that make sense to the clients, and with humour. Humour is considered to be essential to this process. If clients do not laugh at the counsellor's "provocation", that provocation could prove to be destructive. The counselling process itself becomes like children's play[18] but, like that play, it contains a commentary on the interactions that are taking place and the stories inherent in them. Humour can be developed through unexpected but neat accounts of events, reversals, irony and metaphors.[11] It can also develop through the less gentle techniques of sarcasm, ridicule and mimicry. Humorous stories about self, developed in these ways, indicate a flexibility in the approach to life of the elderly client. Telling humorous stories about oneself is recognised as a sign of psychological maturity.

This happy story is not likely to be told unless its tellers sense that there is some meaning to their lives.[19] Some people, as they age, lose this belief when they find that their old sources of meaning are no longer available to them. In their middle years, job-related achievements often fulfilled this sense of purpose, for men especially; and in later years they lose those achievements. However, achievements do not seem to be the only ways in which life can be meaningful for the elderly. Enjoyment of activities for their own sake becomes important. Elderly clients may well need to be encouraged to involve themselves in intellectual activities, supporting causes, creativity and being with people. All of these activities are enjoyed by the elderly not for the achievement they provide alone, but for the happiness they bring.[20] Neither Mr D nor Mrs T needed encouragement of this kind. Mr D, having originally found his sense of meaningfulness in the workplace had long ago expanded into a wide range of opportunities. Mrs T had not even needed to make changes of that kind, since her cooking and knitting, and, above all, being with her family, had continued to provide her with this sense of meaning in her life.

Personal construct therapy provides other techniques for clients which help them to begin telling this story. One involves conducting therapy in as playful a way as possible, so as to help them let go of some of their old stories and be creative with their own lives. Another involves using the process of validation of clients' stories to generate the positive emotions needed for this story.[19] Such validation would not involve confirmation of all stories, but would select those that were empowering. Mr D, who was already telling this story, received support for it in this way from his community nurse. His only area of concern was the losses he had suffered, of his wife and his driving licence. His licence he had lost as a result of an accident in which he had been driving, and he still had no current memory of it. His therapist confirmed his positive and empowering stories about himself, partly through praise from her and partly through encouraging him to seek out validation from other people, such as his son, and from the people who brought him his meals. She also, of course, encouraged him to work through his losses in reminiscence and life review.

Group psychotherapy can also be helpful for supporting and even for beginning to tell this story.[21] There has been a type of this therapy based on theories of the self. It suggests that membership of a therapy group can provide for the elderly opportunities to test their sense of safety, develop their self-esteem and find satisfaction in life, as well as to maintain their sense of identity.[22] Group exercise classes can also be helpful. Even playing games in groups of this kind can be helpful: to establish trust, and to develop imagination, improvisation and group cohesion. Mrs T was, in fact, already involved with a bingo-playing group of friends which provided some of the enjoyment for her version of this story. For elderly people who have lost this capacity to enjoy themselves, group work that provides them with joyful experiences (of sharing, helping, trusting, creating, laughing and being physically active, for example), can reduce the pain of their losses, restore their confidence and renew their investment in living.[23]

Suggested reading

● *Some physical effects of telling the story*

1. Gottschalk, L.A. (1978). Psychosomatic medicine today: An overview *Psychosomatics,* **19**, 89-93.
2. Udelaman, H.D. & Udelaman, D.L. (1983). Current explorations in psychoimmunology. *American Journal of Psychotherapy,* **37**, 210-221.
3. Irwin, M., Daniels, M. & Weiner, H. (1987). Immune and neuroendocrine changes during bereavement. *Psychiatric Clinics of North America,* **10**, 449-465.
4. Boylin, W., Gordon, S.K. & Newurke, M.F. (1976). Reminiscing and ego integrity in institutionalized elderly males. *The Gerontologist,* **16**, 118-124.
5. Hutschnecker, A.A. (1981). *Hope.* New York: Putnam.
6. Nadelson, T. (1990). On purpose, successful ageing and the myth of innocence. *Journal of Geriatric Psychiatry,* **23**, 3-12.
7. Roud, P.C. (1986-87). Psychosocial variables associated with the exceptional survival of patients with advanced malignant disease. *International Journal of Psychiatry in Medicine,* **16**, 113-122.
8. Simonton, O.C., Matthews-Simonton, S. & Creighton, J. (1978). *Getting well again.* Los Angeles: Tarcher.
9. Nahemon, L., McCluskey-Fawcett, K.A. & McGee, P.E. (1981). *Humour and ageing.* New York: Academic Press.
10. Noyes, R. (1981). Treatment of cancer pain. *Psychosomatic Medicine,* **43**, 57-70.

● *Supporting the story*

11. Viney, L.L. (1985). Humour as a therapeutic tool. In A. Landfield & F. Epting (Eds.), *Anticipating personal construct psychology.* Nebraska: University of Nebraska Press.
12. O'Connell, W. (1981). The natural high therapist: God's favourite monkey. *Voices,* **16**, 37-44.
13. Jasnow, A. (1981). Humour and survival. *Voices,* **16**, 50-54.
14. Farrelly, F. & Brandsma, J. (1974). *Provocative therapy.* Port Collins, Colorado: Sheilds.
15. Kuhlman, T.L. (1984). *Humour and psychotherapy.* Homewood, Ill: Brooks-Cole.

16. Saper, B. (1987). Humour as psychotherapy: Is it good or bad for the client? *Professional Psychology: Research and Practice*, **18**, 360-367.
17. Viney, L.L., Benjamin, Y.N. & Preston, C. (1990). Personal construct therapy for the elderly. *Journal of Cognitive Psychotherapy*, **4**, 211-224.
18. Epting, F. (1981). An appraisal of personal construct psychotherapy. In H. Bonarius, R. Holland & S. Rosenberg (Eds.), *Personal construct psychology—recent advances in theory and practice*. London: Macmillan.
19. Epting, F.R. (1984). *Personal construct counselling and psychotherapy*. New York: Wiley.
20. Leslie, R.N. (1982). Counselling the aged. *International Forum for Age Therapy*, **5**, 17-52.
21. Huddleston, R. (1989). Drama with elderly people. *British Journal of Occupational Therapy*, **52**, 290-300.
22. Leszcz, M. (1990). Towards an integrated model of group psychotherapy with the elderly. *The International Journal of Group Psychotherapy*, **40**, 379-490.
23. Saul, S. & Saul, S.R. (1990). The application of joy in group therapy for the elderly. *The International Journal of Group Psychotherapy*, **40**, 353–356.

9 "It is marvellous, being able to do what I want to do when I want to do it"

In this chapter I deal with another self-empowering and enjoyable story that elderly people tell: "It is marvellous, being able to do what I want to do when I want to do it." This story I shall also consider in detail, beginning with a number of different versions of it. Then I describe how elderly people come to tell versions of this story. Analysis of the personal aspects of such story telling examines its account of self and of the age-related events with which it deals, the psychological functions the story provides for its elderly tellers, its implications for their emotions and actions, and the way it links present, past and future. The social aspects of the story to be considered are its interpersonal context, who supports it and to whom does it allocate power. The research literature on the physical effects of telling such a story are reviewed before I consider some ways in which this story can be both initiated and supported.

"It is marvellous, being able to do what I want to do when I want to do it"

This story is about the autonomy of the elderly, their competence, their skills for active, effective coping and their self-esteem. However, it is perhaps most helpful to consider different versions of this tale using other aspects of it. Autonomy, competence and all the other experiences of interest here can also be expressed in terms of the initiatives the elderly take, the effort they make, their abilities as they report them and their capacity to triumph over situations, as well as their construing of themselves as causing events and not just responding to them.

The initiative-based version of this story involves wanting to do things, planning to do them and setting goals. "I like to organise and plan things for myself" shows the capacity of its elderly speaker to take charge. Planning is important for most people, but not always easy for frail elderly people. "Provided you can plan ahead, you can cope with just about any physical problem being older brings." Planning can be important in handling illnesses too. "Now I've had this stroke, I've got to work out which ways of doing things are running away from problems and which I should use to make life easier."

Yet effort is necessary for achieving the promise of these plans. Sometimes elderly clients will focus on their younger days to say "I've been a very active sort of fellow." It's not clear with such a statement whether that capacity is retained; but at least it provides a starting point. Often that history of effort can be helpful. As an elderly man, who had successfully earned his living as a casual labourer, said "I'll get out on my own again. I'll battle on myself, because I'm a fighter." His high self-esteem was apparent there, as it was for this elderly lady who was able to say "Every day is a challenge."

Ability plays an important role too, and the version of this story that is based on it deals with a wide range of abilities. "I've always been good with people, I'll just ask friends and family for help." "I can cope with whatever God sends." "Now that my husband has gone, I'm free to move into a smaller home." "We're lucky that we're pretty financially secure and can cope with inflation." Even when faced with physical and financial constraints of old age, some elderly people can still maintain a strong positive belief in themselves and their own ability. "There's not much you can't do, if you put your mind to it."

Another version of this story about mobility is told by people who see themselves as triumphing over their physical world. "I don't let things get me down" indicates an overcoming of the constraints of ageing. Their self-esteem can be important here too. "I'm a pretty independent type of person." "I'm able to keep myself on a fairly even keel." "Your attitude to things is what I find important. Like, I was just not going to let not having a car any more, stop me from going where I wanted to; and it hasn't." "I make sure my sons come out here to see me every Sunday." While control of others and events is central to this version of the story, so is self-control. Many elderly clients may have been advised, recently, to give up smoking for the sake of their health. A 73-year-old who had smoked two packets of cigarettes a day for 40 years could say, with so much pride, "I haven't touched a cigarette all day."

The other version of this story involves the elderly in perceiving themselves to be at least sometimes the cause of events. "I make my own decisions. I always have. This is a tough neighbourhood, and I've been attacked here twice. But I've chosen to last them out." Making choices are important to the elderly as is staying in control of oneself and one's life. "I've watched my mother and my friends age before me, and I'm taking care of myself. I eat sensibly; I get a bit of exercise, and I keep my mind active with crosswords and the newspapers." Illness of course provides the stimulus for many varieties of this version as it is told by the elderly. For example, a woman in her seventies, spoke of her medication for lower back pain in this way: "I've weaned myself off the tablets. I don't like the side effects they are having, I'd rather put up with the pain." The same theme emerged from a spritely man in his eighties: "I'm not senile and I'm not docile . . . and I'll decide whether I'm going to lose a leg or not."

Two clients tell the story

A man and a woman who told yet another version of this story show some of the different ways in which it can be told. Mr G, at 72 years of age, was a widower, his wife having died some 10 years earlier. He was living at home alone and apparently looking after himself well. However, he was referred to a university-based clinic by a community nurse who thought some closer contact with a therapist might be productive. He had retired from his work as a clerk in an accounting firm only recently and was still enjoying very much the autonomy involved. He told the psychologist who met him at the clinic: "Everything's great now. Things are good. You can lay in bed in the morning and not have to race for the bus for work. And you can go to bed when you like. It's all good now. The hard days are all gone."

Mr G also took great satisfaction in his ability to do the household chores: "I know how to do most things, wash, iron, and do the cooking and the sweeping. You can laugh if you like, but I enjoy them." He was also aware of the autonomy granted by his financial position; which, while he was certainly not rich, met his needs. He had a standard pension from the Federal Government, as well as "a little bit put by". "It's enough to let me have an occasional drink and a smoke with the boys." He was also aware of the advantages of completely owning his own home, free of mortgage, which gave him an independence lacked by many others of his age.

Mrs L, at 76, was living with her husband in special accommodation for the elderly when visited by a social worker who became her therapist. She had been referred following gall bladder surgery. The L's unit was self-contained, with two bedrooms and a kitchen, and was part of a tower complex of similar and more supported accommodation. The retirement village had many levels of accommodation graded in support through to the nursing home level. Mrs L had arranged to have help with the cleaning, but was enjoying providing three meals a day for the two of them and occasional family visitors. "I'm feeling still very spry and able to cope," she said, "but we thought we should think about what the future could bring for us and prepare for it." She had worked in their family shop until she and her husband both retired, and had only good things to say about retirement.

Mrs L, like Mr G, emphasised the importance of financial security: "We saved for our retirement, and with the pension, and the flat we bought when we sold the shop, so we are comfortable now. Of course it helps that we don't play the pokies [poker machines] as much as some of our friends do. And we find we eat less than we used to now that we use up less energy." One of her favourite ways for exercising her relatively recently new autonomy was in being able to help other people. "Now I can do something really useful. I work with the crippled children. They can always do with someone to read to them and tell them stories. And I find it so rewarding mentally to be able to be there for them."

Some personal aspects of the story

Self

The self that is presented in this self-empowering story, "It is marvellous, being able to do what I want to do when I want to do it", is very different from that presented in some of the self-limiting stories. "Sometimes I feel as if life isn't worthwhile" provides a good example for contrast, especially in its helpless version. The tellers of the present, encouraging story are active decision-makers and take charge. They see themselves as having the ability to deal with age-related events. They are also active knowers, capable of reflecting on their own experience and acting on those reflections. They can both receive advice and give it.

Age-related events

Age-related events such as illness and disability do not have big roles in this story, although they are acknowledged. Its focus is much more, like that of the first self-empowering story, "I enjoy myself these days", on the more positive events they experience. These include hobbies and charity work, but also, in the case of Mr G and Mrs L of this chapter, include enjoyment of being able to do quite ordinary household chores, such as meal preparation. The elderly men and women who told this story did not dwell on the physical, psychological, social and financial constraints with which everyone must deal as they age. Certainly, several of the clients who told this story had some financial security, although they were not well off. In general, for the elderly, having some freedom from financial limits can reduce the burden imposed by these other three limits—physical, psychological and social.

The psychological functions of the story

When this story, like the others, is told in the personal style of the tellers it also confirms their identity, but, in this case, it is the identity of a person in touch with their feelings and aware of their own abilities and opportunities. It provides confirmation of their autonomy and competence. It also enables its tellers to take responsibility for some events in their lives. "Being able to do what I want to do" leaves its speakers with some appropriate moral dilemmas about the choices they make. With "when I want to do it" defining the timing of, and probably the situations for some actions, they are taking responsibility for judging the appropriateness of their own actions further. This picture is compatible both with the elderly person as construer and the exerciser of wisdom of personal construct therapy.

Implications of the story for the emotions and behaviour of the teller

This story, like the other self-empowering story I have dealt with, involves awareness of a range of positive emotions. They include pride, self-esteem, self-congratulation and gratification, as well as simple enjoyment. Linked with these emotions are implications for actions of many useful kinds, such as decision-making, as well as mounting and carrying out plans for action based on those decisions. These implications make this story very productive for the elderly people who tell it. These qualities may also make it a story promoting physical health for them. Whether it does, I shall consider shortly.

Past, present and future

This story, "it is marvellous being able to do what I want to do when I want to do it", can be seen as dealing primarily with the present. "Now I can do what I want" is certainly its most powerful message. However, when elderly clients tell this story, I believe that it has implications for their past, and so, in that sense provides links to it. It contrasts old limits with current autonomy. Its implications for the future are less clear. However, as for the story, "I enjoy myself these days", the value of the viable courses of action offered by this story and its hope for its outcomes far outweigh the lack of integrity between present, past and future. Further, all futures are unknown, but that of the elderly is particularly unpredictable; and to acknowledge this can be helpful.

Some social aspects of the story

Its interpersonal context

This story was often told to other people. Sometimes this was to husband or wife and to family members and friends, it was also told to health professionals. In each of these contexts the messages of the story were the same. "I am very happy. I know I can choose. And when I choose what to do, and I can also choose when and where I do it." However, as elderly clients have mentioned, it was also told privately, with no audience at all.

Sources of validation for the story

The sources for validation of this story, like those for the earlier self-empowering story, are both the tellers themselves and the audience they had for the tale. The three groups of listeners provided some support, and so had opportunities to also provide useful feedback about it to its tellers. However, the tellers also sought some other support for it by testing its predictions in the way they behaved. They acted as if they had choices, and events confirmed their construing. This provides, as for the earlier self-empowering story, the best conditions for testing stories.

Power in the story

In this story, power has been allocated solely to the tellers: it has not been handed over to the ageing processes, or to other people, as it had in the past self-defeating story, "Sometimes I feel life isn't worthwhile." Nor are the alienated and detached bodies seen as having more power than elderly people themselves did. This self-empowering story says that they have the power, not only to choose, but to act on their choices and reflect on the possible consequences of their actions.

Some cultural aspects of the story

Information

The information that this story provides is partly self-knowledge for the tellers but also knowledge about the elderly for other people. These others may be family and friends, or health professionals. However, they may also be other people of the teller's own age who can have their horizons expanded greatly when they hear this story. The story conveys that elderly people can plan and make an effort, and have many abilities to do what they want. It also conveys that the elderly can triumph over their physical conditions and disruptive age-related events, and cause changes to occur that involve not only themselves but other people as well.

Values

The cultural values underlying this story are the same from teller to teller. In Western societies one of people's most important rights is autonomy, or freedom of choice, as well as the right to act on that choice, although not without reflection.

These rights, this story says, are also the rights of the elderly. Unfortunately, well-intentioned health and welfare professionals working with elderly clients have tended to emphasise their "maintaining their independence". This cry has been taken up by at least the major English speaking governments as the central value underlying policy on health and welfare for the elderly. This may be partly in the hope of cutting its cost. However, there is an emphasis on this individual-ist value alone, to the exclusion of the more social value represented by intimacy and links with others, which underlies the next self-empowering story, "I have a wonderful relationship with my grandchildren." Discussion of the possible threat to the stories of the professionals and policy makers about their own future "independence", which is posed by including values other than independence, will remain until my final chapter on the stories of the therapists.

Some physical effects of telling the story

Direct evidence about the protective role played by stories of autonomy, compe-tence and control from the elderly is, compared with evidence about the damag-ing role of stories of helplessness, rare as yet. However, there is evidence that the controllability of illnesses affects their outcomes.[1-2] I shall report the results of two studies only. One of these studies has examined the effects of providing increased opportunities for personal responsibility and decision-making for elderly people in nursing homes.[3] Improvements in psychological states resulted, and these effects extended to their physical states as well. The other study found that more illness was reported by the people who experienced the undesirable events which they believed to be beyond their control; and the most illness was reported by those who were uncertain about whether they could control the events that occurred.[4]

There is more evidence pointing to the facilitating role of stories of competence and control during illness and injury. Physically illness management has been effected by this story in at least two ways. The diabetic elderly who tell it con-trol their blood sugar levels better;[5] and such elderly people with chronic pain control that pain better.[6] In rehabilitation, people who feel that they have control over themselves and their lives improve more.[7] The longer ill or injured people are in rehabilitation programmes, the more likely they are to develop stories about their own competence and control.[8,9] Elderly people who initially tell a more competent story later see themselves as achieving greater rehabilitation gains in mobility and interpersonal relationships than do those who do not.[10,11]

Supporting the story

In this story, "It is marvellous, being able to do what I want when I want to do it", the elderly present themselves as active and successful as well as able to deal with age-related events. Further, the events on which they focus tend to be, not illness and disability, but hobbies and charity work, as well as the household chores they can enjoy. This story confirms for them their abilities and opportunities, and yet enables them to take responsibility for some events in their lives. The emotions linked with this story are, amongst others, pride, self-esteem and enjoyment. It associates their future with their present and past, and the capacity for hopeful action that it stimulates makes it very valuable to its tellers.

Socially, this story was often told publicly to others as well as privately to the elderly themselves. This provided the best possible opportunities for testing its usefulness, both through public feedback from others and private reflection on the consequences of acting as this story suggests. This story clearly allocated power to its tellers, being one of the relatively few stories of the elderly which did so. Culturally, it provides information about that power that can be especially useful to others in society, not only others of their age group but younger people planning for their old age. Also, it is based on the strong Western value of independence. Telling of this story by the elderly may be linked with some form of protection from illness as well as with better recovery from it.

Supporting the elderly who tell this story and encouraging others to do so therefore can become important therapeutic goals. I shall now describe some techniques for this purpose, dealing with mainly individual strategies but concluding with group work. These techniques will focus on a number of events of concern to elderly clients. Illness is one such event, so I shall deal with how to make clear how such clients are construing their illness and ensure that their construing gives them some power to deal with it. I shall return to Mrs L at this point. Since all techniques that help people change their construing are useful to personal construct therapists, I shall also look at two cognitive behavioural techniques designed to add to their abilities: skill-learning and thought-stopping. Overuse of alcohol can be another problem for the elderly, so I shall examine techniques for promoting their sense of competence in relation to that. Of course, retelling stories about age-related events through reminiscence is also possible; and Mr G provides an example of this approach. Finally, the role of community-based self-help groups in encouraging the development of this story and supporting older versions of it will be discussed.

The first steps towards promoting control by the elderly of their own health care should be finding out what the illness means to them. What constructs do they use to account for it? Recognising that they take a certain view of their world gives elderly clients some choice about changing that view. They cannot realistically see cancer, for example, as an unmitigated blessing; but it can be viewed as a challenge, as an opportunity to test themselves. Nor, is it necessary to let illness take over their lives. Elderly clients can still, themselves, set the goals to be achieved here. Health care professionals working with cancer sufferers have made several useful suggestions along these lines.[12-14] One involves the use of determinedly positive stories in which cancer cells are visualised as weak and confused and the patient's natural bodily defences as strong and triumphant. If such stories fit with the patient's view of the world then they may be of use; if not, they are not so likely to be employed successfully. Another involves people in developing a story about their "inner guide to health". This guide may take the form of a wise old man or woman, who helps to put people in touch with health-giving power within themselves of which they have been unaware.[15] Mrs L, who was recovering from removal of her gall bladder, was encouraged by her social worker, in support of her other independent stories, to apply this guide to her illness. She was asked to select a wise, old person for this purpose. She chose her own grandmother, her mother's mother, to whom she had been very close. She visualised her as a guide to her own healing powers.

It has also been recommended that elderly clients should be taught certain skills by professionals to help them cope with their handicaps. These skills can lead to a heightened sense of competence.[16] One such skill is self-preparation.[17] If their frailty is progressive, the elderly can learn to anticipate what is to come and test some ways of dealing with it. Thought-stopping is a good technique for dealing with such unwanted short stories which tend to persist.[17] For example, "I'm not going to be able to cope with the pain when it starts again" was an image which one elderly man was not able to get out of his mind. He was able to learn to deal with it by abruptly dismissing it when it troubled him and substituting other more enjoyable stories in its place.

Some elderly clients have difficulties in adjusting their intake of alcohol, as their metabolism slows and their bodies take longer to process it. Such clients, however, can be encouraged to use their capacity to construe loosely for long periods, to reflect on the role alcohol is now filling in their lives.[18] Elderly clients will make only apparently vaguely connected deliberations with many detours, or so it may appear to their therapists. Many of them can use such disconnected construing to arrive at a new set of decisions about, say, their daily beer intake. Of course, if they have arrived at those decisions themselves, the chances of them sticking with them is much greater.[19] Because such clients have been allowed largely to follow their own train of thought, they have arrived at an independent story about their alcohol intake, for which, as I have shown in my analysis of such a story, they are then likely to take responsibility.

The retelling of clients' stories is another viable technique for initiating this story of competence.[20,21] Although Mr G was able to tell the story, "It is marvellous, being able to do what I want to do when I want to do it", about many areas of his life, he was not able to do so about completing his grieving for his wife and opening up the possibility of closeness with other women. He had carefully established himself as "not needing anything from anyone" and claimed "I'm too old to change my ways now. And that's what having a woman around would mean." As he reminisced to his psychologist about his life with his wife, however, he began to recall that their relationship, though very satisfying to him, had left him with considerable autonomy. "I think it's what the young people call 'space'. She gave me 'space' to be me and yet even to change and she was still there for me."[22] He came to see then that he could continue to tell his autonomous story and yet have another rewarding relationship, especially if he continued to live separately.

Group work can also be helpful in initiating and supporting this story of competence and control.[22] Community-based support centres have been set up through local churches and synagogues. Their aims have been to establish better services for elderly clients, make counselling available to them and provide health maintenance programmes for them. Their most important strategy for promoting this story of competence has been to empower the elderly by having them help one another. This group work, then, has gone beyond professionally led support groups, to leaving some of the responsibility with the elderly clients to help with one another's problems. They seem highly likely to respond to this challenge by maintaining their telling of this power-laden story, or at least beginning to tell new stories about their capacities for choice and action, and for reflection on that choice.

Suggested reading

● *Some physical effects of telling the story*

1. Affleck, G., Tennen, H., Pfeiffer, C. & Fifield, J. (1987). Appraisals of control and predictability in adapting to a chronic disease. *Journal of Personality and Social Psychology*, **2**, 273–279.
2. Felton, B.J. & Revenson, T.A. (1984). Coping with chronic illness: A study of illness controllability and the influence of coping strategies on psychological adjustment. *Journal of Consulting and Clinical Psychology*, **3**, 343–353.
3. Langer, E.J. & Rodin, J. (1976). The effects of choice and enhanced personal responsibility for the aged: A field experiment in an institutional setting. *Journal of Personality and Social Psychology*, **34**, 191–198.
4. Suls, J. & Mullen, B. (1981). Life events, perceived control and illness. *Journal of Human Stress*, **7**, 30–34.
5. Peyrot, M. & McMurray, J.F. (1985). Psychosocial factors in diabetes control: Adjustment of insulin-treated adults. *Psychosomatic Medicine*, **47**, 542–547.
6. Litt, M.D. (1988). Self-efficacy and perceived control: Cognitive mediators of pain tolerance. *Journal of Personality and Social Psychology*, **54**, 149–160.
7. Shontz, F.C. (1975). *The psychological aspects of physical illness and disability*. New York: Macmillan.
8. Fry, P.S. (Ed.) (1989). *Psychological perspectives of helplessness and control in the elderly*. New York: North Holland.
9. Giesen, G.B. & Datan, N. (1980). The competent older woman. In N.T. Datan & N.

Lohmann (Eds), *Transitions of ageing*. New York: Academic Press.
10. Affleck, G., Tennen, H., Croog, S. & Levine, S. (1987). Causal attribution, perceived benefits and workability after a heart attack: An eight year study. *Journal of Consulting and Clinical Psychology*, **55**, 29–35.
11. Viney, L.L. & Westbrook, M.T. (1982). Psychological reactions to chronic illness: Do they predict rehabilitation? *Journal of Applied Rehabilitation Counselling*, **13**, 38–44.

● *Supporting the story*

12. Arnkoff, D.B. (1986). A comparison of the ageing and restructuring components of cognitive restructuring. *Cognitive Therapy and Research*, **10**, 147–158.
13. LeShan, L. (1977). *You can fight for your life*. New York: Evans.
14. Simonton, O.C., Matthews-Simonton, S. & Creighton, J. (1978). *Getting well again*. Los Angeles: Tarcher.
15. Weaver, R. (1973). *The old wise woman*. New York: Putnam.
16. Bandura, A. (1984). Recycling misconceptions of perceived self efficacy. *Cognitive Therapy and Research*, **8**, 231–255.
17. Rudestam, K.E. (1980). *Methods of self change*. Belmont, California: Brooks/Cole.
18. Powell, J. (1991). *"Motivational interviewing" with older hospital patients: A personal construct approach*. International Conference on Drugs and Alcohol, Adelaide, Australia.
19. Winter, D. (1992). *Personal construct psychology in clinical practice: Theory, research and applications*. London: Routledge.
20. Viney, L.L. (1989). *Images of illness*. Florida: Kreiger, Second edition.
21. Epting, F.R. (1984). *Personal construct counselling and psychotherapy*. New York: Wiley.
22. Koenig, H.G. (1988). Shepherds Centres: Helping elderly help themselves. *Journal of the American Geriatric Society*, **34**, 70.

10 "I have a wonderful relationship with my grandchildren"

In this chapter I deal with the last of the self-empowering stories that elderly people tell: "I have a wonderful relationship with my grandchildren." I shall begin with a number of different examples of this story, focusing on the importance for the elderly of relationships with other people. These examples will deal with the rewarding relationships they report, not only with their grandchildren, but with others important to them, their spouses and their children, as well as with God. Then two elderly people share something of the meaning of this story for themselves. My last formal analysis of the personal, social and cultural aspects of any story will be made in this chapter. It highlights how helpful stories about good relationships are, in terms of the presentation of themselves by the elderly and the events they experience. Yet it is equally helpful to them in the sources of support they have for it and to whom it allocates power, as well as the cultural information it provides and the values on which it is based. The research literature on the physical effects of this story on its teller are also reviewed, as for earlier self-empowering stories. Some ways in which the story can be supported are also provided.

"I have a wonderful relationship with my grandchildren"

Rewarding relationships are of central importance to the elderly. It can be quite difficult for them to feel good about themselves and their own ways of construing, without such relationships. "I'm so glad I've found this bunch of friends who go to the clubs in the afternoon. They're all about my age, and we've so much in common." Their construing of themselves must be based on how others see them at least to some extent. "I get a real kick out of playing the piano for our group. They seem to enjoy it so much. I play old-time music, and they all tell me how it takes them back to some good times." Most people, and it seems the elderly are no exception, like to feel that some of their good relationships are reciprocal ones, in which one favour deserves another. "When my daughter Jean asked me to mind the little one while she works one day a week, I was really pleased. I felt much better about asking Bob, her husband, to put a railing over the bath for me, which I'd been dreading." Family is often the first source of such rewarding relationships but friends can be too.

Relationships with husband or wife are often very important. Simply to share enjoyable experiences with them can be very satisfying. "Jim and I go down to the Bingo on Tuesday afternoons, and we have such a good time; it doesn't matter whether we win or not, we still have a good time." "My wife has so much more time since she retired; so she's taken up bridge with me, and we make a pretty formidable team." "We find, as we get older, we don't have to have a knees up to have fun. We can get a lot out of just singing around the piano together." "My husband has only recently come to my church and sharing our Christianity has meant a lot in our lives."

Relationships with sons and daughters can be just as rewarding. "My daughter and I are so close, we can always tell what the other's going to say, and it's lovely", said an elderly woman. An elderly man murmured, "I enjoy visiting my son now. We go down the garden, and get away from the women for a bit." Of course these parent–child relationships have not always been good. "My daughter and I used not to get on well, especially when she was a teenager. But now that she's a mother like me, we are much closer and can even laugh together over those bad times." "My son got into drugs for a while and he was impossible. I had to throw him out. But now he's found a lovely girl, and settled down; and I really love seeing him with his little family around him."

Grandchildren are a wonderful source of such satisfying relationships for the elderly. "I do love to just watch my grandchildren grow. Each time I see her she's learned something new. She's a delightful child." "The grandkiddies come over to me once a week, and I love to see them." While pure enjoyment is often the dominant note in these relationships, there are also functions that the elderly can fulfil with their grandchildren in a way that they cannot with other family members. For example, they can be the keeper of the family traditions: "When my first grandchild was born I found the beautiful old christening robe that my mother had, and they've all been christened in it since then." The elderly can also serve as the family watchdogs: "I pointed out to Joyce the other day that Lynette seemed a bit peaky. And when we took her temperature it was 103 degrees! I was so pleased to have picked it up."

For those elderly people for whom God has meaning, relationships with God can be a further important source of happiness. God is seen by some elderly as a friend and companion: "When I let God know what's on my mind, I feel much better for it." God is seen by others as a consultant and adviser: "When I have a problem I lay it at God's feet and I soon find my prayers are answered." A good relationship with God can help elderly clients in dealing with disability, bereavement and even death. This can be particularly so if God is linked by them with eternal life or some other overcoming of the time constraints they experience. "When I find myself getting scared about dying, I remember all the people I love that I'll be joining in heaven—my mum and dad, my older brother and the little one we had who died before her first birthday." There is also evidence that the elderly who report having a good relationship with God also are more satisfied with life than those who do not. "My faith gives me so much—a greater love of my fellow man and a greater enjoyment of the little things in life."

Two clients tell the story

Mr T, at 77, had been very active until recently when rheumatism had begun to slow him down. He had been widowed 8 years earlier, having had an excellent relationship with his wife who died of breast cancer. He admitted that he had "missed her enormously at first." During the past 5 years he had come close to another woman, Jean, who had become a great friend. They were not living together but were sharing lunches, walking and watching TV as well as holidays. They also had had some satisfying sexual intercourse. As he said, "It's not even being able to do it again with someone that's most important, it's the physical closeness, the cuddles, that I missed. So these past five years have been the happiest of my life." Jean, like his wife, had had cancer of the breast and had, in fact, lost a breast. But, as he said, "I love her for what she is inside, not her outside."

Mr T, then, was very happy and contented in terms of his relationship with Jean. He also had good, not intrusive support from his grown children. His happiness was sometimes threatened by a set of constructs he had carried over from his younger, more vigorous days. "I've always been active and useful" is fine of itself, but when he sometimes added: "If I'm not active and useful my life is over", then his integrity was threatened. It was further threatened by the resulting demand he then made of himself: "I must stay healthy." Illness is not inevitable at 77, nor even at 87 years of age. However, Mr T was already experiencing some rheumatism and vulnerability to colds and influenza. He needed to retell this story about himself, so as to make himself less psychologically vulnerable to the effects of physical illness. How his medical practitioner was able to help him, worked through his relationship with Jean, will be seen later in this chapter.

Mrs H, at 68, was living with her husband in their original home, with her children all settled and raising their families near by. She had some problems with high blood pressure. To help her deal with this her community nurse introduced her to systematic relaxation and other management techniques, and encouraged her to revise the story she was telling about her illness. However, in the course of this therapy, her nurse was amazed at her capacity to make the most of her life. And, in closer analysis, it proved to be based very much on her fulfilling relationships with her family and her God. "I'm very lucky to be alive. I have wonderful sons, and wonderful grandsons too. Even though they're teenagers now, they still like to be with us. You'd think they'd drift away. It's really lovely! That's what's so wonderful in my life. It's the love. Everyone needs affection of some kind."

She also had considerable enjoyment in what she still shared with her husband. "We do gardening together and mow the lawns. We go shopping together, and, of course, we go on holiday together. We really enjoy our life." "We've been together now for a long time and we are very happy." And what she shared with God was important to her too. "My God is one of the good things in my life. He's always there when I need Him. He answers my prayers and calms my fears." Mrs H felt herself to be in the centre of a network of loving relationships, in which she was able to both give and receive.

Some personal aspects of the story

Self

This story, "I have a wonderful relationship with my grandchildren", presents its elderly tellers in a very wide range of ways. This range has to be widened to include others as well as grandchildren, which of course it does. Its focus is on the relationship it describes and the enjoyment involved in it; and the identity of the tellers is left undefined in any other way. Its heroes and heroines do not appear to need to make any effort, but if they do, success seems assured. They are pictured as at the centre of a web of satisfying relationships, and these relationships are reciprocal. In other words, grandparents can love and care for grandchildren, and grandchildren can love and care for their grandparents.

Age-related events

The age-related events in focus here, like those for the two earlier self-empowering stories, are positive, enjoyable ones. The constraints of illness and disability has been ousted by the benefits of kinship and friendship. While this story can be about reciprocal relationships with anyone from parent to grandchild and neighbour to God, it is the special ability of the elderly to have grandchildren that makes this last relationship so important to them. That is why I chose as the heading for this chapter "I have a wonderful relationship with my grandchildren."

The psychological functions of this story

Like all the stories elderly clients tell, this story, when told in their personal style, helps to confirm the identities of the tellers. Its most important function, however, is to express the positive feelings of the tellers and, sometime, if their audience is elderly, for them to share it too. Their main emotion is pride: pride in their own capacity to develop and maintain such a relationship, and pride in those same capacities in the other people with whom they are so closely involved.

The implications of the story for the emotions and behaviour of the teller

This story is linked with a range of positive emotions in a way very different from the self-limiting stories that I have dealt with, since the latter were associated with negative feeling such as anxiety and helplessness. The main positive emotion involved here is pride, but there is also happiness and contentment and, most obviously, pure enjoyment. This story also has implications for very positive forms of behaviour from its tellers when they are interacting with others. Its tellers are more likely to approach, reach out to, share with, care for and love others, than those who do not tell it. Like the other self-promoting stories, then, it has many positive implications for the emotions and actions of the elderly clients who tell it.

Past, present and future

While past, present and future are not referred to directly in this story, it does serve to link them well. The story is told in the present tense, implying primarily that it is true now. However, the form of expression also often suggests that this has been the case for some time past; and that it will continue to be so in the future. Its tellers are saying that they have enjoyed their relationship with their grandchildren, do now, and also will do in the future. Further, they have a sense of their own integrity as they tell this story. "I am the same me as I was and will be too."

Some social aspects of the story

Its interpersonal context

While this story was sometimes told by a single elderly client to themselves, to reflect on and confirm their enjoyable relationships, it was most often told to an audience. Sometimes this audience was made up of family members and friends;

sometimes it was of health professionals; and sometimes it was told to the very people with whom the relationships had developed. Its impact of course, differed from audience to audience. With family and friends it was often told to indicate that these relationships were satisfying. With health professionals, it was often pride in self and others that was the chief point of the communication. When it was expressed to the people it involved, a further confirmation of that close relationship was achieved.

Sources of validation for the story

The main source of validation of this story was not its tellers, but those involved in the satisfying relationship at the centre of the tale. The validation source of this story could, then, enable some self-limiting stories to be tested. Another source of external validation for this story was the audience to whom it was told. The listeners, from their observation of the relationship, were able to confirm or deny this account of it.

Power in the story

This story is like the other self-promoting stories of the elderly I have described in allocating considerable power to its tellers. It acknowledges the elderly as able to create good relationships, as having the capacity to enjoy them and being free to reflect on these abilities. The tellers of this story have not handed over their power to either their own ageing bodies, or to family, or health professionals, who may all wish to "help" them. They are involved in powerful, reciprocal relationships, in which they both "help" and "are helped".

Some cultural aspects of the story

Information

The information this story provides is both self-knowledge and knowledge about the elderly for others. In both cases, the elderly tellers provide a view of themselves as confident and happy, and as being supported by as well as supporting others. They tell, also of the special advantages of the elderly over other age groups in their social relationships. Elderly people whose spouses are still with them have special opportunities for building a solid and reliable yet very intimate relationship; and those whose children are now rearing their own families have special opportunities to relate to them as loving colleagues rather than as children needing discipline. Finally, those who have grandchildren have special opportunities to have relationships that are different from the others experienced and yet very rewarding.

Values

The main cultural value of this story is that of the importance of social relationships to human beings. Everyone is seen to have such a right; but not all are able to make use of it. While being close to others is applauded, so, too is independence from others and individual achievement. All societies have to struggle to maintain a balance between these often competing values of interdependence and independence. However, it may be unfortunate for our elderly that Western societies have weighted the balance in favour of independence.

Some physical effects of telling the story

This story of positive interactions with family and friends may have a protective effect with regard to illness.[1-4] Elderly people who tell such a story may be more healthy. They do complain of fewer health problems. They also report fewer problems that are eventually diagnosed as psychosomatic disorders, that is, disorders which, while causing very real physiological damage, have their origins in mental rather than physical events. They may also be less likely to suffer from fewer specific organ impairments, such as heart disease, or at least have organs that are able to resist disease for longer. This protective effect of images of positive interactions is probably the result of their modifying the reactions of the elderly to stress.[5]

The story of satisfying relationships with others may have some protective function for elderly people who are ill. They may suffer less severe symptoms from their illness than those who do not believe themselves to be so fortunate. There have also been studies which suggest that the lasting physical effects of a disease like rheumatoid arthritis may be less severe if the elderly dealing with it are aware of the support available from good relationships. With a chronic disease, like this one, total relief of symptoms is very unlikely to occur. The quality of life which chronically ill people experience, therefore, is likely to be more dependent on the quality of the close relationships available to them than on their physical state.[6,7] Also, for elderly people whose illnesses are not necessarily chronic, having many stories of positive relationships with family and friends may be linked with better recovery from illness-related symptoms. This is true for accident victims, for example, who are more quickly rehabilitated if good relationships are available to them.[8] This also appears to be true for people with heart disease, where physical recovery is possible. Similar information is available about the physical symptoms of cancer. Coping with cancer also seems to be aided by positive interpersonal relationships, whether it be in the initial stages of diagnoses or later, when the elderly are close to death. Confirmation of these findings for all of these illnesses and injuries is available.[9,10]

Supporting the story

In this story, "I have a wonderful relationship with my grandchildren", the elderly tellers present themselves as at the centre of a network of rewarding, reciprocal relationships. The age-related events with which it deals are the specially rewarding relationships that are available only to people in later life. It is a legitimate source of pride, as well as of happiness and contentment. Its major implications for their actions are that they are able to approach, reach out to and, often, love others. It links their present, past and future well. It is told to others as well as self, and provides many opportunities for testing. The people, such as grandchildren, with whom these special relationships have been created are its chief source of validation, but others can also validate them from their posts as observers. The story allocates much power to its elderly tellers. It provides both self-knowledge and knowledge about the abilities and opportunities for the elderly for the wider community. It is based on the value that satisfying social relationships are of central importance to human beings.

The links between this story and both protection from and better coping with illness, together with the psychological functioning of those who tell it, indicate the importance of supporting and even initiating this story from elderly clients. After I examine some constructs about God and spirituality as keys to core, most central and influential constructs, I shall also show with Mrs H how this story was supported and validated. It was used, too, to deal with other problematic construing, with Mr T. Then I describe how good relationships can be initiated and maintained. Because most of this work used individual or marital therapy techniques, I consider those more suited for work with families next. Finally, I show how group therapy can enable elderly clients to develop new relationships, many of which will be rewarding.

With elderly clients, as with all therapy clients, it is important to know what are their most central and influential constructs.[11] These core constructs have a powerful influence on the rest of clients' constructs systems.[12] It is therefore important for therapists not to invalidate them, unless there is time and opportunity for clients to work through the wide range of changes that will then become necessary in the way they view themselves and their lives.[13,14] Therapists will also need to help such clients working through the almost overwhelming anxiety that can be generated in this way. Some constructs can be identified through "laddering" of more peripheral through to the more central. This can be done by asking "Why is each construct important to you?", yielding constructs at higher level of generalisation. However, this procedure can be cumbersome when working with the elderly. More appropriate is asking them to choose and talk about the most important things that have happened to them during their long lives and about their beliefs about God.[11] Mrs H said, in response to the nurse who was visiting her home, "My God is one of the good things in my life. He's always there when

I need Him. He answers my prayers and calms my fears." She proved to have a central construct about a good that was opposed to evil, "about spiritual things and things of the devil." Another of her most central constructs dealt with her occasional fears and frustrations on the one hand and tranquillity and accomplishment on the other.

Elderly clients who do not experience close positive relationships with others may find that they share few of their own stories with others. In fact often their interactions can provide, not validation or support for these stories, but invalidation by the contrast in views. They may also have difficulty in construing others as construers and story-tellers like themselves. Mr T, however, was able to share many stories with his friend, Jean, to have his stories supported by her and, perhaps most importantly, to understand her point of view. His construing of Jean as a fellow construer was apparent in his ready grasp of her concern over her missing breast, it was therefore possible for his medical practitioner to encourage him to use this mutually supportive relationship to test some of his more problematic construings: "If I'm not active and useful, my life is over." After initial tests with his medical practitioner, he agreed to try out a change in this construct with Jean in the context of their excellent relationship. He was able to do so after seeing how the effects of his requirement of himself that he be active and useful were very similar to the effects of Jean's requirement of herself that her body be young and beautiful. He also saw, with Jean's help, that there were many ways to be active and useful, so long as he was alive to be so.

Family can be supportive to the elderly in this way; but they can also, through their shared stories, push towards keeping things as they are.[15] More of this in a moment. First, however, I want to explore how therapists can help them to learn to be supportive. There are listening and responding skills that can be acquired with practice.[13] This process starts with the feelings of the friend or family member and goes on to the feelings of the elderly person. These feelings are an integral part of the stories the elderly are using to make sense of age-related events. They must be recognised and expressed in order to prevent them from distorting communication. What both people will be aiming to establish is effective, as well as open communication. Openness comes through honesty. If this kind of communication is difficult to achieve, then therapy with a professional may be the answer.[13,14] Certainly family and friends should try to support elderly clients in more active participation in their own care. When the elderly are ill, well-informed relatives or friends can be very supportive to them during their convalescence. They can even come to take a role as active members of the health care team.

On other occasions, as I have said, families can maintain stories that make life difficult for elderly clients.[16,17] They do so by hanging on to stories that present elderly clients in ways that they may not want. The job of therapists is, first, to identify who is validating that story and then working with them to retell it.[18] Mrs H was hospitalised in her mid sixties for repairs following the major surgery which she had had 6 years earlier. The repairs had eventually become necessary because she had hurled herself too soon and too strenuously into looking after her husband and three teenage grandsons and contributing to the family business. The story which dominated the whole family in its relationships with her was: "Good women look after other people." Mrs H had accepted this image but, with the help of her therapist was able to modify it. For her, it had become something more like: "Good women care for—that is, love—other people." The problem she found with her family was one of getting them to accept that she could show her love to them in ways other than doing all their laundry for them. Her community nurse agreed with Mrs H that she (the therapist) would see her husband in order to prepare the way for this change.

Of course families are not the only source of support for the self-empowering stories of the elderly. Group work centred on both drama[19] and art,[20] for example, can provide access to networks of supportive relationships. This is partly because it gives often isolated elderly people opportunities to meet others of their own age and chances to practise their interpersonal skills, which may have become rusty during their isolation. So, too, does any group experience, whether led by professionals or peers. Drama therapy can lead to the elderly developing more empathic roles with peers, through the enactment of a wide variety of other roles. It is on such naturally supportive relationships that the self-empowering stories of the elderly are maintained and validation for them received. In art therapy, this can occur not only for the stories that the elderly clients have been able to put into words, but also for the "non-verbal stories" about their vitality, creativity and mastery.

Suggested reading

● *Some physical effects of telling the story*

1. Antonucci, T. & Jackson, J. (1989). Successful ageing and life course reciprocity. In Warnes, A. (Ed.), *Human ageing and late life*. London: Edward Gould.
2. Lieberman, M.A. & Tobin, S.S. (1983). *The experience of old age*. New York: Basic Books.
3. Plank, W. (1989). *Toward a humanistic perspective in gerontology*. Frankfurt: Lang.
4. Smith, P.R. (Ed.). (1991). *The psychology of grandparenthood*. London: Routledge.
5. Hobfoll, S.F. & Walfisch, S. (1984). Coping with a threat to life: A longitudinal study of self, concept, social support and psychological distress. *American Journal of Community Psychology*, **12**, 87–100.
6. Eil, K.O. (1985). Coping with serious illness: On integrating constructs to enhance clinical research, assessment and intervention. *International Journal of Psychiatry in Medicine*, **4**, 335–356.

7. Bloom, J.R. & Spiegel, D. (1984). The relationship of two dimensions of social support to the psychological well-being and social functioning of women with advanced breast cancer. *Social Sciences and Medicine*, 8, 831–837.
8. McFarlane, A.H., Norman, G.R., Streiner, D.L. & Roy, R.G. (1984). Characteristics and correlates of effective and ineffective social supports. *Journal of Psychosomatic Research*, 6, 501–510.
9. McKay, D.A., Blake, R.L. Jr., Colwill, J.M., Brent, E.E., McCauley, J., Umlauf, F., Steakman, G.W. & Kivlahan, D. (1985). Social supports and stress as predictors of illness. *Journal of Family Practice*, 6, 575–581.
10. Markides, K.S. (1983). Aging, religiosity and adjustment: A longitudinal analysis. *Journal of Gerontology*, 38, 621–625.

● *Supporting the story*

11. Leitner, L.M. (1985). Interview methodologies for construct elicitation: Searching for the core. In F. Epting & A.W. Landfield (Eds.), *Anticipating personal construct psychology*. Lincoln: University of Nebraska Press.
12. Neimeyer, R.A. (1987). Core role reconstruction in personal construct therapy. In R.A. Neimeyer & G.J. Neimeyer (Eds), *Personal construct therapy casebook*. New York: Springer.
13. Epting, F.R. (1984). *Personal construct counselling and psychotherapy*. New York: Wiley.
14. Fitting, M.D. (1984). Professional and critical responsibilities for psychologists working with the elderly. *The Counselling Psychologist*, 12, 69–78.
15. Proctor, H. (1981). Family construct psychology: An approach to understanding and treating families. In S. Walrond-Skinner (Ed.), *Developments in family therapy*. London: Routledge and Kegan Paul, pp. 210–217.
16. Neimeyer, R.A. & Neimeyer G.J. (1985). Disturbed relationships: A personal construct view. In E. Button, (Ed.), *Personal construct theory and mental health*. Beckenham: Croom Helm, pp. 195–223.
17. Proctor, H. (1985). A construct approach to family therapy. In E. Button (Ed.), *Personal construct theory and mental health*. Beckenham: Croom Helm, pp. 237–350.
18. Viney, L.L., Benjamin, Y.N. & Preston, C.A. (1988). Constructivist family therapy for the elderly. *Journal of Family Psychology*, 2, 241–258.
19. Johnson, D.R. (1986). The developmental method in drama therapy. Group treatment with the elderly. *Arts in Psychotherapy*, 13, 17–33.
20. Landgarten, H. (1983). Art therapy for depressed elders. *Clinical Gerontologist*, 2, 45–53.

AGE-RELATED EVENTS: RETELLING CLIENTS' STORIES

11 ... about retirement

In the first four chapters of this book I introduced the general principles underlying this form of therapy for the elderly, and in the next six I dealt with specific self-limiting and self-empowering stories of a range of clients. In each of the next four chapters I shall focus on the therapy of just one client. I have selected these clients to illustrate the types of self-defeating stories that they can tell as they confront the most common and often threatening events that age can bring. These events are retirement, illness, bereavement and death. The therapeutic strategies used to give the elderly access to more self-empowering stories will also be described. These more detailed accounts of single clients and their therapy should help to make clearer how personal construct therapy is conducted with elderly clients.

Retirement marks the end of the career path for people in the paid work-force. In most Western societies, retirement is required at a particular age, usually at from 60 to 65 years, which may or may not be the age chosen by the individual worker. It is interesting that a select few in our societies, such as judges and bishops can retire later, while philosophers, historians and scientists tend to be required to retire earlier. People who have retired are, in some respects, similar to people who are unemployed, in that they no longer have the work-associated financial gain, the social support from work associates, nor the hopes and aspirations that work provides. Whether their reaction to their new situation is like that of people who are unemployed, I shall consider in a moment. Many women working at home experience a similar isolation and lack of purpose when all their children finally become independent. They experience this in their forties and have found other sources of social support and self-worth, such as grandchildren, by the time they are elderly. For many men, however, the association of work and self-worth has been with them all their adult lives. They therefore need to establish new sources of meaning for themselves in retirement.

This chapter on personal construct therapy with clients for whom retirement has provided problems begins with some general comments on the psychology of retirement. It is treated both as a normal process of transition through life and as a crisis. The need for validation during such transitions is emphasised. Then the client, Mr J, is introduced. He is a 61-year-old man who has been retired for a year and had been referred to a university-based clinic for therapy for depression. His construing and stories are, initially, listened to and analysed; then the setting of goals with him for his therapy is described. I then provide an account of his therapy with a psychologist and of the outcomes it achieved. In the concluding section of this chapter, I reflect on and evaluate the use of personal construct therapy with people who find retirement difficult.

A psychology of retirement

Retirement as transition

Retirement makes special demands on people who retire to adjust their actions to their new circumstances. Their old ways of coping at work are no longer effective elsewhere.[1] Such people have construed their lives up to that point in certain ways and so told certain stories about themselves. Now they have to change their construing as well as the stories based on it.[2] They have to make a transition.[3] It is quite normal to be in transition, as well as quite common. People in transition are in a period when growth is possible for them, in terms of the new view of their world they can develop. Of course the choices such people face about whether to change their construing can be associated with some emotional disturbances, for example, uncertainty and anxiety.[4] Some people when faced with such feelings react by hanging on to their old constructs and stories.

It seems, from the research literature, that people who have successfully made the transition to retirement differ from others who have no paid work through being unemployed, in reporting less uncertainty.[5] They also show more positive feelings and perceptions of themselves as competent, as well as showing more evidence of being engaged in rewarding relationships with others. Effective reminiscence back to working days can also provide the elderly with sources of personal integrity that enable them to deal better with the full range of transitions that they still face.[6-8]

When the events of retirement lead the elderly to experience overwhelming and interfering negative emotions, such as anxiety, depression and anger, linked with self-defeating actions, then it can be helpful to view them as in crisis. For such a state, crisis intervention therapy is recommended.[9] Such therapy takes a limited number of sessions, usually from as few as one to as many as six, and deals with the present rather than the past. After the clients' main emotions are identified and expressed, these emotions are then used to set priorities for choosing and putting into practice a course of action. Mastery of new skills in clients is encouraged, in order to provide them with grounds for new stories about their own worth. Such therapy also promotes the independence of therapists from clients, at a time when they most need such autonomy.

Retirement may be the earliest life transition in which reminiscence comes to play a large role, as personal construct therapists have noted. People who have recently retired have often suddenly moved out of a situation with work associates who were available both for the telling of some of their personal stories and for the confirmation of certain ways of construing. When such social supports are suddenly no longer available, people search for other audiences and sources of confirmation.[10] Many find that initially this can be achieved, in part by developing new stories for new associates, and also by reminiscing over old work experiences. This form of reminiscing, however, is no longer used when they have effectively made the transition to retirement with its new stories.

Retelling Mr J's stories about his retirement

Listening to Mr J

Mr J, at 66, was living at home with his wife of nearly 40 years, yet he found the adjustment to retirement from working as an accountant difficult. One reason for this was that, although his wife was able to continue with all her usual social and voluntary activities, he was unable to do so because of emphysema. This lung problem may have been caused during his naval service in submarines many years earlier. He was depressed about the state of his lungs, and gradually started to withdraw from social contact, both from his wife, and from their two sons and their family. His wife was very concerned about this. Mr J had made no preparations, other than financial ones, for his retirement. In this crucial period of his life, his sons had recently moved to other cities. Some of the stories he was telling himself and the psychologist he worked with at the clinic initially were as follows. "It seems I have no life of my own now." "I have no identity apart from my wife." "I am just hanging on, with nothing to look forward to." When his depressive feelings overwhelmed him, he would add, "I might as well kill myself." Other stories were about loneliness, anger and guilt, which he only dimly recognised. "At least at work I had things to do." "Of course I shouldn't blame them for retiring me. I was the right age for it." "I even wonder whether I'm to blame for feeling so frustrated now." Although Mr J looked sad, he seemed to have a lot he wanted to share with his therapist. Yet when she asked him how he saw the future, he said: "There is no future for me. I've lost contact with everyone and I don't believe I could link up with people now."

Some of the constructs his therapist noted Mr J. to use were apparent when she invited him to reminisce about his life in the navy. They included dying versus surviving, being cruel versus being a victim, being persecuted versus being protected, having accidents versus being safe, and powerlessness versus strength. He seemed to see himself as dying, persecuted, a victim and having accidents, and powerlessness appeared to be one of his most important constructs. Of course these constructs and the bipolar paths they presented for him were not always as clearly articulated as they are in the account from his therapist. She also asked him about the role of God and religion in his life, and he shared with her his doubts about life's meaning and purpose.

Goal setting for therapy with Mr J

Therapy was presented to Mr J as a series of projects[11] he could engage in to achieve a set of goals. He and his therapist negotiated what those goals were to be. Mindful of suggestions from personal construct therapy, she encouraged him to work towards a greater understanding of his current ways of viewing his life, some new stories that he could base on this greater understanding, and some new actions to support and validate those stories, as well a greater understanding of the choices available to him. He agreed to work towards these goals but expressed doubts as to whether he would be able to achieve them. He was unsure about whether he would be able to produce new stories and so new paths for action, especially with regard to joining in with other people.

His therapist was more confident about these changes in him, partly because she had experienced such change in other depressed men. However, she was also confident because she had evidence, from Mr J's own accounts, of his good relationships with his children and their families until recently. She was planning to encourage his greater understanding of his own construing with some loosening and tightening of his constructs in discussion with her; and to help him replace some of his depressive stories with more enjoyable ones with some cognitive behavioural techniques. His constructs of powerlessness, she hoped, would come to take a less important place in his construct system; while group activities would not only overcome something of his loneliness but would also provide him more choices in how he lived his life in retirement and how he saw himself as a retired person.

The therapy

Because of the likelihood that his depression was due to transitional factors rather than personal ones, his therapist aimed to draw up a contract with Mr J in which they agreed to have only a small number of sessions. Mr J seemed to initially be expecting to meet with her for about 3 months on a weekly basis at the clinic. Because of his loneliness and need to establish sources of social support outside therapy, his therapist suggested only five sessions. Their eventual compromise was to agree to meet for six sessions of an hour each, with re-evaluation of this contract at the end of the fifth session. Because of Mr J's depression and alienation, his therapist offered to see him in his own home, but with the possibility of his visiting her office later.

His therapist was working with Mr J. for him to arrive at a greater understanding of his own construing[12] through recognising the looseness and tightness of his construing and the need to maintain a balance.[13] Early in the first therapy session he had been expressing some anger towards both his previous employers and his workmates. "Towards the end everyone at work was setting me up or ignoring me. They couldn't wait to get rid of the old fogey. And I couldn't wait to get out." This construing was very tight, that is, it gave him very precise predictions about how his colleagues would behave. However, this tightness meant a loss of openness and flexibility in his construing for Mr J. His therapist, in order to loosen his construing about his ex-workmates, asked him to use free association. After he had associated to the word "colleague", as he relaxed in his chair, Mr J was able, on reflection, to loosen some of this construing considerably. "Colleague, workmate, accounts, achievements, doing something." This construing was still too loose for Mr J, so, again, after reflection, he came up with a better balance between loose and tight construing of this topic. "I still don't like my old colleagues and wouldn't want to keep in touch with them. But I can see that they had their reasons for behaving oddly when they saw my retirement looming—like, they had their own careers to consider." Mr J's therapist referred to this example later in the sessions to help him in his growing understanding of his own construing and reconstruing.[14]

Much of the impact of Mr J's depressive stories was likely to be reduced, his therapist considered, by sharing them with her.[15] This meant that she needed to guard against being overcome by those stories herself, since she knew that she had some of those depressive stories in her own repertoire. She needed, however, to listen openly to his stories and acknowledge their content. However, because it was to brief therapy only that they had both agreed, she chose to provide him with some tools with which to cope with them himself. People who tell depressed stories can be encouraged to find different ones by using a range of cognitive behavioural techniques.[16-19] The most useful of these proved to be, for Mr J, focusing on past events that he had enjoyed, either alone or with others, and which he could enjoy in his imagination then.[16] He could have included people, objects, ideas or physical activities. Even imagining enjoyed physical activities can be beneficial to people who are depressed. Mr J was able to think of some such sources of enjoyment that were available to him still, such as completing a crossword puzzle and taking a leisurely walk around the lake. For him, recognition that he could still do these things was one of the first steps away from his depression. It provided him with validation of some positive construing of himself, which was much needed.

Powerlessness versus strength seemed to be a central construct for Mr J, influencing his more peripheral constructs of persecution, being in accidents and being a victim. This proved, however, to be surprisingly easily changed, as he came to understand his own construing more and develop the tools to combat his depressive moods. However, he also used the group activities which his therapist suggested for this purpose. These activities I shall describe in a moment. He was, then, able to let his old central construct give way to a more influential construct about "working with others versus working alone". Both poles of this more important construct could be applied to himself by Mr J in an empowering way. Of course this construing was still based very much on his now completed work experiences, but it could also serve well for reaching out to his family and in wider social activities in the future.

Group activities seemed, to his therapist, to be indicated for Mr J. However, she did not want to promote his dependence on a special therapeutic group, whether run by professionals or peers.[20-22] She considered that he needed some group activities that he could both enjoy and continue to make part of his life. They could cut through some of his loneliness. Also, through the models provided by his fellow retirees at the group, he could gain a greater range of choices about the roles he might play. Mr J initially had a lot of difficulty in choosing a type of activity group he could enjoy. By the fourth therapy session, however, he had decided to try two quite informal groups: an early morning men's swimming group and a weekly afternoon bridge playing group. As his therapy sessions ended he was beginning to use both of these groups to stabilise and confirm his sense of worth, reclaiming his identity through the stories he was now able to tell in these groups. In the men's group, he also found understanding of his construing of himself as powerless and his feelings of depression, some ideas from the group about coping with such feelings and a broader perspective on his life.

Outcomes achieved by Mr J

Mr J was able to test and retell his stories about retirement both with his therapist and with his wider group of fellow swimmers. During the four separate strands of his therapy, which have been separated here but actually occurred almost concurrently, he was able to acknowledge some of his anger, loosen his depression a little, reduce his construct of powerlessness to a less important position in his construct system and begin to overcome something of his loneliness. He continued, however, to suffer some milder bouts of depression. Further work with his sons and their families might have been appropriate, if they had been available. It was not considered necessary with his wife, because she quickly began to respond warmly to the small changes she could see in him during the therapy. His therapist judged it very likely that their relationship would continue to improve without further intervention from her.

The first aspect of his post-retirement life that Mr J began to construe positively was his financial status. Discussions with his swimming and bridge companions made it clear that many of them were worried about their ability to cope financially in the future. He could see that he, using his skills as an accountant, had been able to make and act on a financial plan for himself and his wife that offered as great a degree of security as the current economic recession could provide. "Of course, when you retire, you get a lump sum of superannuation— and, ah, you feel more free, because you don't have to worry about your fortnightly salary and can plan what to do with that lump sum." He also came to see that he could enjoy such an independent existence which provided him with some real choices: "One of the good things about retirement is, that you can do what you want to do each day and more generally in your life too." Although distancing himself from these positive stories by telling them as if speaking for someone else rather than himself, he was finally able to say " I think, when I've got more used to it, that there are some things I am actually going to enjoy about my retirement." Both Mr J and his therapist agreed to finish therapy, as they had planned, after six sessions.

Personal construct therapy for retired clients

Retirement has been described as a transition in which, because so many new events have occurred, old ways of construing and acting are no longer appropriate. Old ways of coping and the telling of old work-based stories no longer provides a sense of self-worth and confirmation of identity. These events can lead to feelings of anxiety, depression and frustration, which in turn can lead to resistance to change. Elderly people making the transition into retirement can choose to make the most of their opportunities to explore new ways of living or to resist any change at all, hanging on to their less effective ways of construing. Retirement, then, can be a period of further psychological growth or one of hanging on to self-defeating ways of construing and coping.

When the anxiety, depression or frustration become too great, to the point of interfering with taking effective action, retirement can be said to have led to a crisis. Crisis intervention therapy for such transitory problem reactions is marked by a number of characteristics. It is brief, with as few as one to six therapy sessions. It involves clients in identifying and expressing their most important distressing emotions. It then deals with the present more than the past, and with actions more than feelings. Finally, it is skill-oriented. It therefore promotes the independence of elderly clients and encourages them to add to their old stories new versions and to find new sources of validation for their new construing.

Mr J was finding the transition to retirement difficult, his depressive and lonely feelings making it hard for him to change some of his construing as he needed. These were the main emotions identified and expressed by Mr J early in therapy, together with some anger and guilt. His current construing and stories were the focus of his therapy, not the past events on which he had based them. All the projects that he and his therapist negotiated together were associated with him acting in some different way. For example, his greater awareness of his own construing was encouraged in order to see how it influenced his actions. The new stories he was to develop were to serve as paths for action, as was the greater range of choices that he was to have. Mr J also learned a number of skills in the course of this brief therapy, such as, how to use some cognitive behavioural techniques to limit his own depressive feelings and how to monitor his own role as a construer and potential reconstruer. He also began to replace his stories of helplessness and constructs of powerlessness with those about his own present freedom of choice and even, eventually, of enjoyment.

This account of personal construct therapy with a man who has recently retired has shown it be useful but not magical. The main reason Mr J's depressive feelings, for example, were dealt with so quickly is because they arose in reaction to a particular event of retirement. They were the result of transition. Some elderly people feel depressed for much more personal and long-standing reasons, and they need more therapy sessions, with somewhat different content. In the next chapter, I shall describe how a somewhat older woman was helped to deal with the ongoing stress of severe, chronic illness.

Suggested reading

• *A psychology of retirement*

1. Carp, F.M. (1972). *Retirement*. New York: Behavioural Publications.
2. Golan, N. (1981). *Passing through transitions*. New York: Free Press.
3. Gould, R.L. (1978). *Transformations*. New York: Simon & Schuster.
4. Viney, L.L. (1980). *Transitions*. Sydney: Cassell.
5. Viney, L.L. & Tych, A.M. (1985). To work or not to work: An enquiry of men experiencing unemployment, promotion and retirement. *Psychology and Human Development*, **1**, 57-66.
6. Richter, R.L. (1986). Allowing ego integrity through life review. *Journal of Religion and Ageing*, **2**, 1-11.
7. Gubrium, J.F. (1976). *Time, roles and self in old age*. New York: Human Sciences Press.

8. Sherman, E. (1987). Reminiscence groups for community elderly. *Gerontologist*, **27**, 569-572.
9. Aguilera, D., Messick, J.M. & Farrell, M.S. (1970). *Crisis intervention*. St. Louis: Mosby.
10. Winter, D. (1985). Group therapy with depressives: A personal construct theory perspective. *International Journal of Mental Health*, **13**, 67-85.

● *Retelling stories about retirement: therapy*

11. Viney, L.L. (1993). Goals in psychotherapy: Some reflections of a constructivist therapist. In L. Leitner & G. Dunnett (Eds.), *Critical issues in personal construct therapy*. Malabar, Florida: Krieger.
12. Neimeyer, G.J. & Neimeyer, R.A. (1992). Intervening in meaning: Defining the boundaries of constructivist assessment. In G.J. Neimeyer (Ed.), *Case book in constructivist assessment*. New York: Sage.
13. Epting, F.R. (1984). *Personal construct counselling and psychotherapy*. New York: Wiley.
14. Fransella, F. & Dalton, P. (1990). *Personal construct counselling in action*. London: Sage.
15. Rowe, D. (1978). *The experience of depression*. Chichester: Wiley.
16. Beck, A.T., Emery, G. & Greenberg, R.L. (1985). *Anxiety disorders and phobias: A cognitive perspective*. New York: Basic Books.
17. Gallagher, D. & Thomson, L.W. (1982). Treatment of major depressive disorders in older adult outpatients with brief psychotherapies. *Psychotherapy*, **19**, 482-490.
18. Thompson, L.W., Gallagher, D. & Breckenridge, I.S. (1987). Comparative effectiveness of psychotherapies for depressed elderly. *Journal of Consulting and Clinical Psychology*, **55**, 385-390.
19. Thompson, L.W., Davies, R., Gallagher, D. & Kranzc, S. (1985). Cognitive therapy with older adults. *Clinical Gerontologist*, **5**, 245-279.
20. Griffin, M. & Waller, M. (1985). Group therapy for the elderly: One approach to coping. *Clinical Social Work Journal*, **13**, 261-271.
21. Leszcz, M. (1990). Towards an integrated model of group psychotherapy with the elderly. *The International Journal of Group Psychotherapy*, **40**, 379-490.
22. Rook, K.S. (1984). Promoting social bonding: Strategies for helping the lonely and socially isolated. *American Psychologist*, **39**, 1389-1407.

12 ... about illness

While many elderly people have made the transition to retirement without problems, they find it difficult to deal with physical illness. For those who have experienced no serious illness when younger, there has been no opportunity to develop the constructs necessary to deal with such a life-affecting event. Now they are more likely than younger people to experience both acute illnesses, which are short but may be life-threatening, and more long-lasting chronic illnesses, such as those caused by rheumatism, strokes and heart conditions. This chapter therefore deals with illness. Illness is less common than the loss of others and subsequent mourning, which I discuss in the next chapter. Dealing with one's own death, which all human beings have to do, is examined in the last chapter of this section.

Elderly clients experiencing the symptoms of both acute and chronic illness try to make sense of what is happening to them. They construe their illnesses and tell stories about them. The meanings that they convey are seen by personal construct therapists as central to how people react to illness, and consequently to recovery and rehabilitation. In the second section of this book, I have emphasised, in my accounts of self-defeating and self-empowering stories of the elderly, that the former tend to be linked with poor recovery and rehabilitation, while the latter have more beneficial physical effects for them. It is within this conceptual framework that I shall be describing therapy with elderly people who are ill.

This chapter begins with a brief personal construct psychology of illness, including stories told by elderly people and others, about their own illness and their construing of it. This account will also examine some of the main emotional responses of the elderly to illness and links between psychology and illness. To conclude this section I deal specifically with the stories told by the elderly about illness. I then go on, as I did in Chapter 11, to describe therapy with one elderly client, Mrs C, who had recently had a stroke. She was frightened and confused, and her husband was becoming frustrated and angry in his dealings with her. A general account will be given of her situation, and then her stories and constructs reviewed. Again, as in Chapter 11, I shall consider goal-setting with Mrs C, from the point of view of her therapist, a counsellor and herself. Then I shall describe a range of strategies which helped her to retell her stories to some extent. These included behavioural techniques, skill retraining, shared reconstruction and learning to relate to others again. Some of the outcomes achieved by Mrs C and her therapist will also be described.

A psychology of illness

Stories and illness

When the elderly are ill, they try to see meaning in that illness. In personal construct terms, they use constructs to spell out these meanings. In fact they do not actually respond to the symptoms of their illness, but to their constructs about them.[1] Often they build these constructs together into integrated stories about their illness which then determine how they react to them. The central message to them from personal construct therapy is that, since they have developed, even created, their own constructs and stories about the illness, they have the power to change them.[2] Some culturally shared stories about tuberculosis in the nineteenth century and cancer in the twentieth, for example, show how such stories can go far beyond accurate description of either disease. Tuberculosis was described as painless, cancer as painful. Tuberculosis was given almost aphrodisiac properties, while cancer was desexualising. Even the stories about their treatment differed, people with tuberculosis being wooed and coaxed, while people with cancer were assaulted (for example, in stories of the "bombardment" of cancer cells).

During this decade more attention has been paid to people's stories about illness. For example, researchers have tried to understand what it is like to have the symptoms of certain illnesses and how to construct one's own stories about them.[3] They have come to recognise that people build these stories out of ordinary, everyday experiences and not out of specialist medical experiences.[4] Also these stories stem from beliefs about links between symptom and disease which people held long before their current symptoms became apparent. A team of researchers which has been working on these stories for almost two decades describes them as common-sense models of illness.[5] They have found four factors to be important to the development of these illness stories. The first of these factors consists of the identifying characteristics of the illness, such as the location of the symptoms, how they are felt and seen, how long they last and the language with which they are expressed. The other factors that they consider to influence the development of such stories by people who are ill are their perceptions of the causes of the illness, its course over time and its likely outcomes.

The emotional responses of the elderly to illness

People's emotional responses to illness have been identified and compared, and found to be highly consistent for many different types of illness and different age groups.[6-7] One of its major emotions is anxiety, a reaction to the many threats that severe illness poses.[2] In fact different sources of such anxiety have proved important in elderly people's reactions to situations related to chronic illness. After they are discharged from hospital, bodily mutilation is often important to them. So, too, if their rehabilitation is not progressing well, are feelings of isolation. Further, if their illness produces handicaps in communication (as in some kinds of strokes or deafness), then vague, general anxiety is common. Elderly clients who are ill, then, have many reasons to be anxious.

In reaction to the frustrations of attempts to use their old ways of coping and expressing themselves by the symptoms of their illness, people are also likely to be angry.[2] Their anger is not, however, expressed directly but rather indirectly or passively. This may be because of the constraints often caused by their increasing dependence on others, particularly family, friends and the health professionals available to them. They also seem to turn this anger in on themselves, so that depressive feelings result, with much self-blame and pessimism. Expressing the anxiety and depression has, however, been linked with better rehabilitation, whereas indirectly expressed anger has been linked with poor rehabilitation.

Also characteristic of elderly people's reaction to illness are feelings of helplessness.[2] Such feelings have been linked with poor rehabilitation. Since there are so many situations that the elderly who are ill experience, in which they are "done to" rather than being "the doer", this is hardly surprising. People's sense of competence has also been seen to be reduced by illness, and this is particularly marked in the elderly. It seems to be easier for young people who are severely ill to maintain their sense of control and also of those of their own abilities that remain intact. Elderly people seem more likely to be overwhelmed by illness-related events, and to develop many constructs about themselves as helpless and very few about themselves as competent.

Psychological factors and illness

Psychological factors contribute both to the development of illness in people and their recovery from it, in both the middle-aged and the elderly.[2] While these links have been apparent for some time, it is only recently that researchers have begun to show how such links may be made. They can be seen in the gastro-intestinal system, cardiovascular system and immune system. In the elderly, for example, their telling of pessimistic stories has been linked with poor immune system functioning, resulting in more risk of infection.[8] This is not to say that one of these states necessarily caused the other. It should also be added that poor immune system function in the elderly has also been linked with poor health, use of many medications, problems in sleeping, depression and the drinking of alcohol in the form of beer or spirits.

Because such links between mind and body have been established, it is well for therapists with elderly clients to monitor any psychological contribution to their illnesses or their responses to it.[9] One client's headaches may be linked to her ongoing battles with the daughter with whom she lives. Another client's high blood pressure may be worsened by stress. A third client's overwhelming sense of helplessness in the face of her severe illness may make any hope for her future impossible and so limit her chances of successful rehabilitation. However, it is also well for therapists to be careful that such an assessment does not bring blame for the illness from family and even some health professionals. Clients do not see themselves as being able to choose how tense or overwhelmed they feel. It is the job of their therapists to show them that this can be so.

Illness stories of the elderly and their sense of integrity

Illness and injury make it difficult for the elderly to maintain a sense of integri-ty.[10] I identified integrity as very important to the personal construct psychology of the elderly that I described in Chapter 2, and to the self-promoting stories I considered in Chapters 8, 9 and 10. Illness often provides the elderly with expe-riences that make it hard for them to continue to tell stories about themselves as being content and concerned with a wider perspective than simply the here and now, two of the hallmarks of personal integrity.[11] For example, physical disabili-ties make it difficult for the elderly to trust and hope. Disabilities also limit the freedom of the elderly, so how do they then maintain their autonomy? Their capacities to take initiative and to feel confident are also frustrated by many ill-ness-related events. If such basic construing of self is threatened, how can a sense of integrity be maintained? The more healthy the elderly clients can main-tain themselves the better their chances of retaining their sense of integrity.[12]

When the elderly become ill, especially, but also when they become frail, their capacity to trust is put to the test. They need to be able to trust the physicians, nurses and family members in whose hands they place themselves. They also need to be able to trust anyone with whom they will engage in effective therapy. This is an important criterion for selecting elderly clients for therapy. And what makes such trust possible? Essentially, they are relying on the integrity of those others on whom they depend, health professionals, families and therapists.

Retelling Mrs C's stories about her illness

Listening to Mrs C

At 63 years, Mrs C was referred for therapy, having had a quite severe stroke 6 months earlier. She was referred by the community nurse because of the over-whelming and debilitating anxiety she was still experiencing. When her counsellor first met Mrs C in her own home that anxiety was apparent to her, in Mrs C's sweating palms and continually worried facial expression. So, too, was the extent of the interference with her cognitive functioning from the brain damage caused by the stroke. This included loss of her abilities to read, spell, write (all but her name) and recognise numbers and, apparently, her capacity to relearn and retain information. At 6 months after the stroke, it was too early to tell which of these capacities might return. It was also too early to tell whether her high level of anxiety was more related to the confusion with which these losses left her, or to some stories that she was telling to herself about herself.

Mrs C seemed to her counsellor to be overweight, unkempt in hair and clothes, and rather sweaty. She was extremely anxious in the presence of her counsellor initially; although this anxiety diminished a little when the two of them retired to her kitchen and she was able to talk to her directly without her husband being present. Mr C's love for his wife was apparent, but so, too, was his disgust that she was not responding more quickly to the rehabilitation techniques being used with her. "I think she should try harder." He was putting a lot of pressure on her to respond, perhaps in part because of his frustration with being "stuck at home with her". His normally social life style, based on their local club, was being limited by her requests that he stay home with her. Since, without number recognition she would not have been able to tell the time by herself, her dependence on him, for the moment, was seen by her counsellor as necessary and not manipulative. Again, in the privacy of her kitchen, Mrs C reported that she could not remember having sex with her husband; "I don't really like it." Mr C reported that in bed with him, "she is just like a young girl."

Not surprisingly, the stories Mrs C was telling about herself were self-defeating. One set dealt with her loss of normal abilities to function in the everyday world. "I can't do anything", she said, making it very hard for her to make any progress in any way at all. Another of those stories extended this all-encompassing plot to all possible future occasions: "I'll never do anything again." She was feeling both helpless and hopeless. She was also refusing to go out, even with Mr C, and this refusal was tied to another set of stories of hers about embarrassment and shame. It became clear that she was very aware of the slowness of her speech and other lack of response to others, when she had been able to speak as quickly and clearly as they did before the stroke. "I feel awful when I'm with other people, so stupid and slow." "Whatever do they think of me. I'll never go out again." Here, too, she was tying herself into a totally self-defeating set of stories.

When her counsellor listened to Mrs C, she was aware that these stories were based on two main constructs. One such construct was her confusion. "I'm not able to get a grip on things." She told of her struggles to handle the telephone, for example, and how each time she would try to phone she would "make a total mess of it." Her other major construct was one of rejection. She saw herself as "unlovely" and "unloved." Her current physical appearance was quite unattractive. Her husband, her closest person, was, in fact, rejecting her. Her construing here was, then, not necessarily inaccurate, but nevertheless could be changed.

Goal-setting with Mrs C

Given Mrs C's anxiety, confusion and stories of incapacity, her counsellor believed it to be essential that she commit herself to achieving some relatively simple and concrete goals in therapy. Their contract was that they both would work hard towards achieving a more comfortable lifestyle for Mrs C. This was not so much negotiated together as planned by the counsellor. Her prime focus with Mrs C was on action projects, designed with the aims of eventually increasing her awareness of her construing, giving her some alternative stories and providing opportunities in the future for choice. To accomplish this, she arranged with Mrs C initially twice-weekly half-hour sessions at home, to be followed by weekly and finally fortnightly visits. Eventually 12 such visits were made before Mrs C and her therapist agreed to finish therapy. Her counsellor then followed up this therapy with some monthly supporting telephone calls.

The therapy

Mrs C's anxiety, if caused by her illness and its resulting symptoms, was entirely appropriate. However, that anxiety itself had become extremely threatening to her. Her fear of having panic attacks was almost as great as the fear she experienced during them. Also, as I have said, anxiety is linked with more illness,[13] with which Mrs C did not need to have to deal. It was therefore important that she learn some skills for managing that anxiety. In her current state, her counsellor judged, the more complex of techniques, such as systematic relaxation, would be too difficult for her. She therefore told her about the effects of breathing deeply on levels of anxiety.[14,15] Initially, Mrs C was encouraged to experience the effect on her anxiety when she took, say, 20 deep breaths, breathing so that her lungs expanded as much as possible. She later learned to take some breaths of this kind before answering the telephone, to ward off, or at least to limit, the anxiety of any subsequent panic attack.

Because not being able to tell the time made her particularly dependent on others, her consellor asked Mrs C to work with her towards being able to do so. Initially, Mrs C was very anxious, but her counsellor showed her respect for her and her expectation that Mrs C would cope. She was to learn to read the hour hand of her kitchen clock, as well as a quarter to and a quarter past the hour and half past the hour.[16] This was an attempt by her counsellor to invalidate those entrapping stories of Mrs C's that she "couldn't do anything" and "never will do anything", and to find more encouraging stories to take their place.[17,18] Her counsellor anticipated that Mrs C would have forgotten how to tell the time in this way by her next visit; and that was indeed the case. However, she was prepared to repeat the training simply and calmly as many times as it took for Mrs C to learn it. The counsellor reported to Mr C their work on this problem, asking him to help his wife to learn it and emphasising that this simple form of time-telling only was involved. He, however, ignored this part of the story, and continued to quiz her on times like 4.25 and 6.05. The counsellor clarified this several times for him and continued practising these skills with Mrs C. By their sixth session, Mrs C was remembering it quite well and, as a consequence, feeling a little pleased with herself, for what she felt was the first time since her stroke.

Had the relationship between Mr and Mrs C been more robust at that time, working with them together in family therapy might have been appropriate.[19,20] However, given its state, the counsellor chose to work individually with Mr C to achieve some of the same goals. Clearly, he needed to express his anger and frustration and to explore his own construing, so as to find some alternative stories. In the three sessions they had together, the expression of his anger needed little encouragement. He was furious and disappointed with his wife for "letting me down". He felt "trapped" at home with her. He resented the loss of male companionship that her "demands" for him to stay home with her inflicted. He also proved to be experiencing a little guilt about some of his feelings about his wife. The counsellor encouraged him to share his construing with her, and make clear that she could see his point of view. She also helped him to organise other family members to be with Mrs C on two weekly afternoons and on Friday night, while he spent time with his men friends at his club, playing "the pokies" [poker machines] and cards, and drinking the occasional beer. She then took the opportunity, offered by their alliance, to keep him a little more in touch with Mrs C's point of view too, especially in regard to the frightening, and to him, frustrating, sexual encounters.

Mrs and Mr C expressed considerable conflict over some dresses Mr C had bought for her since her stroke. She had not even taken the label off them, let alone worn them. She confided to the counsellor that she felt that they were unsuitable for her, but also that she was now far too unattractive to wear them. The counsellor then gently confronted this story with an alternative story of her own. "If you had an accident and chopped off the end of your finger, would you be any less of a person." The relevance of this for her own position struck Mrs C at once; and her counsellor used this chance to mention getting her hair cut and set, as it had not been done since before the stroke. Mrs C countered that she would not be able to give instructions about it to a hairdresser quickly enough; but Mrs C and the counsellor were able to find a photograph of her before the stroke to take as a guide. The counsellor then made an appointment for her nearby telling the hairdresser that Mrs C was recovering from being very ill. This excursion, although traumatic for Mrs C, raised her own and her husband's confidence in her considerably. Even the counsellor began to see her with new eyes. Shared reconstructing by client and therapist was occurring.

Her counsellor would not have completed her sessions with Mrs C without making sure that she had support from people other than herself in developing her self-promoting stories.[21] Mr C, who had previously confirmed only her most self-defeating stories, was becoming more able to do so; but his anger and frustration might surge up again, making this less likely. Some neighbours seemed more suitable for this purpose than the family members, given their initial lack of support of Mr and Mrs C in this time of crisis. One neighbour was an elderly widow, the other, a mother at home with young children. Her therapist encouraged Mrs C to invite each of these neighbours separately for a cup of tea about once a week. While Mrs C feared their ridicule of her continuing slowness and clumsiness, she soon found them able to provide her with quite non-critical company and confirmation for those stories.

Outcomes achieved by Mrs C

After her therapy sessions were completed, Mrs C was still suffering from some major physical and psychological effects of the stroke. She had, as well as the achievements I have described, succeeded in learning to identify and use numbers again. It was still likely to be more than a year, however, before she would have recovered as much as she ever would. She was to continue to visit a rehabilitation unit periodically for monitoring and, when judged necessary, further rehabilitation. Her therapy had, however, roused her from the despair that had been overwhelming her. She had begun to tell at least some stories about herself that were encouraging and was revising much of how she had come to construe other people.

In coming to use some simple tools to deal with her anxiety, she was able to say "I don't feel so overwhelmed by panic now." Her early experiences in the therapy with relearning how to tell the time helped her to be able to say "It's hard; but maybe if I keep trying, I'll get there . . . well sometimes." The reconstruction that led to her admitting "When I look in the mirror, I do feel more like my old self. Before I didn't dare look at all." And with her revised contacts with her neighbours, she was able to agree "It feels good to have a bit of company in." She and Mr C were beginning to reconstrue their relationship, a process that would need to continue as some of her abilities returned to her.

Personal construct therapy for elderly clients who are ill

When elderly people are ill, they particularly need to make sense of what is happening to them. They use constructs based on past experiences to make events meaningful, and even combine these constructs into stories. I have mentioned some common stories about tuberculosis and cancer. Elderly people who are ill actually build their own, common-sense accounts of their illnesses, based in part on the symptoms and the cause of them, but also on their own past experiences of other illnesses and others' constructs about these illnesses. The emotions which illness stimulates in the elderly are similar across many illnesses and also like those of younger people. Elderly people who are ill experience considerable anxiety and depression, which, though distressing, can be helpful in recovery if expressed well. However, they also experience considerable helplessness and indirectly expressed anger, neither of which aid recovery.

Such links between psychological and bodily functioning have often been found. Association between mind and body can now be seen in a variety of the bodily systems of the elderly: the gastro-intestinal, cardiovascular and immune systems. Therapists working with the elderly are advised to monitor such links in their clients. Their physical health should be monitored closely. The symptoms of their illness and their resulting disability or lethargy can make it hard for elderly people to maintain any sense of integrity. Such outcomes of illness can serve to blight hope in the elderly, limit their autonomy, cut off their initiative and make any sense of competence or identity very difficult for them to maintain. With the building blocks for their integrity being knocked out in this way by illness, it can be very hard for them to keep any sense of their own integrity.

At 63, Mrs C was referred to her therapist some 6 months after a quite severe stroke. She had lost much spelling, writing and recognition of and use of numbers, and apparently her capacity to relearn. When her therapist first met her, she saw her as overweight, unattractive and unkempt. Mrs C could not tell the time, and could remember nothing of having had sex with her husband before her stroke. She was generally anxious but also experiencing panic attacks, and her husband was angry and resentful. Mrs C's main stories were self-defeating ones: "I can't do anything" and "I'll never do anything again." Her main constructs were about the confusion underlying her anxiety and the rejection she was experiencing from her husband and others.

The goals that her therapist planned to achieve with Mrs C mainly involved action. Their agreed aim was to make life more comfortable for Mrs C. At the same time, however, these action strategies were used to help her become aware of some of the traps her constructs provided for her, and to develop some alternative stories and a wider range of choices. Their actual therapy involved Mrs C in learning to use deep breathing to begin to control the level of her anxiety, as well as to tell the time to the quarter hour. Some parallel individual therapy sessions with Mr C also helped him to express and accept his own feelings, understand a little of Mrs C's construing, and plan some ways in which he might spend some time away from her at their club. Mrs C also did some shared reconstruing with her therapist which led to her successful visit to the hairdresser. She was also encouraged to reach out in a limited way to her neighbours. This therapy did seem to cut through her despair. It helped her control her panic attacks, and it led to her telling some much more encouraging stories about herself: "It's hard . . . but I'll get there" and "I do feel more like my old self." Her learning how to tell the time and improve her appearance with her therapist led to this story retelling, while her renewed contacts with her neighbours provided opportunity to confirm these new stories.

This chapter about personal construct therapy with an elderly client who was ill, has shown many of the losses with which she, and others like her, have to deal. Mrs C had lost many abilities such as spelling and writing. She had also lost much of her mobility and something of her ability to speak clearly to others. She had lost, too, contacts with neighbours and friends, and was in danger of losing her initially good relationship with her husband. She had much to mourn. Mourning is in fact the topic of my next chapter, and the chief task of the client I describe in it. However, the loss in that chapter is of a much loved person and the retelling of the client's stories are necessary for effective mourning. Chapter 13 is about personal construct therapy for elderly clients who are bereaved.

Suggested reading

● *A psychology of illness*

1. Viney, L.L. (1986). Physical illness: A guidebook for the kingdom of the blind. In E. Button (Ed.), *Personal construct theory and mental health*. Beckenham: Croom Helm.
2. Viney, L.L. (1989). *Images of illness*. Florida: Krieger, Second edition.
3. Bishop, G.D. & Converse, S.A. (1986). Illness representations: A prototype approach. *Health Psychology*, **5**, 95–114.

4. Gannick, D. & Jesperson, M. (1984). Lay concepts and strategies for handling symptoms of disease. *Scandinavian Journal of Primary Health Care*, 2, 67–76.
5. Leventhal, H., Nerenz, D.R. & Steele, D.J. (1982). Illness representations and coping with health threats. In A. Baum & J. Singer (Eds.), *A handbook of psychology and health*. Hillsdale, New Jersey: Lawrence Erlbaum.
6. Prohaska, T.R., Keller, M.L., Leventhal, E.A. & Leventhal, H. (1987). Impact of symptoms and ageing attributions on emotions and coping. *Health Psychology*, 6, 495–514.
7. Viney, L.L. (1990). A constructivist model of psychological reactions to illness and injury. In G.J. Neimeyer & R.A. Neimeyer (Eds.), *Advances in Personal Construct Psychology*. New York: JAI Press.
8. Kamen-Siegel, L., Rodin, J., Seligman, M.E. & Dwyer, J. (1991). Explanatory style and cell-mediated immunity in elderly men and women. *Health Psychology*, 10, 249–255.
9. Gouldsmith, E.M. & Good, R. (1991). All in the mind? The psychologicalisation of illness. *The Psychologist*, 14, 449–453.
10. Erikson, E.H., Erikson, J.M. & McKinnick, H.Q. (1986). *Vital involvement in old age*. London: Norton.
11. Erikson, E.H. (1963). *Childhood and society*. New York: Norton.
12. Viney, L.L., Benjamin, Y.N. & Preston, C. (1988). Promoting independence in the elderly: The role of psychological social and physical constraints. *Clinical Gerontologist*, 24, 71–82.

● *Retelling stories about illness: therapy*

13. Viney, L.L. (1989). *Images of illness*. Florida: Krieger, Second edition.
14. Greer, S. & Moorey, S. (1987). Adjunct psychological therapy for patients with cancer. *European Journal of Surgical Oncology*, 13, 511–516.
15. Forester, B., Kornfeld, D.S. & Fleiss, J. (1982). Effects of psychotherapy on patient distress during radiotherapy for cancer. *Psychosomatic Medicine*, 44, 118–126.
16. Yesavage, J.A. (1984). Relaxation and memory training in 39 elderly patients. *American Journal of Psychiatry*, 141, 778–781.
17. Babbins, L.H., Dillon, J. & Merovitz, S. (1988). The effects of validation therapy on disoriented elderly. *Activities, Adaptation and Ageing*, 12, 73–86.
18. Viney, L.L. (1989). Psychotherapy as shared reconstruction. *International Journal of Personal Construct Psychology*, 3, 423–442.
19. Proctor, H. (1985). A construct approach to family therapy. In E. Button (Ed.), *Personal construct theory and mental illness*. Beckenham: Croom Helm.
20. Viney, L.L., Benjamin, Y.N. & Preston, C. (1988). Constructivist family therapy with the elderly. *Journal of Family Psychology*, 2, 241–258.
21. Neimeyer, R.A. & Neimeyer G.J. (Eds.) (1987). *Personal construct therapy casebook*. New York: Springer.

13 ... about bereavement

This chapter on personal construct therapy for the elderly who are bereaved follows two on retirement and illness and precedes one on dying. In each I describe some of the helpful ways of making good psychological sense of these often distressing events with which the elderly are likely to be faced. I then go on to describe a bereaved client and the use of personal construct therapy with her. Loss of spouse or other loved people are not the only losses to be borne by the elderly. Elderly clients can also suffer loss of physical functioning, such as sight and hearing, and sexual function, as well as loss of health, work, relationships and brain function. There can even be a loss of aspects of the old self to be mourned.

Elderly clients who have lost someone close to them, and indeed all people in mourning, first experience shock and numbness. They then go on to show signs of psychological strain, as well as the feelings of anger, anxiety, guilt, sadness, depression and even despair. They can also deny either the loss itself, or some aspects of the person who has been lost. This denial response is usually only temporary, as is the common idealisation of the person they have lost. Bereavement, then, leads to an almost incredible range of emotions for the elderly, and often these emotions are experienced by them with an intensity which they have never known before. There is considerable evidence that some of their psychological processes during bereavement represent their struggle to deal with this situation. There is also evidence that support from others can help them to mourn more effectively. Sadly, this is often a time when they are least able to reach out to others, because isolation and alienation can be important to their bereavement response.

In this chapter, then, I provide a psychology of bereavement, beginning with some of the effects of it on the elderly that research has revealed. I then deal with the psychoanalytic approaches to bereavement, stressing separation, and the concept of bereavement as transition is also described. These approaches are then compared with the personal construct approach to bereavement, in which loss is seen as triggering dislocation of the construct system of those who grieve. I then describe the processes of therapy with Mrs Z, who had recently lost her husband. As in the last two chapters, I show what can be learned from listening to Mrs Z, especially to her stories and her constructs. Then the goal setting processes of the therapy are considered, from the viewpoints of both Mrs Z and her welfare worker, before the therapy itself are described. Then an account of the outcomes achieved by Mrs Z is provided, as is an evaluation of the role of personal construct therapy with bereaved, elderly clients.

A psychology of bereavement

Some physical effects of bereavement on the elderly

Both the physical and psychological health of the elderly can be threatened by bereavement.[1] There is evidence, for example, that those who are in mourning have the functioning of their immune systems affected.[2] In other words, while grieving, because of this physiological change, they are more susceptible to colds and influenza, and indeed any viral infections. Their own reports have supported this finding, the bereaved elderly being more likely to report illness and illness of greater severity, take many medications and rate their own health as poorer than those who are not bereaved.[3] This situation is made worse when bereaved spouses have already been depressed when the death occurs.[4] Such depression is linked with a much more complicated course for their mourning. Of course, that depression may have been the result of inability to handle the many losses already experienced by the elderly.

Psychoanalytic approaches to bereavement

Those who take a psychoanalytic approach to bereavement, while aware of the range and intensity of the emotional responses involved in it, have focused on the human need for attachments and its loss in any separation. Bereavement can then be seen as either attempts to restore that closeness[5] or as attempts to reduce it.[6] Defensive strategies such as denial and idealisation can play a part in these processes, together with the entire range of other defences. The focus then is on the ability of bereaved people to maintain their identity and integrity in the face of loss.[7] Of course, as I have noted, the death of the spouse is by far from being the only loss that needs to be mourned in this way.

Stages of bereavement

A number of approaches to bereavement, psychoanalytic and others, have indicated that there are certain stages that the bereaved should move through as they mourn. One such psychoanalytic approach indicates that yearning occurs first, then emotional disorganisation and despair, to be followed eventually by reorganisation.[5] Another, less psychoanalytic, approach focuses on shock and numbness, followed by depression, then anger, before a final acceptance of the loss can occur.[8] These accounts can be useful in that they acknowledge the appropriateness of emotional disorganisation and anger in the bereaved, and are of concern when they start to be understood by health professionals as prescribing the precise order in which certain aspects of bereavement should occur.

Bereavement as transition

Just as retirement, and illness too, can be viewed as periods of transition for the elderly who experience them, so can bereavement.[9] From this perspective, mourning involves the elderly bereaved in learning, as each change in their new world of loss is made real to them, that they need to develop a new set of assumptions about themselves and that world. The change to be adapted to here is primarily loss of a loved one, but also of the less major losses linked with it, such as of old roles and of old social standing. The bereaved need to reassess their view of their world and their interaction with it. This view of bereavement is very close to the personal construct view now to be presented, as can be seen when a simple substitution of the terms "stories" and "constructs" for the "assumptions" of this account is made.

Bereavement as dislocation of the construct system

The personal construct therapy account of bereavement does view the loss as triggering disruption of some of the personal constructs of the bereaved.[10] After the death, the bereaved elderly will still be trying to interpret and anticipate events. This interpretation has been based on the system of personal constructs that they have built as a result of earlier experiences, many of which may have been validated by the newly lost loved one. The psychological states that accompany bereavement then are the result of the need to change parts of their personal construct systems. Such changes are the products of construct dislocation (or disorganisation) and adaptation (or adjustment to the loss) and can occur in any order.

Psychological states that are evidence of this construct dislocation include shock and numbness, anger, guilt, sadness and despair.[11] For example, shock can be described as an overwhelming and sudden awareness of the need to reconstrue events. Guilt can occur when the bereaved feel that their actions involving other people do not fit with their expectations based on their most central constructs about themselves.

In contrast, the adaptation of the bereaved to construct dislocation involves the two inseparable processes of assimilation and accommodation.[11] The bereaved try to assimilate or change the events with which they are confronted, by denying their existence or insisting that other people agree with their interpretation of events. Two of the psychological processes that represent this assimilation are denial and idealisation. Accommodation involves the active elaboration of their personal construct system, which is actually the main goal of personal construct therapy. Thus it involves the creation of alternative viable stories by those in mourning. From this perspective then, the bereaved elderly can be seen as active participants in their own mourning.

Retelling Mrs Z's stories about her loss

Listening to Mrs Z

Mrs Z was referred to a welfare worker because of the possibility of debilitating depression, her second husband, Mariano, having died of cancer only a year earlier. The Z's had arrived together from Spain some 6 years before, having been then married for 20 years. Mrs Z had also had a small stroke more recently. She cried almost continually during the first two therapy sessions, in despair and lamenting the loss of a perfect partner. She talked, through her sobs, of how generous he had been with her, how caring and how gentlemanly. She also spoke of how difficult she found it to be alone in their house and how she dreaded the long nights. She felt herself to be extremely lonely and isolated, and was regretting that they had not had children together. It later transpired that she alone had made this choice, for reasons which will become apparent. Her son from her first marriage was still in Spain. She received some support from her priest and congregation, as well as God, but felt much guilt about this.

While Mrs Z still had extensive family both in Australia and Spain, she did not regard most of them as supportive, because of the pressure she experienced from them to spend her newly inherited money on them or at least leave it to them when she died. They were also trying to encourage her, she reported, to sell the house of which she was so proud. Most of them she considered to be "greedy", although later she came to identify some family who were "needy" and so, she felt, more deserving of her help. As therapy progressed also, her early idealisation of her husband became much more realistic. It seemed that since they had been in Australia he had often been as she described, but back home in Spain he had been mean, demanding and patriarchal. She referred to him as "a tyrant" and confessed that she had refused to have children with him, even though he wanted them, because she had not wanted to mix their genes. Now, she said, she thought she could have raised their children to be more like her than him.

At the beginning of her therapy, two sets of stories seemed to hold particular importance for Mrs Z. The first set dealt with her despair and isolation. "My life is over" trapped her into giving up all hope for the future and so also giving up any reason to make an effort. The other pair of this set, "I am alone", was based on the assumption that, if she did try to reach out to others, there would be no-one there. Her continuing despair and isolation could have been ensured by these stories. Her second and somewhat contradictory set assumed that such reaching out might be possible, but that it must be only by giving and not by receiving. These stories were: "I must be good" and "I must help others". Her own expectations of herself to be "good" could therefore only be met by giving to others.

She also had a number of constructs which were interfering with her functioning. For example, she spoke of herself as "disabled". The residual effects of her stroke were already minor and involved only a small limp which need not have interfered with her mobility at all; but it was doing so to a considerable degree because of use of this construct in relation to herself. She also had some suspicions about the extent to which she should trust others. Her description of herself as "unprotected" showed how vulnerable and dependent on others she felt. Similarly her other construct of "being used" conveyed a sense that she felt, at least at times, that she was at the mercy of others and exploited to meet their needs.

Goal-setting with Mrs Z

Mrs Z and her welfare worker decided together from the start to use the full 10 therapy sessions that were available for this service at that time. They met for approximately an hour and a half a week in the client's home, in her "best room" with her "best coffee cups". Mrs Z saw a relatively large number of sessions as appropriate partly because of the intensity of the emotions she was experiencing and their threat to overwhelm her. She was particularly frightened of her depression and loneliness, and blamed herself a good deal for them. "I should be handling things better." It seems likely that she could not really believe in the likelihood of greater emotional calm, and even enjoyment for herself, that her welfare worker said could result from the therapy, because her depression and isolation would have made this difficult. However, she was able to find the courage to embark on this therapeutic journey with both an unknown destination and an unknown companion.

Her welfare worker, while mindful of Mrs Z's view of their therapy, worked towards four specific goals that she believed could be achieved with her. The first of these focused on two of the constructs that Mrs Z was using quite often, describing herself as "unprotected" and "used", and yet at the same time she was expressing a desire to be more "independent". Her notion of independence was, at that time, very poorly defined. Her therapist could see ways to use reminiscence to allow her both to mourn to express her sadness and yet to define this important but confusing construct further.[12] Two stories of Mrs Z's had given her the second goal: "My life is over" and "I am alone." These stories were preventing this elderly client from functioning more effectively, and necessitated the development of alternative stories with new sources of validation.[13] Her construct of "disabled" was also to be loosened,[14] while her stories about "helping" and "being good" were also to be found alternatives, if it proved appropriate, during the 10 sessions.

The therapy

When Mrs Z's welfare worker began to explore with her the meanings that "independence" held for her, they were confused and involved both positive and negative emotions.[15] This proved, in part, to be because her husband, Mariano, had encouraged her to be independent, but only as he was dying; and her meanings were confused with his. He had, as her reminiscences began to show, treated her almost as a vassal before they came to Australia, and she did not want to have that kind of relationship with her family. The reminiscences provided opportunities to come to grips with the anger she had been experiencing at Mariano. They also gave her the chance to again get in touch with some old sources of support for some of her more useful stories of independence. This reminiscence also provided the opportunity to mourn the loss of much of her relationship with Mariano that had been good, and express more fully her sadness.[16–18] Her further explanation of some alternative stories of independence was encouraged by working through some of her most feared aspects, and encouraging her to try them out in actuality, for example, travelling alone and negotiating with her health professionals.

Her welfare worker's next goal had much to do with the loneliness that worried Mrs Z: "My life is over. I am alone."[19,20] As a therapist she was planning to work towards eventual reorganisation of Mrs Z's daily life, so that it would contain regular and satisfying contact with others. Of course this could only be achieved when her mourning process was concluded, which would still take some time, but at least some advances could be made to old friends and new groups of people tested. Between the third and fourth therapy sessions Mrs Z attended a family funeral. This funeral confirmed her growing sense of independence: "I think now I did the right thing with Mariano's funeral." It has also helped her to feel more able to reach out, for example, to invite one of her brothers to come to Australia on holiday at her expense. She also began to organise her days so as to fill the empty spaces. She gradually became able to sit at the table, where she and Mariano used to eat together, without much pain. The nights, however, remained difficult for her. She also, late in their sessions, was able to ask her therapist if there were any elderly shut-in people close to home that she could visit, because it made her sad to think that these people could not get out.

Mrs Z's construct of being "disabled" by her stroke was very much linked with her fears about being dependent, for example, through the story "Now I can't do anything". Her welfare worker therefore worked towards Mrs Z's greater decision-making in relation to her own health. She believed that any recovery she had made from her stroke was due to a naturopath, but was now experiencing some difficulty with the diet that he had recommended. She had had some nausea and mild diarrhoea. Her welfare worker encouraged Mrs Z to take one of a range of possible decisions about what to do about this: continue his diet, go back to him and describe its effects, consult a medical practitioner, or take over her own health care (so long as no major health problems emerged). She opted for the latter course, and was even able to find herself a masseur with whom she was very pleased. Mrs Z was also involved in discussions evaluating the implications of the minor impairment that remained and making yet more decisions about what activities were still available to her and how she might still improve. The latter goal, of course, underlay her successful search for a masseur. If she had been working with a psychoanalytic therapist, these losses of hers—this stroke-related impairment, and her loss of Mariano—would have been understood more in terms of their drain from the energy that she had been appropriately investing in her self, ego or identity.[17]

Two of Mrs Z's most influential stories were this linked pair: "I must be good" and "I must help others". Her therapist worked with her to examine these stories and related ones about "being responsible" and "meeting God's expectations", again in terms of their implications for her own behaviours.[21] These discussions involved her making further distinctions between the "needy" and "greedy" members of her family and choosing to take more responsibility for the former; and she was able to act on this distinction. She also went away to pray and to reflect on these stories of hers, and referred them to a late session saying: "I feel that perhaps God knows how much I've suffered and been a slave, and is giving me a little time to enjoy myself and be my own boss." This revision of her tale of what God wanted,[22] enabled her to make some trips to the city to buy new furniture for herself, which she thoroughly enjoyed and about which she felt no guilt. She was then ready to finish therapy within the planned number of sessions.

Outcomes achieved by Mrs Z

Although Mrs Z on entering therapy had found her welfare worker's suggestions that she might be able to enjoy herself unconvincing, this did occur. Her own account of her life at the end of therapy was:

All I can say is that I enjoy life. My family and friends help with this. That makes me happy. Otherwise there is nothing much that I enjoy, just sitting in the sun and reading. And I'm fairly healthy now. That's the main thing I think. I can move about and enjoy life. And that's God's main purpose, isn't it . . .

It is clear that she had achieved something of her own vague goals in therapy.

Of the goals that her welfare worker as therapist anticipated their dealing with, all showed some gains. Mrs Z was still saddened by the loss of her husband, but had done some effective mourning, especially in expressing her anger about him. Her stories about her own independence were much clearer and more feasible, and she was making some of the independent actions she had most feared. Her stories about loneliness and her life being over now had a well-developed range of alternatives that were well supported by friends, church acquaintances, an exercise group, and even by God. Her sense of being alone had lessened, but she was still crying a little when alone to express her sadness. Her "disabled" self had become a much more healthy and active self, taking responsibility for monitoring and maintaining her own health. As for being responsible for others, she had been able to achieve a more realistic assessment of the needs of her family and free herself from constructs which required her to help them financially. She was even able to reconstrue her relationship with God to feel more "cared about" and "secure".

Personal construct therapy with elderly bereaved clients

Elderly clients who are bereaved are likely to have reacted initially to their loss with shock and numbness. They are, however, then overtaken by some of the wide range of intensely experienced emotions I have identified. These include anger, anxiety, guilt, sadness, depression and despair. For a time they may also deny that loss or idealise their memory of the person they have lost. There is evidence, then, of continuing psychological struggle for the bereaved. Support from others while grieving can be helpful to them, even if it is only in listening to accounts of the death or of life with the loved one. However, it seems that the elderly bereaved are not always able to reach out at this time because of the despair, depression and isolation they feel. This can be dangerous because bereavement can affect the health of the elderly.

Psychoanalytic approaches view relationships with others in terms of the opposing processes of attachment and separation. Mourning then becomes either a process of reattachment after loss, or of detachment to adjust to that loss. Stage approaches to bereavement, while helping to identify some aspects of mourning that have been ignored, such as anger, can be restrictive, with their prescribed order for particular emotions to be expressed. The transition approach to bereavement, closer to the personal construct approach, views it as a period of great change requiring the bereaved to develop new assumptions about themselves and their worlds.

For the personal construct approach, dislocation of the construct system by the loss is seen as being the reason why these emotions are experienced and at such intensity. However, there are also processes of adaptation by which the bereaved can restore some of their previous ability to interpret and anticipate. This can be by assimilation, in which the changes are made to the loss-related events, through denial or idealisation. However, it can also occur through accommodation, in which it is the bereaved's constructs that are changed through elaboration. It is this process of elaboration of constructs, or the retelling of stories, that is central to personal construct therapy.

Mrs Z's husband had been dead for about a year when she was referred for therapy. She had also had a minor stroke since his death. Her depression and loneliness, accompanied by guilt and sometimes despair were appropriate to someone in mourning. She was also initially idealising her husband in their "perfect" relationship, that same husband she later came to call a "tyrant". In fact, she had refused to have children with him because of how he behaved with others. She was also experiencing pressure from her family whom she saw as wanting financial support from her. In this situation, she construed herself as "used", and, because of her stroke, "disabled". Her main stories, very self-limiting ones, were to do with "life being over" and "being alone", and she also told of some "being good" and helping others that led to further difficulties with her family.

Because of Mrs Z's despair and other strong emotions she was probably unable to believe at the beginning of her therapy that it could be useful to her. Her goals, as a result, were vague. Her therapist, however, had four goals in mind when they started. These were to encourage Mrs Z to mourn and to work out a more viable construct of "independence", develop together alternative stories to "my life is over", loosen her "disabled" construct and find alternative constructs for "used". Reminiscence was employed to achieve the first goal, with expression of sadness, guilt and anger, together with securing of some old sources of support for Mrs Z's more viable stories of independence. Her therapist then encouraged Mrs Z to act on these related stories by travelling alone and making her own decisions. Her loneliness was approached by searching for other viable alternatives, and again supported by the encouragement of a range of activities involving Mrs Z in making approaches to others. Loosening of Mrs Z's construct of "disabled" was achieved through, at first verbal and later actual, demonstrations of the great amount she could still do. New endings for her old stories about her family and God were also developed through repeatedly testing them and reflecting on the results of these tests.

At the end of this therapy Mrs Z was often contented and even able to enjoy life. She was still sometimes sad and lonely. She had done some effective mourning, although more remained to be done. She had, in particular, identified and expressed her anger at her husband. Her work on establishing her "indepen-dence" had begun, with a better defined construct now being tested by indepen-dent acts which were in turn helping to elaborate that construct further. Her loneliness was being somewhat countered by social contacts, some of which she was beginning to initiate herself. Her "disabled" stories had almost been replaced by "active, responsible" stories. Her stories about doing good by help-ing others, were being added to by more self-promoting stories of being "given to" and being "kept safe". She apparently gained much from her therapy.

I have provided accounts of personal construct therapy with elderly clients who have retired, been ill and mourned in this section of the book. These have been based on personal construct accounts of retirement, illness and bereavement. Similarly, in the next chapter, I shall focus on personal construct therapy for the elderly who are dying.

Suggested reading

● *A psychology of bereavement*

1. Dorian, B. & Garfinkel, P.E. (1987). Stress, immunity and illness—A review. *Psychological Medicine*, **17**, 393–407.
2. Gelser, D.S. (1989). Psychosocial influences on human immunity. *Clinical Psychology Review*, **9**, 112–130.
3. Thompson, L.W., Breckenridge, J.N., Gallagher, D. & Peterson, J. (1984). Effects of bereavement on self perceptions of physical health in elderly widows and widowers. *Journal of Gerontology*, **39**, 309–314.
4. Gilewski, M.J., Farberow, N.L., Gallagher, D. & Thompson, C.J. (1991). Interaction of depression and bereavement on mental health in the elderly. *Psychology and Coping*, **6**, 67–75.
5. Bowlby, J. (1980). Loss, sadness and depression. In J. Bowlby (Ed.), *Attachment and loss*. New York: Hogarth.
6. Brink, T.L. (1985). The grieving patient in later life. *Psychotherapy Patient*, **2**, 117–127.
7. Raphael, B. (1984). *The emotion of bereavement*. London: Hutchison.
8. Kozma, A. & Stones, M. (1980). Bereavement in the elderly. In G. Shoenberg (Ed.), *Bereavement counselling*. London: Greenwood.
9. Parkes, C.M. (1981). Psychosocial care of the family after the patient's death. In S. Margolls, H.C. Raether, A.H. Kutscher, J.B. Powers, I.B. Seeland, R. Debellis & D.J. Cherico (Eds.), *Acute grief: Counselling the bereaved*. New York: Columbia.
10. Woodfield, R. & Viney, L.L. (1985). A personal construct approach to bereave-ment. *Omega*, **16**, 1–13.
11. Viney, L.L. (1986). The bereavement process: A new approach. *Bereavement Care*, **4**, 27–32.

● *Retelling stories about loss: therapy*

12. Viney, L.L., Benjamin, Y.N. & Preston, C. (1988). Mourning and reminiscence: Parallel psychotherapeutic processes for the elderly. *International Journal of Ageing and Human Development*, **28**, 237–249.

13. White, M. & Epson, D. (1990). *Narrative means to therapeutic ends*. London: Norton.
14. Epting, F.R. (1984). *Personal construct counseling and psychotherapy*. Chichester: Wiley.
15. Bannister, D. (1975). Personal construct psychotherapy. In D. Bannister (Ed.), *Issues and approaches in psychological therapies*. London: Wiley.
16. Essa, M. (1986). Grief as a crisis: Psychotherapeutic interventions with the elderly bereaved. *American Journal of Psychotherapy*, 40, 243–251.
17. Hildebrand, H.P. (1982). Psychotherapy with older patients. *British Journal of Medical Psychology*, 55, 19–28.
18. Sorensen, M.H. (1986). Narcissism and loss in the elderly. Strategies for inpatient older adult groups. *International Journal of Group Psychotherapy*, 36, 533–547.
19. Andersson, L. (1985). Intervention against loneliness in a group of elderly women. An impact evaluation. *Social Science & Medicine*, 20, 355–364.
20. Epting, F.R. & Neimeyer, R. (Ed.) (1984). *Personal meanings of death*. London: Hemisphere.
21. Winter, D.A. (1992). *Personal construct psychology in clinical practice*. London: Routledge.
22. Viney, L.L. (1990). The construing widow: Dislocation and adaptation in bereavement. *Psychotherapy Patient*, 3, 207–222.

14 ... about dying

This is the last of four chapters focused on personal construct therapy with clients who are dealing with some of the most common events with which the elderly are faced. These events are retirement, illness, bereavement and dying. From my constructivist point of view, retirement has been seen as a transition, illness, especially the chronic illness which is frequent in the elderly, as a source of severe stress, and bereavement as a loss requiring a complex process of mourning. These transitions, stresses and losses have all been considered as events that have made carrying on with the old ways of construing difficult for the elderly people who experience them. I shall now provide a similar account of the process of dying, using a single case to illustrate both why change needs to occur and how personal construct therapy can help in making the changes that are necessary.

For elderly people who recognise that they are close to death, a series of re-adjustments of their ways of making sense of their world becomes necessary. Death is their final transition,[1] which can make it especially important to them that they deal with it as well as possible. In this sense, approaching death may be said to be similar to approaching retirement. Yet it also can be linked with the other two events on which I have focused in this section of this book. Elderly people who are dying often have to cope with illness that is the cause of their dying. They also must, when dying, anticipate bereavement as part of that process. When the elderly die, their loved ones will lose them, but they may be about to lose their loved ones too. So this transition of dying also involves losses to be mourned.

The process of dying seems to begin with what has been called the crisis of knowledge, when a person begins to realise how close they are to their own death.[2] It is often then that the fears of dying that they may have been warding off all their lives can make their appearance. These fears can be about dying alone or about avoiding undignified pain and distress. They can also, of course, be about the great uncertainty of life after death. Acceptance does come to many who are dying, but only if they make the necessary adjustments to the role they have filled, in relation, for example, to their families. Perhaps the fears of dying that often emerge during this process might not be so strong or so common, if Western societies as a whole were more accepting of death. It is a completely natural process and yet it is avoided and even denied by Western cultures, with only a few exceptions. As a result, elderly people who are otherwise ready to die may have never experienced with another the entire process of dying, and they may never have even seen a dead body, due to the "protection" of mourners routinely given by hospital staff and undertakers.

In this chapter I provide a brief psychology of dying. It contains descriptions of some different styles of dying, and of people's emotional reactions to it. Some of the metaphors and stories about dying which are shared by Western cultures are explored, as are the roles of religious belief and of integrity in the death of the elderly. This section of the chapter concludes with a personal construct account of dying. Then I show how Mrs F, a 69-year-old woman, came to retell her stories about dying. The results of listening to Mrs F, both to her account of her current situation and history, and to her main constructs and stories, are then provided, together with a description of the goal-setting achieved jointly by Mrs F and her therapist, a nurse. Their therapy involved a change of situation, tools for dealing with Mrs F's fears about death, as well as elaboration of her stories and even a change from what had been one of her most central constructs to replace it with others that were more appropriate. The outcomes achieved by Mrs F and her therapist will also be described, before I evaluate the use of personal construct therapy with elderly clients who are dying.

A psychology of dying

Some styles of dying

There are many different styles of dying. Some of these styles cannot be controlled in any way by the people who are dying. For example, because of what happens to the body during the process of dying, it can be either "eruptive" or "congealing".[3] Coronary occlusions can lead to a more sudden and disruptive death, whereas lung disease can lead to a much slower and swamping death. Elderly clients may need to be prepared for both. However, there are other aspects of dying over which they can have much more control. For example, just as they have chosen to live their lives as continually extending and expanding, they can choose that their death be the same.[4] Similarly, clients who have lived their lives as shrinking and contracting, can make their deaths the same. As people have lived, so they die. If there is considerable pain and discomfort as their bodies break down, it is important that they have the appropriate medications and acceptance that leave them free to make these choices.

Emotional reactions to dying

Dying has been found to be linked with the very emotions that might be expected, given my description of the dying process.[5] People who were to die within 3 months have shown themselves to have sad, depressive feelings over their coming loss compared with those who were ill but did not die so soon. They also have some specific fears, especially about the ways in which their bodies were breaking down.[6] They show the acceptance of death that has been described in two ways. Firstly, they express more contentment and enjoyment than the other patients, and, secondly, they show less anxiety in the personal construct sense. In other words, they seem to have found the constructs and stories needed to allow them to make sense of their current situation.

Some common metaphors and stories about dying

Death has been represented in our societies by many metaphors with powerful meanings.[7] These metaphors may have been all the more powerful because of the common denial and avoidance of death. If death is seen as a person, it can be as a gentle comforter or as a grim reaper. The dying person has also been represented by a series of figures: the hero, the wiseman, the fool and the martyr. All elderly people, as they come to die, will contain in their construct systems some of these shared cultural constructs. Each has its special dominant emotions and paths of action. Yet there is also a set of metaphorical stories, that these people may have chosen to live their lives by.[4] If so, these will be very influential in their dying. For example, elderly clients who have seen their lives as a game of cards, will still be playing to win or lose when dying. Those who have seen their lives as a series of natural cycles, each with their own meaning, will see death in the same way. Similarly, those who have seen their lives as a story, the meaning of which is their contribution to life, will want to make a worthy final contribution to this history as they approach death.[4]

Religious faith and dying

The chief fears that elderly people express about dying are fears of physical pain, the as yet unknown risks of dying, the threat to integrity that dying could pose and the uncertainty of life after death.[6] The main coping strategy used to deal with these fears, together with exercising self-control and talking to friends and family about them, has been prayer. Talking with God can provide opportunities to make the pain meaningful, confront the risks, confirm the integrity and give more certainty about life after death.[8] The modifying role that can be played by religious faith—whether it be Christian, Jewish, Muslim, Hindu or Buddhist—in making sense of one's own death should not be underestimated. This factor provides an explanation of research findings for groups of elderly people that would otherwise be hard to explain. For example, expressions of satisfaction with life by the elderly have been linked with church attendance.[9] This contentment seems likely to be linked with the benefits of prayer.

The integrity of the elderly and death

The hard-won integrity of the elderly can be threatened by the approach of death, but it can also be quite central to the response of the elderly to it.[10] If they can maintain a sense of unity both within themselves and within their own lives and the lives of others, this can put a perspective on death that makes it less threatening for them.[11] Indeed many of the more basic aspects of human development which underlie integrity become important too.[12] The hope provided by trust can be as much needed, in the face of death, as the wisdom of integrity. Indeed as death approaches, all of these old constructs, such as having autonomy, initiative, competence, a capacity to relate to others and a sense of identity and generativity, take on new meanings. It is necessary for the elderly to resolve all the conflicts of life before they can be ready to resolve the conflicts of death.

A personal construct psychology of dying

People who are dying, like the bereaved, are faced with the need to change some of their most trusted ways of making sense of their world. Because they must face the fact that life may continue without themselves as part of it, they need to make adjustments both in their systems of constructs and in the stories they have based on them. If these constructs are resistant to change, then difficulties can arise. Those with such constructs may become confused and yet unable to try out new ways of construing. They are then limited to just reshuffling their old ideas, a frustrating state. Some of the change needed can be encouraged by other people working with those who are dying. Family members can be helpful in supporting this change, but sometimes they have constructs, about those who are dying, that they want to hang on to for a little longer. This is a situation in which health professionals, such as nurses, can be helpful, by validating those changes in their construing that become necessary.

It needs to be acknowledged, however, that the very constructs that dying people are adjusting at this time may not be clearly expressed in words. When people die, trust, as I have said, is important. Some of this trust needs to be with health professionals, that they will continue to accept and help them. This trust may also be with family members, in a belief that they will behave in the ways expected of them. More of that trust is needed in self, that those who are dying will die as they want to—bravely, contented or lovingly, whichever it might be. Yet another part of that trust, for most people who are dying, is in believing that they make up a part of some being greater than the individual. Whether this is God's plan or the universe, it gives both their lives and deaths meaning. Yet all of these forms of trust are only rarely put into words. Much more often they are only vaguely grasped by those dying and only apparent to those who observe them in their acceptance of death.

Retelling Mrs F's stories about dying

Listening to Mrs F

Mrs F was referred for therapy as she was dying with advanced breast cancer in a general hospital. She was 69 years of age. This cancer had made its original appearance in her breast over 9 years earlier, but a combination of surgery and other treatments had kept it in remission. Mrs F reported having felt obliged, for a long time, to care for whichever members of her family needed care. When her father, for example, was ill for years before his death, it was she, not her three brothers and sisters, who looked after him. Her mother, in her late eighties, was now becoming more frail and needing more supervision. And she, even with her cancer, was finding herself providing this care. Her husband had recently become depressed, and she was finding this difficult to deal with.

Her account of her illness was as follows.

> When I first found out I had cancer, I went to live with my eldest daughter. So, we were living together quite happily there. And then I thought, well, I was on my feet and . . . er . . . I hadn't had any reoccurrence or any bad health for five years, and I thought, no, it would be best. It was time they were on their own. So, I said to her "Well, I'll get a Housing Commission house, and you can go and start on your married life with your husband five years late." And she said "No, are you sure?" And I said "No, it's about time I moved." I flew the coop you know. So I said "You stand on your own two feet now that you know that I'm OK."

And then the cancer returned.

> It was about three or four years later that I found out I had secondary cancer, advanced breast cancer. And that was the one that really knocked me through a loop, after thinking I had beaten the disease. But it wasn't to be. So I was wondering, where in the devil is the justice in the world, you know, after all that. And I thought, well, at least I can cope with it, more so than somebody else; so that was why it was put on my shoulders . . .

Mrs F was living, at the time of referral, in a family situation with very few resources to help her adjust to the nearness of death for her. She was also being hospitalised frequently for short periods. Her husband was depressed. Her mother was frail. Her brothers and sisters had, for decades, been confirming her in the roles of supporter and comforter to the rest of them. Even her grown daughters, she saw as still reliant on her. After her first bout with cancer it was not herself but her daughter she reported as needing to "stand on her own two feet." The very person in the family who would have been the one to support and be with Mrs F was Mrs F herself!

The sadness of her husband was one of the things she found most difficult to deal with. The story she told about it was: "His unhappiness drags me down." A number of intertwined and complex meanings are conveyed in this metaphor. Approaching death was presenting her with one of the greatest challenges of her life which had been full of challenges, and she was preparing herself to rise to it. Her husband, however, she saw as weighing her down. She must have feared sinking into that pit of depression with him and out of which the link could be almost overwhelming. The image is one of her swimming along bravely with the sudden weight of her husband making any progress difficult. This story needed to be retold.

One of Mrs F's most central constructs seemed, not surprisingly, to focus on her being "a caring and capable person". These constructs had been repeatedly validated by her family and friends. They had enabled her to live a full and rewarding life; however, they could provide a trap for her in death. Because they had been so important to her, she was needing to hang on to them as other certainties let her down. Even in her relationship with God, in which many otherwise active and capable people allow themselves to be supported, she saw herself as "more of a doer than a taker". Central to her relationship with God was "being a giver of my time" to help others. So that even in this relationship, some changes in construing were needed to help her approach her death with dignity.

Goal-setting with Mrs F

Goal-setting with a person with Mrs F's central construct of herself as "caring and coping" had to be approached with some sensitivity. Her nurse-therapist was aware that it would be easy, in this situation, to invalidate these constructs while validating nothing else in their place. She decided that the best way was to support, at least for a time, Mrs F's view of herself as the carer and coper, and so to enlist her from the start as a fellow carer and coper to plan together how they might make use of their time. So a set of shared, specific goals was set up from the first of their sessions, and the number of sessions was left to Mrs F to decide.

The goals involved making choices of a range of arrangements for professional health care that could be made now that she was in the terminal phase of cancer.

They also involved discussing some of the fears about her death that she felt she could not share with her family, as well as elaborating her understanding of her husband's emotional state. These later elaborations would, hopefully, lead to her telling new stories about him. She also agreed to look at some of the ways in which she might be able to see herself that did not involve her in the carer role. This evaluation and possible loosening of some of her most important constructs was going to need to be not only with those about her family relationships but also those about God.

The therapy

For someone at this stage of the physical decline with cancer, a range of health services was available to Mrs F. Her therapist helped her to explore these options: staying at home with pain medication provided by visiting nurses, staying in a hospital with other ill people where the same medication would continue to be available, or moving to a hospice for the dying. Mrs F was drawn by the hospice's philosophy of being there to help patients take control of their own death,[13] compared with the demands of her family to still care for them and the constraints of the general hospital. Her nurse-therapist supported this choice by Mrs F for two reasons. She believed that the autonomy of the patient which marked the philosophy of this hospice would be compatible with Mrs F's stories about herself, as it has proved to be for other people who are dying.[14–17] However, she was also pleased that this move of Mrs F's to new accommodation would mean that her day-to-day relationships would be with new health professionals, and in this case some voluntary workers, who would not have her role as a "coping carer" firmly fixed in their minds as her family did. They would listen to her attentively.

It was also important to help Mrs F get in touch with some of her fears about her own death. Her nurse-therapist felt that this could be done best by exploring some of the meanings it had for her.[18] For Mrs F it was quickly coming to mean a release from pain and discomfort, which she could only welcome. But it also meant being cut off from her loved ones, while some unfinished business remained. Her nurse-therapist's aim here was to help Mrs F construct a set of stories about death that would permit her to be comfortable with herself and what she believed was to come. Given her central role as a carer, Mrs F's unfinished business was largely with her family members. For example, she wanted her daughters to know how proud she had become of them, and she was concerned that there might not be time to make sure that they understood. She was also afraid that the pain might, as it had before, become too much for her. This fear was reduced by the readily availability of pain medication in the hospice.

Her story about her husband dragging her down was also to receive some attention. Mrs F and her nurse-therapist explored the reasons that she felt her husband was unhappy,[19] and they proved to extend far beyond her own illness.[20] Some ways to help him were further elaborated, in particular, ways in which other members of their family could do so. The reasons why she apparently felt responsible for him, given that she had a lot herself to deal with, were also discussed. The focus of Mrs F and her nurse-therapist lay on her own feelings independent of his feelings. The therapist encouraged her to still be supportive of her husband up to a point, but to keep much of her now precious energy for meeting her own needs.

Mrs F was particularly confused by the need to change, in some ways at least, her most central construct[21] of herself as a "carer". She felt, by this time, too ill and weak, for example, to care for her mother; but she was not ready to acknowledge that another member of the family could take on this role in her place. In fact she clung more closely to the family carer role when she described how her sister could not take on the responsibility of their mother because "she is really an alcoholic". However, spontaneously, while talking with her therapist, she began to rehearse handing over that responsibility, and by the end of that session she had done so in imagination, if not yet in fact. In this session she had loosened her construing of her family roles considerably. It may be that her ability to share her feelings with her therapist encouraged her to reconstrue herself in a role more suited to her recently altered circumstances. She became able to discuss her sister's role in her mother's care with other family members.

Another therapeutic process which may have helped to get Mrs F to this point of reconstruction was a "balancing of the books" which her nurse-therapist had undertaken with her through reminiscence.[22,23] It was when she realised how much she had done for others through her church, for example, that she began to accept that she did not need to go on "doing for" God but could afford to think a little about what he might do for her. This led her to think about her own death as a part of life, with its books balanced.[24] She also began to consider death as an alternative with advantages, when compared with the diminished life she was currently experiencing. Much of her construing about life and death was not verbalised directly, but her therapist was able to identify some of her preverbal constructs through observing her more relaxed behaviour and her reduced emotional involvement in some of the topics with which she had at first been so involved.

Outcomes achieved by Mrs F

Mrs F was calmer and more content at the end of her therapy, which was concluded jointly by the two participants after only five sessions. There were still times when she began to focus again on how to reorganise her family so that they could cope after she had gone. There were still times when she was sad about current events and a little frightened about dying. Yet her quality of life did seem to improve. Of course this might have in part been because she was now in a specialised palliative care unit, attended by staff who were neither so frightened nor so frustrated by people who are dying, as her earlier health professionals may have been. She was also considered by her nurse-therapist as likely to benefit greatly from an environment in which she was encouraged to take control of her own death.

However, her therapy gave her specifically the opportunity to explore with her therapist her major fears about dying. One of these proved to be a fear that the pain before death might become unbearable for her. Her nurse-therapist handled this fear, partly through Mrs F's expression of her feelings about it, but also by encouraging her to raise this issue again with the health professionals who would now care for her until she died. She was able to take the risk of retelling her story about her husband "dragging me down", to take more responsibility for her own feelings but less responsibility for his feelings. She also needed to reconsider some of her most central construing of herself as carer, to at least allow that other people might be able, given how ill she was, to take on some of her responsibilities. She was even able to change a little her view of herself as a giver and not a taker in her relationship with God.

Personal construct therapy with the elderly who are dying

The process of dying is usually considered to begin with the realisation by those who are dying that they are close to death. They may then explore a range of specific fears about what death may bring, but, if they make appropriate adjustments, arrive at an acceptance of death. People often die as they have lived. It follows, then, that elderly people may make their deaths either an opening up or a shutting down of their lives. At this time their dominant emotions can be sadness and depression, but also some enjoyment of the good things in their lives. They have a range of metaphors and stories about death and the dying which they share with the other members of their culture. These stories can affect how they die, as can their religious faith and their personal integrity.

As well as these culturally shared constructs and stories, there are also the personal constructs and stories of each elderly person who dies, which determine death's course. The approach of death calls into question many of these constructs and stories, especially those that were based on old roles with others that are no longer appropriate, as the elderly become weaker or face a future in which they will no longer be experiencing participants. Some elderly people who are dying are readily able to reconstrue as it becomes necessary, but others hang on to their old ways of making sense of their worlds. Similarly, some of the members of their family who have remained close to them are able to change their construing of the elderly and so can validate new ways of construing for them. However, other family members cling for as long as they can, to their old, shared constructs, making any reconstruction for the elderly very difficult indeed. This difficult situation is further complicated by the fact that many of the constructs important to accepting one's own death, for example trust, may not have been put into words but remain at a preverbal level as they shape one's response to death.

Mrs F, at 69 years of age, was experiencing a severe reoccurrence of breast cancer that was no longer considered treatable. She saw her family as demanding and herself as their sole carer. In the main story she told about her husband, she saw his unhappiness dragging her down. Her most central constructs to describe herself were that she was "caring and capable", which could be a trap for someone who was too ill to be capable. Her account of her relationship with God, in which she saw herself as "more of a doer than a taker", also provided this trap. She clearly needed to revise some of her constructs and retell some of her stories before she could come to accept death.

Her therapist worked initially to engage her in therapy as "a carer and capable" of taking care of herself. This approach avoided invalidating some of her most important constructs by offering her help. They drew up together a set of goals, which included choosing a health care service and exploring some of her fears about death. She was also to consider retelling her story about her husband, and loosening her construing of herself as a capable, carer with both her family and with God. This was partly accomplished by approaching death as a time to "balance books", which for Mrs F seemed very near to being ready to be closed.

After her therapy, Mrs F was calmer and more contented than she had been initially. Although she was still sometimes sad and confused, she had been exploring effectively with her therapist a number of sources of fears, including her fear of pain. Mrs F was able to raise this directly with the hospice staff, who were eager to review their arrangements with her and discuss further any points of doubt. She was also able to retell her story about her husband dragging her down, taking more responsibility for her own feelings but less for his feelings. She began to construe others as being able to take her place as the family carer and to begin to hand over this set of responsibilities. Balancing her books enabled her to do so, not only with her family, but with other people and even with God.

This chapter on personal construct therapy for people who are dying has been the last of four showing how this therapy can be used with elderly people who are retired, ill and bereaved, as well as approaching death. In these chapters, some self-limiting stories of the clients can be identified, as can the more self-empowering stories they often come to tell after therapy. Up to now, however, I have focused on the stories of elderly clients, and how they can affect the way those clients live their lives, as well as how they affect their responses to therapy. It is now time, however, to look at how the stories of therapists affect therapy with the elderly. From a constructivist perspective, the therapists of elderly clients have many stories about that therapy and the elderly who participate in it; and these stories can have a powerful impact on therapy with the elderly. I shall now consider, then, the stories of therapists, and their implications for how therapy with the elderly is conducted.

Suggested reading

● ... *about dying*

1. Viney, L.L. (1980). *Transitions*. Sydney: Cassell.
2. Kastenbaum, R. & Aisenberg, R. (1977). *The psychology of death*. New York: Springer.

● *A psychology of dying*

3. Prichard, E., Tallmor, M., Kutscher, A.H., Debellis, R. & Hale, M.S. (1984). *Geriatrics and thanatology*. New York: Praeger.
4. Salmon, P. (1985). *Living in time*. London: Dent.
5. Viney, L.L. & Westbrook, M.T. (1986). Is there a pattern of psychological reactions to chronic illness which is associated with death? *Omega*, **17**, 171–183.
6. Fry, P.S. (1990). A factor analytic investigation of home-bound elderly individual's concerns about death and dying, and their coping responses. *Journal of Clinical Psychology*, **46**, 737–748.
7. Keleman, S. (1974). *Living your dying*, San Francisco: Random House.
8. Meissner, W.W. (1987). *Life and faith*. Washington, DC: Georgetown University Press.
9. Markides, K.S. (1983). Aging, religiosity and adjustment: A longitudinal analysis. *Journal of Gerontology*, **38**, 621–625.
10. Pegg, P.F. & Metzger, E. (Eds.) (1981). *Death and dying: A quality of life*. London: Pluman.
11. Stedeford, A. (1984). *Facing death*. London: William Heinemann.
12. Erikson, E. (1982). *The life cycle completed*. New York: Norton.

● *Retelling stories about dying: therapy*

13. Rinaldi, A. & Kearl, M.C. (1990). The hospice farewell: Idealogical perspective of its professional practitioners. *Omega*, **21**, 283–300.
14. Hendon, M.L. & Epting, F.R. (1989). A comparison of hospice patients with other recovering and ill patients. *Death Studies*, **13**, 567–578.
15. Viney, L.L., Walker, B., Roberts, T., Tooth, B., Lilley, B. & Ewan, C. (in press). Dying in palliative care units and in hospital: A comparison of cancer patients' quality of life. *Journal of Consulting and Clinical Psychology*.
16. Wallston, K.A., Burger, C., Smith, R.A. & Baugher, R.J. (1988). Comparing the quality of death for hospice and non-hospice cancer patients. *Medical Care*, **26**, 177–182.

17. Kubler-Ross, E. (1981). *Living with death and dying*. London: Souvenir Press.
18. Siegelman, E.Y. (1990). *Metaphor and meaning in psychotherapy*. New York: Guilford.
19. Epting, F. (1981). An appraisal of personal construct psychotherapy. In H. Bonarius, R. Holland & S. Rosenberg (Eds.), *Personal construct psychology and recent advances in theory and practice*. London: Macmillan.
20. Viney, L.L. (1989). *Images of illness*. Malabar, Florida: Krieger, Second edition.
21. Leitner, L.M. (1985). Interview methodologies for construct elicitation: Searching for the core. In F. Epting & A.W. Landfield (Eds.), *Anticipating personal construct psychology*. Lincoln: University of Nebraska Press.
22. Agnew, D.P. (1986). Psychotherapy of the elderly: The life validation approach in psychotherapy with elderly patients. *Journal of Geriatric Psychiatry*, **16**, 87–92.
23. Coleman, P. (1986). Issues in the therapeutic use of reminiscence in elderly people. In I. Hanley & M. Gilhooley (Eds.), *Psychological therapies for elderly people*. London: Croom Helm.
24. Richter, R.L. (1986). Attaining ego integrity through life review. *Journal of Religion and Ageing*, **2**, 1–11.

LEARNING FROM THE ELDERLY

15   The stories of therapists

Those who are fortunate enough to work therapeutically with the elderly have many opportunities to learn from them. Therapists, whether they are welfare workers, social workers, nurses, psychologists, counsellors, or medical practitioners, can learn by listening to clients' self-limiting stories of depression, anxiety and isolation. They can learn even more from listening to the self-empowering stories of the elderly about enjoyment, autonomy and rewarding relationships with others. Therapists can even learn from clients' stories of retirement, illness, bereavement and dying, most therapists having experienced few of these events as yet. They can learn from clients' wisdom, through the more distant and yet more integrated perspective the elderly can take on events, from the love that they give and receive from friends and family, and from their courage in facing the losses and blows that will come to us in later years. In other words, the stories of the elderly can be very valuable to others, although this is rarely acknowledged today in most Western societies.

It is time, in this final chapter of my book, to recognise that therapists, too, have stories, just as our elderly clients do. Therapists have developed them from a number of different sources. My focus, for the moment, is on the stories of therapists about elderly clients. They come from direct interactions with elderly people in general and from important relationships with older members of their own families. They come from formal training in the psychology of the elderly and from professional training as helpers. And, more difficult to detect, they come from shared constructs and stories of the Western cultures in which most therapists function today. These stories can be helpful to elderly clients; but they can also be extremely unhelpful. Those stories that are helpful enable therapists to validate the self-promoting stories of clients, and to invalidate their self-limiting ones. However, those that are unhelpful tend to have the opposite effects, which can be quite harmful to clients.

I begin this chapter about the stories of therapists about the elderly with some helpful and unhelpful stories arising from the sources I have just described: interactions with the elderly in general, relationships with elderly family members, academic and professional training, and the cultures in which therapists live and work. I consider the need to become aware of the stories of therapists who work with elderly clients about the elderly in general, the lack of such awareness and some of the ways in which therapists can deceive themselves. I then move on to some other strategies that can be used to deal with these stories: setting aside some of the therapists' stories, choosing and adhering to an appropriate set of ethical standards, listening respectfully to the elderly clients' stories, and monitoring and changing the stories of therapists are ways of dealing with them. The chapter then ends with nine guidelines that I suggest should be kept in mind by therapists when they are working with elderly clients. These guidelines are based on the work of fellow constructivist therapists; and they are also based on my own use of personal construct therapy with elderly clients as it is reported in this book.

Some stories of therapists about the elderly: helpful and unhelpful

From interactions with elderly people

From their daily interactions with elderly people, therapists sometimes do develop stories about them that are later useful in therapy. Some examples follow. "Even if you are elderly, it is possible to live a contented life." "The pride elderly men take in the lives they have led, is often appropriate." "To watch the love of a grandmother in her face as she looks down at her grandchild is a wonderful thing." "Elderly people often have their act together in a way that we younger people don't." These stories are all based on appreciation of elderly people they have met. Therapists who tell them can easily help to validate the contented, proud, loving and integrated stories of their elderly clients.

Daily interactions with elderly people can also, unfortunately, provide a quite different set of stories about the elderly for therapists. These stories are based less on an appreciation of the strengths and opportunities that the elderly have and more on the losses they see them suffering. "When you get old, you also get senile." "The elderly become helpless, in the face of pressures from family and community." "Most elderly people get frail and disabled." "When you're old, you loose all your friends and family." "Old people have to know that they are getting closer and closer to death. I don't know that I could cope with that." These stories make it hard for the therapists who tell them to encourage their elderly clients to tell more self-promoting stories.

From family relationships with the elderly

Many therapists have spent their own early years, when they were forming some of their own most powerful stories, in close relationships with grandparents. Also, as such therapists reach their professional prime, their own parents are also likely to be becoming elderly. They therefore may have the opportunity to develop stories about relationships with the elderly which are either positive or negative, depending on the quality of those relationships. If these relationships have been rewarding, these kinds of stories result. "I can trust elderly people." "To be honest with the elderly is best." "My gran was always there for me, when no-one else was, so I know that some elderly people can be strong and reliable." These stories are based on earlier happy, successful relationships that these therapists have had, and they help to support the stories about good relationships told by their elderly clients.

Some therapists, however, have had some poor relationships with elderly family members, either as children with their grandparents, or as adult offspring of elderly parents. Such experiences have led to these kinds of stories. "I don't trust anyone over the age of sixty." "It is best to hold back some information from elderly people, because you never know how they'll take it." "Sometimes you have to protect elderly people from knowing the worst. It could knock them over completely." These stories are based on poor relationships with elderly family members. They make it difficult for the therapist who tell them to validate those stories about good relationships told by their clients.

From academic sources

Therapists develop stories, not only from their own personal experiences but also from their professional training. In this section of this chapter I want to focus on the psychology of the elderly that is presented to therapists in training, and in the next section I shall focus on the stories that can result from that professional training. Therapists who can easily validate self-promoting stories for their elderly clients have often been exposed to other professionals acknowledging the abilities of the elderly. They tell these types of stories. "Elderly people can thrive, so long as they've got appropriate physical and social supports." "People who have survived into their eighties often have incredible strength." "The wisdom of the elderly can't be denied." Their clients are fortunate.

Often training courses for professional therapists include very little information about the elderly, however, leaving therapists at the mercy of their personal and cultural stories about them. Yet this may be better than when the professional training is based on a need to diagnose and treat. "Depression in the elderly is often in epidemic proportions, and needs antidepressive medication. Life events are of little importance." "Lower back pain in the elderly is likely to lead to the syndrome of inappropriate illness behaviour." Such stories about the elderly interfere with the effective formation of therapeutic relationships with elderly clients, and they can lead to therapists who undermine their stories about themselves as happy contented human beings who are still able to take part in fruitful interpersonal relationships.

From professional training

The training of therapists will also have involved exposure to a range of different approaches to therapy, all with their different assumptions about people in general and the elderly in particular. Some such assumptions lead to stories that emphasise the capacity of elderly clients to work effectively in therapy and to achieve goals in therapy that are rarely available to other clients. "I find elderly clients to be particularly well motivated in therapy perhaps because they are aware that they have only limited time within which to work." "Older patients are then beyond the shame and embarrassment that could interfere with the work of younger patients." "An eighty-year-old knows that they want from life and whether they are getting it or not. That cuts out so much nonsense." Therapists who, because of the professional role models they have adopted and the approaches to therapy they choose, tell stories of this kind. They can also easily believe that elderly clients will make good use of therapy. As a consequence, they can get those clients to believe that story too.

Other approaches to therapy, unfortunately, take a much less positive view of the elderly client's chances of benefiting from therapy. Therapists who have been trained in this way or exposed to model therapists using this approach are more likely to tell these kinds of stories. "Elderly people are set in their ways." "By seventy, people are not as flexible as they once were." "The old are too rigid to gain from therapy." "By seventy, it's too late for people to change." When they tell these stories, even if it is as a result of their professional training, therapists find it hard to believe that elderly clients will make good use of therapy. They therefore find it hard to convince their elderly clients that this is so. In this situation, the stories of neither therapist nor client are going to lead to good therapy.

From the culture in which the therapist works

The Western culture can be a difficult one in which to conduct therapy with elderly clients. In other cultures, such as the Chinese, in which the elderly are respected for their wisdom, therapists are more likely to be able to tap into a shared fund of stories of this type. "Grandmother is the most important member of our family. We all ask her advice before we make difficult decisions." "Men who have lived long are full of knowledge." Therapists who tell such stories will be able both to respect and admire their elderly clients, and validate the self-promoting stories of those clients. However, they may also have difficulty in working well with them because they have had relatively little experience of life.

Much more common in Western cultures are stories about the elderly that belittle and undermine them. "Once men retire from work, they should just drop out gracefully. Their time is over." "Once you're over eighty, you're not much use to anyone." "Grandma lives in a flat underneath us, but we don't take much notice of her." These stories are not helpful to elderly clients. They can lead therapists working with the elderly to feel that they risk lowering their own professional status by doing so. They can also lead them to believe that their own efforts in therapy will achieve little, which is bad for their morale. Their clients may well learn from them in therapy only that the elderly should be despised and ignored.

Becoming aware of therapists' stories about the elderly

The need for awareness

Given the wide range of stories that can be held by therapists about their elderly clients, and the helpfulness of some and the unhelpfulness of others, it is clearly important for therapists to try to be as aware of their own stories as possible.[1] Personal construct therapy can be particularly useful in this regard, because it emphasises how everybody constructs stories in order to make sense of their worlds and to gain support for their own identities.[2] It also requires that clients and therapists should both be understood in terms of the same concepts, so that, if clients are viewed as telling stories, so too are therapists. This approach also provides a number of ways of monitoring these stories of therapists. One such therapist has even gone so far as to devise a repertory grid with the purpose of helping therapists understand better how they construe the elderly.[3] Their stories about the elderly are thus revealed.

The lack of awareness

There is, however, a marked lack of awareness of the stories therapists tell about elderly clients and the implications these have for them. In fact, relatively few training programmes in clinical and counselling psychology, for example, even mention the elderly, let alone require supervised practical experience with them.[4] Avoidance of elderly clients by mental health professionals is common, both in training and later in practice.[5] Two emotional reactions of potential therapists to the elderly seems to be most likely to be responsible for this. One is that the elderly can present a severe threat to the younger, healthy, cognitively alert therapists, who are reminded that they too may be older, ill and even cognitively impaired one day.[6,7] The second emotional reaction of therapists, likely to lead to their avoidance of elderly clients, may be guilt.[8] In this reaction, again recognising that they are younger, healthier and more cognitively alert, they feel guilt because elderly clients do not share some of these enviable attributes. The most central and influential constructs held by such potential therapists require of them that they share their good fortune with others, and these particular attributes they cannot share.

Opportunities for self-deception by therapists

Given the culture in which Western therapists work, there are many stereotypes and myths about the elderly that they can deceive themselves with, so that therapy for elderly clients becomes to them neither necessary nor appropriate. These myths and stereotypes are often linked with descriptions of the elderly which degrade them, for example "old man" or "little old lady". Such deceptions enable potential therapists to see the elderly as senile, generally incompetent,[9,10] having lost their sexual potency, alienated,[11] ill, and lacking control and flexibility.[12] If this is the natural state of the elderly, psychotherapy cannot be helpful to them. Potential therapists who believe this are therefore spared coming to terms with their own anxieties and guilt.

How to deal with therapists' stories

Setting aside some of the therapist's stories

Therapists come to therapy with the elderly telling many stories about them, based on their everyday and family interactions, as well as on their professional training and culture. It is therefore important that therapists identify the stories and articulate them as clearly as possible, as well as considering carefully their possible impact on the course of therapy.[13] It is for this reason, especially when these stories come from earlier family relationships, that psychoanalytic therapists encourage their professionals in training to experience therapy themselves from the point of view of the client.[14] They can then become more aware of both the content of these stories and their impact on relationships, especially on the therapeutic relationships. Psychoanalytic therapists would also be concerned with the verbalisation of some of these stories that have not been verbalised before.[15] Personal construct therapists also recommend personal therapy for potential therapists.[16] They are less concerned, however, with finding causes for the current actions of therapists than with making explicit the alternate paths that the stories of potential therapists offer them.

Personal construct therapists have also identified another set of stories that are told by therapists and need to be monitored.[17] These are the stories that people tell at different phases of their life span. It is difficult for young and middle-aged therapists to understand, for example, the stories of integrity of the elderly, because they have not experienced such integrity themselves yet. This is very different from working with children or adolescents; therapists can remember something of what it was like to be at that age. Not only, then, is making journeys into this unknown territory with elderly clients difficult, but it can be interfered with by the stories that are so much more important to younger therapists because of their phase in life span. Young therapists are focused on stories of identity and sharing, and middle-aged therapists have moved on to stories of generativity. Both sets of stories can interfere with therapists being able to hear those about integrity.

Choosing an appropriate ethical position

As I have acknowledged earlier, there is a good deal of confusion about what are the most appropriate ethics to govern work with the elderly. Yet to function well with elderly clients, therapists need to take an explicit position on what ethic they are following.[18] Current discussions of the ethics governing health and welfare services for the elderly have pitted autonomy against sociality. Other commentators have asked that a more humane ethic be followed.[19] Should therapists encourage their clients to be independent? Should they encourage them to have meaningful relationships? Should they work towards both autonomy and sociality? If so, which, if compromises are necessary, should take precedence over the other? Such are the ethical dilemmas presented to therapists working with the elderly.

I, as a personal construct therapist, have answered these questions in the following way. In constructivist terms, elderly clients are active construers.[20] So, too, are the therapists who work with them. It is therefore appropriate to apply the abilities, values and information of both sets of construers in this therapeutic relationship to arrive at a shared ethic. Elderly clients are certainly consulted about their preferences in this area. This source of information is very important to their joint decision-making; but therapists are sometimes in a position to provide yet other information, which may not have been available to clients before. Negotiating this shared ethical stance can be difficult, because clients and therapists often, being of different generations, have different values. Such negotiation, however, is possible; and it provides a secure basis for therapeutic story retelling.

Listening respectfully to the stories of the elderly

One good way to deal with the interfering stories of therapists, in general, is to ask those therapists to listen respectfully to the stories of their elderly clients. This then becomes their primary goal, with formulating plans for psychotherapy and even acting on those plans, as secondary goals. Personal construct therapists use a form of listening that they call credulous listening, to which respect is central. Therapists who listen credulously do not set aside their own constructs and stories entirely. This would be impossible. They make sure, however, that their clients' constructs and stories provide the main frame of reference for the therapeutic interactions, rather than their own. They also try to engage their clients in very close relationships with them. These strategies, too, are difficult, but very useful for therapists dealing with elderly clients.

Changing the stories of therapists

Changing some of the more harmful stories of therapists about the elderly is often necessary. Two major ways to achieve this come to mind. The first is that therapists' stories will change as they work in therapy with elderly clients. It is very difficult for a therapist to avoid changes in his or her own stories when involved so intimately and openly in the life story of another.[21] Elderly clients can teach much to therapists. Hopefully, they can especially provide them with experiences which will naturally lead to their respecting elderly people more. This respect will grow as they recognise the courage and wisdom of their elderly clients. Therapists, who are open and credulously listening, do not change their stories as much in therapy as clients do, but they are constantly in the process of revising their own constructs and stories about clients.

Sometimes, however, therapists, for various reasons, deceive themselves about their own stories.[22] They are, after all, only human. There are a wide range of difficulties that therapists bring on themselves without any help from clients. However, it is always possible to use personal construct therapy with such self-deceiving therapists. Therapists can, then, apply this story-telling therapy to themselves, as well as seeking therapists who can work with them using it.[16] It also provides a helpful set of concepts for peer supervision in small groups, another very important tool for understanding and limiting many of the potentially harmful effects of therapists' stories about the elderly.

Some guidelines for therapists working with the elderly

It now seems appropriate to suggest some guidelines for therapists dealing with professional issues that arise when they work with the elderly. Therapists may well want to keep this list somewhere handy so as to serve as a source of reflection and discussion.

1. Therapists should identify the ethical values on which their work with clients is based, and be able to say which of these are most important to them.
2. Therapists should work to understand the ethics and values of their elderly clients, which may well be different from theirs.
3. Therapists should try to understand the stories of elderly clients, because they cannot do so from their own direct experience but only indirectly through those clients.
4. Therapists can work effectively with elderly clients if they have stories that empower them.
5. Therapists need to have the informed consent of their clients to therapy, even though making clear what therapy involves for them may be difficult.
6. Therapists should protect the privacy of their elderly clients.
7. Therapists need to respect their elderly clients, as well as the stories they tell and the constructs they use.
8. Therapists should encourage elderly clients to develop their social supports, since such supports will provide confirmation for their more self-promoting stories after therapy ends.
9. Therapists need to monitor continually their own ability to work with elderly clients, so as not to harm them. Supervision, both from experts and from peers, helps in this process. Personal therapy may also be helpful.

Learning from the elderly

Learning by therapists from elderly clients can occur in three main ways, as this book has shown. They can learn from the courage and wisdom of their stories in adversity. They can also learn how useful stories can be to elderly clients, as well as to therapists themselves. Learning from the stories of the elderly has occurred, for example, from understanding how they came to deal with a range of stressful, age-related events. As the client I described moved through the transition of retirement, a form of crisis intervention therapy became possible with him. He emerged from his depression and isolation into some sense of his own autonomy and ability to enjoy himself. The client who was ill, dealing with the interacting patterns of stroke-related helplessness and anxiety, was able in therapy to glimpse her old self and achieve some small, but significant to her, relearning. The client who was dealing with the reconstructions of bereavement, initially told dependent and lonely stories, but was able to retell them at times to allow some contentment in her life. Finally, the client who was dying also needed to reconstrue, but this time it was her own role as the main family support that she needed to give up; and she began to acknowledge that, given her frailty, this was acceptable.

It has also been apparent in this book how useful stories can be to the elderly, even though they may be rarely told. This became clear in the three self-empowering stories that I examined at some length: "I enjoy myself these days", "It is marvellous being able to do what I want to do when I want to do it", "I have a wonderful relationship with my grandchildren". The advantages such stories gave to their elderly tellers included a sense of self as actively enjoying life, of old age as having certain compensations, of identity, of enjoyable emotions and some viable courses of action, as well as of integration of their present, past and future. These psychological advantages have been complemented by the social advantages of allocating oneself power and having opportunities to test and confirm their stories. The cultural advantages consisted of the passing of information and the exploration of values or ethics. The disadvantages of the self-limiting stories of the elderly that I have considered have been profound. Therapy of course provided opportunities for elderly clients to retell these stories so as to be more self-empowering.

Therapists have also learned, as shown in this chapter especially, how useful stories can be to them. Being aware of and monitoring their own stories about the elderly can be highly valuable to therapy with them. Therapists develop these stories from their daily interactions with the elderly, from family relationships, from their academic and professional training and from their cultures. If they are able to emerge from these experiences with stories of the elderly as integrated, wise, well motivated for therapy and to be respected, then they are likely to provide support for their clients own self-promoting stories. If, however, they emerge from these experiences with stories of the elderly as helpless, not to be trusted, needing medical diagnosis and physical treatment, unlikely to change in therapy and to be ignored, then they run some risk of supporting their clients' own self-defeating stories.

Therapists can learn, however, to become aware of their own stories, once they acknowledge the need for it. They can also acknowledge some of the threats that the elderly pose for them or the guilt they feel. They can even acknowledge some of their own self-deceiving stories about the elderly, which have made it possible for them to avoid working with them. The more harmful stories of therapists about the elderly can be dealt with in personal therapy or in learning to set aside those stories that are central to earlier phases of the life span. Their own ethical stances can also be identified by therapists and negotiated with their clients. Therapists can also focus on listening credulously and respectfully to their elderly clients. This process, of itself, will often change some of therapists' more harmful stories, as they share so intimately the lives of their clients.

Suggested reading

● *Becoming aware of therapists' stories about the elderly*

1. Viney, L.L. (1989). Psychotherapy as shared reconstruction. *International Journal of Personal Construct Psychology*, **3**, 1423–1442.
2. Winter, D.A. (1992). *Personal construct psychology in clinical practice.* London: Routledge.
3. Vacc, N. (1987). Gerontological counselling grid: Making judgements about older adults. *Counsellor Education and Supervision*, **26**, 310–336.
4. Cohen, L.D. & Cooley, S. (1983). Psychology training programs for direct services to the ageing. (Status report: 1980.) *Professional Psychology*, **14**, 720–728.
5. Gatz, M. & Pearson, C.E. (1988). Ageism revisited and the provision of psychological services. *American Psychologist*, **43**, 184–188.
6. Hildebrand, P. (1986). Dynamic psychotherapy with the elderly. In T. Handly & M. Filhouly (Eds.), *Psychological therapies for the elderly.* London: Croom Helm.
7. Nadelson, T. (1990). On purpose, successfully ageing and the myth of innocence. *Journal of Geriatric Psychiatry*, **23**, 3–12.
8. Schneider, J. (1981). *Self care and the helping professions.* In P.F. Pegg and E. Metzf (Eds.), *Death and dying.* London: Pitman.
9. Henig, R.M. (1981). *The myth of senility.* New York: Anchor.
10. Rabbitt, P. & Abson, J. (1991). Do older people know how good they are? *British Journal of Psychology*, **82**, 132–151.
11. Shanas, E. (1979). Social myth as hypothesis: The case of the family relations of old people. *The Gerontologist*, **19**, 3–9.
12. Giles, H. (1991). "Gosh, you don't look it!" A sociolinguistic construction of ageing. *The Psychologist*, **4**, 99–119.

● *How to deal with therapists' stories*

13. Kelly, G.A. (1985). *The psychology of personal constructs.* New York: Norton.
14. Kottler, J.A. (1991). *On being a therapist.* San Francisco: Jossey Bass.
15. Myers, W.A. (1984). *Dynamic therapy for older patients.* New York: Jason Aronson.
16. Winter, D.A. (1992). *Personal construct psychology in clinical practice.* London: Routledge.
17. Viney, L.L., Benjamin, Y.N. & Preston, C. (1990). Personal construct therapy for the elderly. *Journal of Cognitive Psychotherapy*, **4**, 211–224.
18. Fitting, M. (1986). Ethical dilemmas in counselling elderly adults. *Journal of Counselling and Development*, **64**, 325–327.
19. Spielman, B.J. (1986). Rethinking paradigms in geriatric ethics. *Journal of Religion and Health*, **25**, 142–155.
20. Epting, F.R. (1984). *Personal construct counselling and psychotherapy.* New York: Wiley.
21. Leitner, L.W. (1990). Terror, risk and reverence: Experiential personal construct psychotherapy. *International Journal of Personal Construct Psychology*, **3**, 201–211.
22. Knight, B. (1986). *Psychotherapy with older adults.* London: Sage.

Some definitions of personal construct terms

Abstraction In abstraction, people's approaches to their worlds become more general, less related to the physical world and have a higher level of conceptualisation.

Anger Anger is experienced when people get no confirmations for their predictions about events and try to extract some.

Anxiety Anxiety is experienced when people become aware that they do not have the constructs to make the interpretations and predictions about events that they need.

Bipolar constructs When constructs are used, they imply that both similarities and differences are perceived between events. They are therefore bipolar, providing a choice between two opposing predictions and courses of actions.

Concretisation In concretisation, people's approaches to their worlds become more specific, more related to the physical world and have a lower level of conceptualisation.

Constructs These are the tools by which people make sense of their lives. They are interpretations that aid in understanding the past and present and predicting the future. They are based on comparisons of events in terms of their similarities and differences.

Construct systems In construct systems, people's constructs are recognised as influencing one another and being influenced.

Core constructs Constructs which are referred to as core are those by which we make sense of our selves, which are the most central, stable and sustaining.

Crisis When people faced with situations new to them react with interfering negative emotion and self-defeating action, they are in crisis.

Emotions   Emotions vary with people's success in interpreting their worlds. When interpretation is effective they experience positive emotions; when it is not they experience negative emotions.

Enactment   Enactment involves role play based on particular events (or relationships) to encourage reconstruing of those events and develop new courses of actions.

Guilt   Guilt arises with awareness that one's actions do not fit with one's most central constructs about oneself.

Hostility   Hostility is experienced when people try vigorously to confirm their disconfirmed interpretations and predictions.

Integration   The constructs and events that make up stories should be linked together.

Integrity   The integrity of the elderly is based on a sense of trust and autonomy, as well as on a range of other constructs. It provides them with meaning to their lives, as well as wisdom about themselves and others.

Invalidation   When people's predictions of events, which they have based on their construing, are disconfirmed, distressing emotions result.

Laddering   Laddering involves asking the question "why?", in order to discover the more abstract and influential implications of the meanings that people use.

Loose construing   Construing that is loose leads to predictions about events which can change but are recognisably related to each other.

Narratives   Narratives are stories in which events or constructs are integrated. They provide order and meaning in people's lives.

Objectivity   An objective psychology is one which views people from a predominantly external perspective.

Preverbal construing   Construing that is preverbal takes place even when there are no words with which to talk about it.

Pyramiding   Pyramiding involves asking the questions of "how?" or "what?", in order to discover the more concrete and specific implications of the meanings that people use.

Reconstruction   Any reinterpretation of the meaning of events is reconstruction.

Repertory grid techniques   Repertory grid techniques are used for assessing the content of people's personal meanings and how they use them.

Self-characterisation   Self-characterisation is a simple technique for assessing the content and relative importance of people's personal meanings.

Stories   Stories are narratives in which events or constructs are integrated. They provide order and meaning in people's lives.

Subjectivity   A subjective psychology is one which views people from a predominantly internal perspective.

Threat   People experience threat when they recognise the possibility of major changes to their core constructs.

Tight construing   Construing that is tight leads to unvarying predictions about events.

Transition   When in transition, people need to adjust their construing and actions to situations that are new to them.

Validation   When people's predictions about events, which they have based on their construing, are confirmed, enjoyable emotions occur.

References

Affleck, G., Tennen, H., Croog, S. & Levine, S. (1987). Causal attribution, perceived benefits and workability after a heart attack: An eight year study. *Journal of Consulting and Clinical Psychology*, **55**, 29–35.

Affleck, G., Tennen, H., Pfeiffer, C. & Fifield, J. (1987). Appraisals of control and predictability in adapting to a chronic disease. *Journal of Personality and Social Psychology*, **2**, 273–279.

Agnew, D.P. (1986). Psychotherapy of the elderly: The life validation approach in psychotherapy with elderly patients. *Journal of Geriatric Psychiatry*, **16**, 87–92.

Aguilera, D., Messick, J.M. & Farrell, M.S. (1970). *Crisis intervention.* St. Louis: Mosby.

Alonzo, A.A. (1984). An illness behaviour paradigm: A conceptual exploration of a situational–adaptation perspective. *Social Science and Medicine*, **24**, 499–510.

Andersson, L. (1985). Intervention against loneliness in a group of elderly women. An impact evaluation. *Social Science and Medicine*, **20**, 355–364.

Antonucci, T. & Jackson, J. (1989). Successful ageing and life course reciprocity. In A. Warnes (Ed.), *Human ageing and late life.* London: Edward Gould.

Arnkoff, D.B. (1986). A comparison of the ageing and restructuring components of cognitive restructuring. *Cognitive Therapy and Research*, **10**, 147–158.

Avorn, J. (1983). Biomedical and social determinants of cognitive impairment in the elderly. *American Geriatrics Society Journal*, **31**, 137–143.

Babbins, L.H., Dillion, J. & Merovitz, S. (1988). The effects of validation therapy on disoriented elderly. *Activities, Adaptation and Ageing*, **12**, 73–86.

Baltes, P.B. & Danish, S.J. (1980). Intervention in life span development and ageing: Issues and concepts. In R.R. Turner & H.W. Reese (Eds.), *Life span developmental psychology: Intervention.* New York: Academic Press.

Bandura, A. (1984). Recycling misconceptions of perceived self efficacy. *Cognitive Therapy and Research*, **8**, 231–255.

Bannister, D. (1975). Personal construct psychotherapy. In D. Bannister (Ed.), *Issues and approaches in psychological therapies.* London: Wiley.

Bannister, D. (1987). A PCT view of novel writing and reading. In F. Fransella & L. Thomas (Eds.), *Experimenting with personal construct psychology.* London: Routledge and Kegan Paul.

Bannister, D. & Fransella, F. (1985). *Inquiring man.* Beckenham: Croom Helm.

Beck, A.T., Emery, G., Greenberg, R.L. (1985). *Anxiety disorders and phobias: A cognitive perspective*. New York: Basic Books.

Belsby, J.K. (1990). *The psychology of ageing: Theory, research and intervention*. California: Brooks Cole.

Berger, J.W. (1989). Developing the story in psychotherapy. *American Journal of Psychotherapy*, **43**, 248–259.

Berman, L. & Sokowska-Ashcroft, I. (1986). The old in language and literature. *Language and Communication*, **6**, 139–144.

Bishop, G.D. & Converse, S.A. (1986). Illness representations: A prototype approach. *Health Psychology*, **5**, 95–114.

Blazer, D.G. (1989). Current concepts: Depression in the elderly. *New England Journal of Medicine*, **320**, 164–166.

Blazer, D.G. (1989). The epidemiology of depression in later life. *Journal of Geriatric Psychiatry*, **22**, 35–52.

Bloom, J.R. & Spiegel, D. (1984). The relationship of two dimensions of social support to the psychological well-being and social functioning of women with advanced breast cancer. *Social Science and Medicine*, **19**(8), 831–837.

Blumberg, B., Flaherty, M. & Lewis, J. (Eds.) (1980). *Coping with cancer*. Washington, DC: US Department of Health and Human Services.

Blumenthal, J.A., Thompson, L.W., Williams, R.B. & Kong, Y. (1979). Anxiety-proneness and coronary heart disease. *Journal of Psychosomatic Research*, **23**, 17–21.

Bowlby, J. (1980). Loss, sadness and depression. In J. Bowlby (Ed.), *Attachment and loss*. New York: Hogarth.

Boylin, W., Gordon, S.K. & Newurke, M.F. (1976). Reminiscing and ego integrity in institutionalized elderly males. *The Gerontologist*, **16**, 118–124.

Brink, T.L. (1985). The grieving patient in later life. *Psychotherapy Patient*, **2**, 117–127.

Britton, B. & Pellergrini, I.D. (1990). *Narrative thought and narrative language*. Hillsdale, New Jersey: Erlbaum.

Brody, E. (1966). The ageing family. *The Gerontologist*, **6**, 201–206.

Brody, H. (1987). *Stories of sickness*. New Haven: Yale.

Brubaker, T.H. (Ed.) (1983). *Family relationships in later life*. Beverly Hills, California: Sage.

Butler, R.N. (1963). The life review: An interpretation of reminiscence in the aged. *Psychiatry*, **26**, 19–29.

Butler, R.N. & Lewis, M.I. (1977). *Ageing and mental health*. Saint Louis: Mosby.

Carp, F.M. (1972). *Retirement*. New York: Behavioural Publications.

Carp, F.M. & Carp, A. (1981). Mental health characteristics and acceptance/rejection of old age. *American Journal of Orthopsychiatry*, **5**, 230–241.

Chapman, S.L. & Brena, S.I. (1982). Learned helplessness and responses to nerve blocks in chronic low back pain patients. *Pain*, **14**, 355–364.

Charatan, F.B. (1986). An overview of geriatric psychiatry. *New York State Journal of Medicine*, **86**, 630–634.

Churchill, L.R. & Churchill, S.W. (1982). Story-telling in medical arenas: The art of self-determination. *Literature and Medicine*, **1**, 73–79.

Cohen, G.D. (1984). Psychotherapy with the elderly. *Psychosomatics*, **25**, 455–463.

Cohen, L.D. & Cooley, S. (1983). Psychology training programs for direct services to the ageing. (Status report: 1980.) *Professional Psychology*, **14**, 720–728.

Cohler, B.J. (1982). Personal narrative and life course. In P. Baltes & O.G. Brim (Eds.), *Life span development and behaviour*, Vol. 4. New York: Academic Press.

Coleman, P. (1986). Issues in the therapeutic use of reminiscence in elderly people. In I. Hanley & M. Gilhooley (Eds.), *Psychological therapies for elderly people*. London: Croom Helm.

Colthart, N.E.C. (1991). The analysis of an elderly patient. *International Journal of Psychoanalysis*, **72**, 209–219.

Combs, G. & Freedman, J. (1990). *Symbol story and ceremony: Using metaphor in individual and family therapy*. London: Norton.

Cooper, J. & Goethals, G.R. (1981). The self concept and old age. In S.B. Kiesler, J.N. Morgan & U.K. Oppenheimer (Eds.), *Ageing: Social change*. New York: Academic Press.

Cumming, E. & Henry, W.E. (Eds.) (1961). *Growing old: The process of disengagement*. New York: Basic Books.

Curtis, J.R., Geller, G., Stokes, E.J., Levine, D.M. & Moore, R.D. (1989). Characteristics, diagnosis, and treatment of alcoholism in the elderly. *Journal of the American Geriatric Society*, **37**, 310–316.

Cytrynbaum, S., Blum, L., Patrick, R., Stein, J., Wadner, D. & Wilk, C. (1980). Midlife development: A personality and social systems perspective. In L.W. Poon (Ed.), *Ageing in the 1980's*. Washington, DC: American Psychological Association.

Dalton, P. & Dunnett, G. (1992). *A psychology for living: Personal construct theory for professionals and clients*. Chichester: Wiley.

Dean, K. (1986). Lay care in illness. *Social Science and Medicine*, **23**, 275–284.

Dennett, D.C. (1983). The self as a centre of narrative gravity. In D.L. Johnson & P.M. Cole (Eds.), *Consciousness and self*. New York: Praeger.

Department of Community Services (1986). *Nursing homes and hostels review*. Canberra: Australian Government Publishing Service.

Derogatis, L.R., Abeloff, M.D. & Melisaratos, N. (1979). Psychological coping mechanisms and survival time in metastatic breast cancer. *Journal of the American Medical Association*, **242**, 1504–1508.

Dorian, B. & Garfinkel, P.E. (1987). Stress, immunity and illness—A review. *Psychological Medicine*, **17**, 393–407.

Dunn, U.K. & Sacco, W.P. (1989). Psychiatric evaluation of the Geriatric Depression Scale and the Jung Self-Rating Depression Scale using an elderly community sample. *Psychology and Ageing*, **4**, 125–126.

Dush, D.M., Hirt, M.L. & Schroeder, H. (1983). Self statement modification with adults: A meta analysis. *Psychological Bulletin*, **94**, 408–422.

Eil, K.O. (1985). Coping with serious illness: On integrating constructs to enhance clinical research, assessment and intervention. *International Journal of Psychiatry in Medicine*, **4**, 335–356.

Ellis, A. (1984). The essence of R.E.T.—1984. *Journal of Rational-Emotive Therapy*, **2**, 19–26.

Epting, F.R. (1981). An appraisal of personal construct psychotherapy. In H. Bonarius, R. Holland & S. Rosenberg (Eds.), *Personal construct psychology—recent advances in theory and practice*. London: Macmillan.

Epting, F.R. (1984). *Personal construct counseling and psychotherapy*. Chichester: Wiley.

Epting, F.R. & Neimeyer, R. (Eds.) (1984). *Personal meanings of death*. London: Hemisphere.

Erikson, E. (1982). *The life cycle completed*. New York: Norton.

Erikson, E.H. (1950). Transactions of June 8–9, 1950 meeting. In M.J.E. Senn (Ed.), *Symposium on the healthy personality*. New York: Macey Foundation.

Erikson, E.H. (1963). *Childhood and society*. New York: Norton.

Erikson, E.H. (1964). *Insight and responsibility*. New York: Norton.

Erikson, E.H. (Ed.) (1978). *Adulthood*. New York: Norton.

Erikson, E.H. (1982). *The life cycle completed*. New York: Norton.

Erikson, E.H., Erikson, J.M. & McKinnick, H.Q. (1986). *Vital involvement in old age*. London: Norton.

194 References

Essa, M. (1986). Grief as a crisis: Psychotherapeutic interventions with the elderly bereaved. *American Journal of Psychotherapy*, 40, 243–251.

Evans, R.L. (1986). Cognitive telephone group therapy with physically disabled elderly persons. *Gerontologist*, 26, 8–11.

Farrelly, F. & Brandsma, J. (1974). *Provocative therapy*. Port Collins, Colorado: Sheilds.

Feffer, M. (1988). *Radical constructivism: Rethinking the dynamics of development*. New York: New York University Press.

Feinstein, D. (1990). Bringing a mythological perspective to clinical practice. *Psychotherapy*, 27, 388–396.

Felton, B.J. & Revenson, T.A. (1984). Coping with chronic illness: A study of illness controllability and the influence of coping strategies on psychological adjustment. *Journal of Consulting and Clinical Psychology*, 3, 343–353.

Ferraro, K.F. (1992). *Gerontology: Perspectives and issues*. New York: Springer.

Fischer, K.W. (1980). A theory of cognitive development: The control and construction of hierachies of skills. *Psychological Review*, 87, 427–431.

Fitting, M.D. (1984). Professional and critical responsibilities for psychologists working with the elderly. *The Counselling Psychologist*, 12, 69–78.

Fitting, M.D. (1986). Ethical dilemmas in counselling elderly adults. *Journal of Counselling and Development*, 64, 325–327.

Forester, B., Kornfeld, D.S. & Fleiss, J. (1982). Effects of psychotherapy on patient distress during radiotherapy for cancer. *Psychosomatic Medicine*, 44, 118–126.

Fransella, F. (1972). *Personal change and reconstruction: Research and treatment of stuttering*. London: Academic Press.

Fransella, F. (1984). Kelly's constructs and Durkheim's representations. In R. Farr & S. Moscovici (Eds.), *Social representations*. Towerbridge: Redwood Burn.

Fransella, F. (1985). Individual psychotherapy. In E. Button (Ed.). *Personal construct theory and mental health*. Beckenham: Croom Helm.

Fransella, F. & Dalton, P. (1990). *Personal construct counselling in action*. London: Sage.

Frogatt, A. (1985). Listening to the voices of older women. In A. Butler (Ed.), *Ageing: Recent advances and creative responses*. London: Croom Helm.

Fry, P.S. (Ed.) (1989). *Psychological perspectives of helplessness and control in the elderly*. New York: North Holland.

Fry, P.S. (1990). A factor analytic investigation of home-bound elderly individual's concerns about death and dying, and their coping responses. *Journal of Clinical Psychology*, 46, 737–748.

Gallagher, D. & Thomson, L.W. (1982). Treatment of major depressive disorders in older adult outpatients with brief psychotherapies. *Psychotherapy*, 19, 482–490.

Gallagher, D.E. & Thompson, L.W. (1983). Effectiveness of psychotherapy for both indigenous and nonindigenous depression in older adult outpatients. *Journal of Gerontology*, 38, 707–712.

Gannick, D. & Jesperson, M. (1984). Lay concepts and strategies for handling symptoms of disease. *Scandinavian Journal of Primary Health Care*, 2, 67–76.

Gatz, M. & Pearson, C.E. (1988). Ageism revisited and the provision of psychological services. *American Psychologist*, 43, 184–188.

Gelser, D.S. (1989). Psychosocial influences on human immunity. *Clinical Psychology Review*, 9, 112–130.

German, P.S. & Burton, C.C. (1989). Clinicians, the elderly and drugs. *Journal of Social Issues*, 19, 221–243.

Giesen, G.B. & Datan, N. (1980). The competent older woman. In N.T. Datan & N. Lohmann (Eds), *Transitions of ageing*. New York: Academic Press.

Giles, H. (1991). "Gosh, you don't look it!" A sociolinguistic construction of ageing. *The Psychologist*, 4, 99–119.

Gilewski, M.J., Farberow, N.L., Gallagher, D. & Thompson, L.V. (1991). Interaction of depression and bereavement on mental health in the elderly. *Psychology and Ageing*, **6**, 67–75.

Glidewell, J.C. (1972). A social psychology of mental health. In S.E. Golann & C. Eisdorfer (Eds.), *Handbook of community mental health*. New York: Appleton–Century–Crofts.

Golan, N. (1981). *Passing through transitions*. New York: Free Press.

Goldstein, S.E. (1979). Depression in the elderly. *Journal of the American Geriatrics Society*, **27**, 38–42.

Gottschalk, L.A. (1978). Psychosomatic medicine today: An overview. *Psychosomatics*, **19**, 89–93.

Gould, R.L. (1978). *Transformations*. New York: Simon & Schuster.

Gouldsmith, E.M. & Good, R. (1991). All in the mind? The psychologicalisation of illness. *The Psychologist*, **14**, 449–453.

Greenbaum, J. & Rader, L. (1989). Marital problems of the "old" elderly, as they present at a mental health clinic. *Journal of Gerontological Social Work*, **14**, 111–116.

Greer, S. & Moorey, S. (1987). Adjunct psychological therapy for patients with cancer. *European Journal of Surgical Oncology*, **13**, 511–516.

Greer, S., Morris, T. & Pettingale, K.W. (1982). Psychological response to breast cancer: Effect on outcome. *Lancet*, **111**, 785–787.

Grieger, R.M. (1985). The process of rational-emotive therapy. *Journal of Rational-Emotive Therapy*, **3**, 138–148.

Griffen, M. & Waller, M. (1985). Group therapy for the elderly: One approach to coping. *Clinical Social Work Journal*, **13**, 261–271.

Gubrium, J.F. (1976). *Time, roles and self in old age*. New York: Human Sciences Press.

Guidano, J.F. (1991). *A redefinition of cognitive therapy: Using affect in the exploration of self*. New York: Guilford Press.

Gutterer, S.M. (1989). Story-telling: A valuable supplement for poetry writing in the elderly. *Arts in Psychotherapy*, **16**, 127–131.

Hanley, I. (1980). Psychological treatment of emotional disorders in the elderly. In Fraser Watts, F.N. (Ed.), *New developments in clinical psychology*, Vol. 2. London: British Psychological Society.

Hareven, T. & Adams, K. (1982). *Ageing and life course perspectives*. London: Tavistock, 1982.

Harper, C.M., Newton, P.A. & Walsh, J.R. (1989). Drug-induced illness in the elderly. *Postgraduate Medicine*, **86**, 245–256.

Hartsfield, J. & Clopton, J.R. (1985). Reducing presurgical anxiety: A possible visitor effect. *Social Science and Medicine*, **25**, 529–533.

Hendon, M.L. & Epting, F.R. (1989). A comparison of hospice patients with other recovering and ill patients. *Death Studies*, **13**, 567–578.

Henig, R.M. (1981). *The myth of senility*. New York: Anchor.

Hermans, H.J.M., Kempen, H.J.G. & Van Loon, R.J.P. (1992). The biological self: Beyond individualism and rationalism. *American Psychologist*, **47**, 23–32.

Herr, J. & Weakland, J. (1979). *Counselling elders and their families*. New York: Springer.

Hess, T.M. (1990). *Ageing and cognition*. New York: North Holland.

Hildebrand, H.P. (1982). Psychotherapy with older patients. *British Journal of Medical Psychology*, **55**, 19–28.

Hildebrand, P. (1986). Dynamic psychotherapy with the elderly. In T. Handly & M. Filhouly (Eds.), *Psychological therapies for the elderly*. London: Croom Helm.

Hobfoll, S.F. & Walfisch, S. (1984). Coping with a threat to life: A longitudinal study of self, concept, social support and psychological distress. *American Journal of Community Psychology*, **12**, 87–100.

Huddleston, R. (1989). Drama with elderly people. *British Journal of Occupational Therapy*, **52**, 290–300.

Hutschnecker, A.A. (1981). *Hope*. New York: Putnam.

Irwin, M., Daniels, M. & Weiner, H. (1987). Immune and neuroendocrine changes during bereavement. *Psychiatric Clinics of North America*, **10**, 449–465.

Jasnow, A. (1981). Humour and survival. *Voices*, **16**, 50–54.

Johnson, D.R. (1985). Expressive group therapy with the elderly: A drama therapy approach. *The International Journal of Group Psychotherapy*, **35**, 109–127.

Johnson, D.R. (1986). The developmental method in drama therapy: Group treatment with the elderly. *Arts in Psychotherapy*, **13**, 17–33.

Johnson, M. & Carpenter, L. (1980). Pre-operative anxiety. *Psychological Medicine*, **10**, 361–367.

Jung, C. (1934). *The development of personality*. Princeton, New Jersey: Princeton University Press.

Kamen-Siegel, L., Rodin, J., Seligman, M.E. & Dwyer, J. (1991). Explanatory style and cell-mediated immunity in elderly men and women. *Health Psychology*, **10**, 249–255.

Kane, R.L. (1981). *Assessing the elderly*. Lexington, Massachusetts: Heath.

Kaplan, B.H., Cassel, J.C. & Gore, S. (1977). Social support and health. *Medical Care*, **15**, 47–58.

Kastenbaum, R. (1983). Can the clinical milieu be therapeutic? In E.D. Bowles & R.J. Ohta (Eds.), *Ageing and milieu*. New York: Academic Press.

Kastenbaum, R. & Aisenberg, R. (1977). *The psychology of death*. New York: Springer.

Keating, D.P. & Rosen, H. (1991). *Constructivist perspectives on developmental psychopathology and atypical development*. Hillsdale, New Jersey: Erlbaum.

Keleman, S. (1974). *Living your dying*. San Francisco: Random House.

Keller, J.F. & Brownley, M. (1989). Psychotherapy with the elderly: A systemic model. *Journal of Psychotherapy and the Family*, **5**, 29–46.

Keller, J.F., Croake, J.W. & Brooking, J.Y. (1975). Effects of a programme in rational thinking on anxieties in older persons. *Journal of Counselling Psychology*, **22**, 54–57.

Kelly, G.A. (1955). *The psychology of personal constructs*. New York: Norton.

Kelly, G.A. (1967). A psychology of the optimal man. In A.H. Mahrer (Ed.), *The goals of psychotherapy*. New York: Appleton–Century–Crofts.

Kelly, G.A. (1969). Personal construct theory and the psychotherapeutic interview. In B. Maher (Ed.), *Clinical psychology and personality*. New York: Wiley.

Kendig, H.L. (Ed.) (1986). *Ageing and families: A support networks perspective*. Sydney: Allen & Unwin.

Kleinman, A. (1988). *The illness narratives*. New York: Basic Books.

Knight, B. (1986). *Psychotherapy with older adults*. London: Sage.

Koenig, H.G. (1988). Shepherd's Centres: Helping elderly help themselves. *Journal of the American Geriatric Society*, **34**, 73.

Kohlberg, L. (1973). Stages and ageing in moral development—Some speculations. *Gerontologist*, **13**, 497–502.

Kottler, J.A. (1991). *On being a therapist*. San Francisco: Jossey Bass.

Kozma, A. & Stones, M. (1980). Bereavement in the elderly. In G. Shoenberg (Ed.), *Bereavement counselling*. London: Greenwood.

Kubler-Ross, E. (1981). *Living with death and dying*. London: Souvenir Press.

Kuhlman, T.L. (1984). *Humour and psychotherapy*. Homewood, Ill: Brooks-Cole

Kuypers, J.A. (1974). Ego functioning in old age: Early adult life antecedents. *International Journal of Ageing and Human Development*, **5**, 157–179.

Lachman, M.E. (1986). Locus of control in ageing: A case for multi-dimensional and domain specific assessment. *Psychology and Ageing*, **1**, 12–18.

Landgarten, H. (1983). Art therapy for depressed elders. *Clinical Gerontologist*, **2**, 45–53.

Langer, E.J. & Rodin, J. (1976). The effects of choice and enhanced personal responsibility for the aged: A field experiment in an institutional setting. *Journal of Personality and Social Psychology*, **34**, 191–198.

Leitner, L.M. (1982). Literalism, perspectivism, chaotic fragmentalism and psychotherapy techniques. *British Journal of Medical Psychology*, **55**, 307–317.

Leitner, L.M. (1985). Interview methodologies for construct alienation: Searching for the core. In F.R. Epting & A.W. Landfield (Eds.), *Anticipating personal construct psychology*. Lincoln: University of Nebraska Press.

Leitner, L.M. (1990). Terror, risk and reverence: Experiential personal construct psychotherapy. *International Journal of Personal Construct Psychology*, **3**, 62–69.

LeShan, L. (1977). *You can fight for your life*. New York: Evans.

Leslie, R.N. (1982). Counselling the aged. *International Forum for Age Therapy*, **5**, 17–52.

Leszcz, M. (1990). Towards an integrated model of group psychotherapy with the elderly. *The International Journal of Group Psychotherapy*, **40**, 379–490.

Leventhal, H., Nerenz, D.R. & Steele, D.J. (1982). Illness representations and coping with health threats. In A. Baum & J. Singer (Eds.), *A handbook of psychology and health*. Hillsdale, New Jersey: Lawrence Erlbaum.

Levinson, D.J. (1978). *The seasons of a man's life*. New York: Ballantine.

Lewis, M.I. & Butler, R.N. (1974). Life review therapy: Putting memories to work in individual and group psychotherapy. *Geriatrics*, **29**, 165–174.

Lieberman, M.A. (1978). Adaptive processes in later life. In N. Datan & L.H. Ginsberg (Eds.), *Life span developmental psychology*. New York: Academic Press.

Lieberman, M.A. & Birdwise, N.G. (1985). Comparisons among peer and professionally-directed groups for the elderly: Implication for the development of self help groups. *International Journal of Group Psychotherapy* **35**, 155–175.

Lieberman, M.A. & Tobin, S.S. (1983). *The experience of old age*. New York: Basic Books.

Linn, J.G. & Husaini, B.A. (1985). Chronic medical problems, coping resources, and depression: A longitudinal study of rural Tennesseans. *American Journal of Community Psychology*, **6**, 733–742.

Litt, M.D. (1988). Self-efficacy and perceived control: Cognitive mediators of pain tolerance. *Journal of Personality and Social Psychology*, **54**, 149–160.

Loupland, N., Couplan, J. & Giles, H. (Eds.) (1991). *Sociolinguistics and the elderly: Discourse, identity and ageing*. Oxford: Blackwell.

Lynch, J.J. (1977). *The broken heart*. New York: Harper & Row.

Mace, N. & Rabins, P.U. (1981). *The 36-hour day*. Baltimore: Johns Hopkins.

Mahoney, M.J. & Gabriel, T.J. (1987). Psychotherapy and the cognitive sciences: An evolving alliance. *Journal of Cognitive Psychotherapy*, **1**, 39–59.

Mahoney, M.J. & Lyddon, W.J. (1988). Recent developments in cognitive approaches to counselling and psychotherapy. *The Counselling Psychologist*, **16**, 190–234.

Mair, J.M.M. (1988). Psychology as story telling. *International Journal of Personal Construct Psychology*, **1**, 125–137.

Mair, J.M.M. (1989). *Between psychology and psychotherapy*. London: Routledge.

Mair, J.M.M. (1990). Telling psychological tales. *International Journal of Personal Construct Psychology*, **3**, 27–36.

Markides, K.S. (1983). Aging, religiosity and adjustment: A longitudinal analysis. *Journal of Gerontology*, **38**, 621–625.

Marmar, G.R., Easton, L. & Gallagher, D. (1989). Absence and outcome in late life depression. *Journal of Nervous and Mental Disease*, 177, 464–472.

Marshall, V.W. (1980). *A sociology of ageing and dying*. Belmont, California: Wadsworth.

Matheny, K.B. & Cypp, P. (1983). Control, desirability, and anticipation as moderating variables between life change and illness. *Journal of Human Stress*, 2, 14–23.

Mazor, R. (1982). Drama therapy for the elderly in a day care centre. *Hospital and Community Psychiatry*, 33, 577–579.

McAdams, D.P. (1985). *Power, intimacy and the life story*. Homewood, Illinois: Dorsey Press.

McFarlane, A.H., Norman, G.R., Streiner, D.L. & Roy, R.G. (1984). Characteristics and correlates of effective and ineffective social supports. *Journal of Psychosomatic Research*, 6, 501–510.

McKay, D.A., Blake, R.L. Jr., Colwill, J.M., Brent, E.E., McCauley, J., Umlauf, F., Steakman, G.W. & Kivlahan, D. (1985). Social supports and stress as predictors of illness. *Journal of Family Practice*, 6, 575–581.

McLeish, J.A.P. (1983). *The challenge of ageing*. Toronto: Douglas and McIntyre.

Meichenbaum, D. (1977). *Cognitive-behaviour modification: An integrative approach*. New York: Plenum Press.

Meissner, W.W. (1987). *Life and faith*. Washington, DC: Georgetown University Press.

Moorey, S. & Greer, S. (1987). *Adjuvant psychological therapy: A manual for the treatment of patients with cancer*. London: Cancer Research Campaign Psychological Medicine Group.

Moran, J.A. & Gatz, M. (1987). Group therapies for nursing home adults: An evaluation of two treatment approaches. *The Gerontologist*, 27, 588–591.

Myers, W.A. (1984). *Dynamic therapy for older patients*. New York: Jason Aronson.

Myers, J.E. & Salmon, H.E. (1984). Counselling programs for older persons: Status, shortcomings and potentialities. *The Counselling Psychologist*, 12, 39–53.

Nadelson, T. (1990). On purpose, successful ageing and the myth of innocence. *Journal of Geriatric Psychiatry*, 23, 3–12.

Nahemon, L., McCluskey-Fawcett, K.A. & McGee, P.E. (1981). *Humour and ageing*. New York: Academic Press.

Nash, C. (Ed.) (1990). *Narrative in culture*. New York: Routledge, Chapman & Hall.

Natale, S.M. (1986). Loneliness and the ageing client: Psychotherapeutic considerations. *Psychotherapy Patient*, 2, 77–93.

Neimeyer, G.J. (1987). Personal construct assessment, strategy and technique. In R.A. Neimeyer & G.J. Neimeyer (Eds.), *Personal construct therapy casebook*. New York: Springer.

Neimeyer, G.J. & Neimeyer, R.A. (1993). Intervening in meaning: Defining the boundaries of constructivist assessment. In G.J. Neimeyer (Ed.), *Case book in constructivist assessment*. New York: Sage.

Neimeyer, R.A. (1985). Personal constructs in clinical practice. In P.C. Kendall (Ed.), *Advances in cognitive-behavioural research and therapy*. New York: Academic Press, pp. 275–339.

Neimeyer, R.A. (1986). Personal construct therapy. In W. Dryden & W.L. Golden (Eds.), *Cognitive-behavioural approaches to psychotherapy*. London: Harper & Row.

Neimeyer, R.A. (1987). An orientation to personal construct therapy. In R.A. Neimeyer & G.J. Neimeyer (Eds.). *Personal construct therapy casebook*. New York: Springer.

Neimeyer, R.A. (1987). Core role reconstruction in personal construct therapy. In R.A. Neimeyer & G.J. Neimeyer (Eds.), *Personal construct therapy casebook*. New York: Springer.

Neimeyer, R.A. (1988). The origin of questions in the clinical context. *Questioning Exchange*, **2**, 75–80.

Neimeyer, R.A. & Neimeyer, G.J. (1985). Disturbed relationships: A personal construct view. In Button, E. (Ed.), *Personal construct theory and mental health*. Beckenham: Croom Helm.

Neimeyer, R.A. & Neimeyer, G.J. (Eds.) (1987). *Personal construct therapy casebook*. New York: Springer.

Neito, D.S., Raymond, T. & Horsley, D.L. (1989). Principles of therapeutic intervention with elders and their families. *Journal of Psychotherapy and the Family*, **5**, 13–27.

Neugarten, B.L., Havighurst, R.J. & Tobin, S.S. (1968). Personality and patterns of ageing. In B.L. Neugarten (Ed.), *Middle age and ageing*. Chicago: University of Chicago.

Newman, J., Engel, R. & Jensen, J. (1990). Depressive symptom patterns among older women. *Psychology and Ageing*, **5**, 101–118.

Newton, E. (1979). *This bed my centre*. Melbourne: McFee Gribble.

Noyes, R. (1981). Treatment of cancer pain. *Psychosomatic Medicine*, **43**, 57–70.

O'Connell, W. (1981). The natural high therapist: God's favourite monkey. *Voices*, **16**, 37–44.

Oberleder, M. (1966). Psychotherapy with the ageing: An art of the possible. *Psychotherapy*, **3**, 139–142.

Parkes, C.M. (1981). Psychosocial care of the family after the patient's death. In S. Margolls, H.C. Raether, A.H. Kutscher, J.B. Powers, I.B. Seeland, R. Debellis & D.J. Cherico (Eds.), *Acute grief: Counselling the bereaved*. New York: Columbia.

Pegg, P.F. & Metzger, E. (Eds.) (1981). *Death and dying: A quality of life*. London: Pluman.

Peterson, J.A. (1973). Marital and family therapy involving the aged. *The Gerontologist*, **46**, 27–31.

Peyrot, M. & McMurray, J.F. (1985). Psychosocial factors in diabetes control: Adjustment of insulin-treated adults. *Psychosomatic Medicine*, **47**, 542–547.

Plank, W. (1989). *Gulag 65: Towards a humanistic perspective in gerontology*. Frankfurt: Lang.

Powell, J. (1991). *"Motivational interviewing" with older hospital patients: A personal construct approach*. International Conference on Drug and Alcohol, Adelaide, Australia.

Powell, J.E. (in press). Literature review: Alcohol and drug use by elderly people. *Australian Psychologist*.

Prichard, E., Tallmor, M., Kutscher, A.H., Debellis, R. & Hale, M.S. (1984). *Geriatrics and thanatology*. New York: Praeger.

Proctor, H. (1981). Family construct psychology: An approach to understanding and treating families. In S. Walrond-Skinner (Ed.), *Developments in family therapy*. London: Routledge and Kegan Paul.

Proctor, H. (1985). A construct approach to family therapy. In E. Button (Ed.), *Personal construct theory and mental health*. Beckenham: Croom Helm.

Prohaska, T.R., Keller, M.L., Leventhal, E. A. & Leventhal, H. (1987). Impact of symptoms and ageing attributions on emotions and coping. *Health Psychology*, **6**, 495–514.

Quinn, W.H. & Keller, J.F. (1981). A family therapy model for preserving independence in older persons: Utilization of the family of procreation. *American Journal of Family Therapy*, **9**, 79–84.

Rabbitt, P. & Abson, J. (1991). Do older people know how good they are? *British Journal of Psychology*, **82**, 132–151.

Radley, A.R. & Green, R. (1985). Styles of adjustment to coronary graft surgery. *Social Science and Medicine*, **20**, 461–472.

Radley, A.R. & Green, R. (1986). Bearing illness: Study of couples where the husband awaits coronary graft surgery. *Social Science and Medicine*, **23**, 577–585.

Raphael, B. (1984). *The emotion of bereavement*. London: Hutchison.

Reeder, L.Q. (1973). Stress and cardiovascular health: An international cooperative study—I. *Social Science and Medicine*, **7**, 573–584.

Reiss, D. (1981). *The family's construction of reality*. Cambridge: Harvard University Press.

Renshaw, D.C. (1984). Geriatric sex problems. *Journal of Geriatric Psychiatry*, **17**, 123–138.

Richter, R.L. (1986). Allowing ego integrity through life review. *Journal of Religion and Ageing*, **2**, 1–11.

Riegel, K.F. (1975). Adult life crises: A dialectic interpretation of development. In N. Datan & L.H. Ginsberg (Eds.), *Life-span development psychology: Normative life crises*. New York: Academic Press.

Rimm, D.C. & Masters, J.C. (1979). *Behaviour therapy*. New York: Academic Press.

Rinaldi, A. & Kearl, M.C. (1990). The hospice farewell: Idealogical perspective of its professional practitioners. *Omega*, **21**, 283–300.

Rodin, J. (1980). Managing the stress of ageing: The role of control and coping. In S. Levine & H. Ursin (Eds.), *Coping and health*. New York: Plenum.

Rodin, J. & Langner, E. (1977). Long term effects of a control relevant intervention with the institutionalized aged. *Journal of Personality and Social Psychology*, **35**, 897–902.

Rogers, C.R. (1980). Growing old—or older and growing. *Journal of Humanistic Psychology*, **20**(4), 5–16.

Rogers, D. (1982). *The adult years: An introduction to ageing*. Englewood Cliffs, New Jersey: Prentice Hall.

Rolland, J.S. (1987). Chronic illness and the life cycle: A conceptual framework. *Family Process*, **26**, 203–221.

Rook, K.S. (1984). Promoting social bonding: Strategies for helping the lonely and socially isolated. *American Psychologist*, **39**, 1389–1407.

Rosenthal, M. (1984). Geriatrics: A selected up-to-date bibliography. *American Geriatrics Society Journal*, **32**, 64–79.

Roud, P.C. (1986–87). Psychosocial variables associated with the exceptional survival of patients with advanced malignant disease. *International Journal of Psychiatry in Medicine*, **16**, 113–122.

Rowe, D. (1978). *The experience of depression*. Chichester: Wiley.

Rowe, D. (1982). *The construction of life and death*. Chichester: Wiley.

Rowe, D. (1987). *Beyond fear*. London: Fontana.

Rudestam, K.E. (1980). *Methods of self change*. Belmont, California: Brooks/Cole.

Russell, C. (1981). *The ageing experience*. Sydney: Allen & Unwin.

Salmon, P. (1985). *Living in time*. London: Dent.

Salvendy, J.T. (1989). Special populations in brief group psychotherapy: Experiences with the elderly. *European Journal of Psychology*, **3**, 138–144.

Saper, B. (1987). Humour as psychotherapy: Is it good or bad for the client? *Professional Psychology: Research and Practice*, **18**, 360–367.

Sarbin, T. (Ed.) (1986). *Narrative psychology: The storied nature of human conduct*. New York: Praeger.

Saul, S. & Saul, S.R. (1990). The application of joy in group therapy for the elderly. *The International Journal of Group Psychotherapy*, **40**, 353–355.

Schneider, J. (1981). *Self care and the helping professions*. In P.F. Pegg & E. Metzf (Eds.), *Death and dying*. London: Pitman.

Seligman, M.E.P. & Garber, J. (Eds.) (1980). *Human helplessness: Theory and applications.* New York: Academic Press.

Shanass, E. (1979). Social myth as hypothesis: The case of the family relations of old people. *The Gerontologist,* 19, 3–9.

Shapiro, A.P. (1978). Behavioural and environmental aspects of hypertension. *Journal of Human Stress,* 4, 9–17.

Sherman, E. (1981). *Counselling the ageing: An integrative approach.* New York: Free Press.

Sherman, E. (1987). Reminiscence groups for community elderly. *The Gerontologist,* 27, 569–572.

Sholomska, S.A.J., Chevron, E.S., Prusoff, D. & Berry, C. (1983). Short-term interpersonal therapy (IPT) with the depressed elderly: Case reports and discussion. *American Journal of Psychotherapy,* 37, 552–566.

Shontz, F.C. (1975). *The psychological aspects of physical illness and disability.* New York: Macmillan.

Siegel, D.E., Shore, G.K. & Gordon, E. (1984). *Building support networks for the elderly.* Beverly Hills, California: Sage.

Siegelman, E.Y. (1990). *Metaphor and meaning in psychotherapy.* New York: Guilford.

Siegrist, J.S. & Halhuber, M.J. (Eds.) (1981). *Myocardial infarction and psychosocial risks.* New York: Springer.

Simonton, O.C., Matthews-Simonton, S. & Creighton, J. (1978). *Getting well again.* Los Angeles: Tarcher.

Smith, P.R. (Ed.). (1991). *The psychology of grandparenthood.* London: Routledge.

Sontag, S. (1977). *Illness as metaphor.* London: Allen Lane.

Sorensen, M.H. (1986). Narcissism and loss in the elderly. Strategies for inpatient older adult groups. *International Journal of Group Psychotherapy,* 36, 533–547.

Specht, R. & Craig, G.J. (1982). *Human development: A social work perspective.* New Jersey: Prentice Hall.

Spielman, B.J. (1986). Rethinking paradigms in geriatric ethics. *Journal of Religion and Health,* 25, 142–155.

Starr, J.W. (1983). Toward a social phenomenology of ageing: Studying the self process in biographical work. *International Journal of Ageing and Human Development,* 16, 255–270.

Stedeford, A. (1984). *Facing death.* London: William Heinemann.

Sterns, H.L. & Sanders, R.E. (1980). Training and education of the elderly. In R.R. Turner & H.M. Reese (Eds.), *Life span developmental psychology: Intervention.* New York: Academic Press.

Stever, J.L. (1984). Cognitive-behavioural psychodynamic group psychotherapy in treatment of geriatric depression. *Journal of Consulting and Clinical Psychology,* 52, 180–189.

Suls, J. & Mullen, B. (1981). Life events, perceived control and illness. *Journal of Human Stress,* 7, 30–34.

Szapocznck, J., Kurtines, M.M., Santisban, D. & Perez-Vidaz, A. (1982). New directions in the treatment of depression in the elderly. *Journal of Geriatric Psychiatry,* 15, 257–281.

Taylor, C. (1984). *Growing on: Ideas about ageing.* New York: Van Nostrand.

Templer, D.I. & Cappelle, Y.G. (1986). Suicide in the elderly: Assessment and intervention. *Clinical Gerontologist,* 5, 475–487.

Thompson, L.W., Breckenridge, J.N., Gallagher, D. & Peterson, J. (1984). Effects of bereavement of self-perceptions on health in elderly widows and widowers. *Journal of Gerontology,* 39, 309–314.

Thompson, L.W., Davies, R., Gallagher, D. & Krantz, S. (1986). Cognitive therapy in older adults. *Clinical Gerontologist*, **5**, 245–279.

Thompson, L.W. & Gallagher, D. (1984). Efficacy of psychotherapy in the treatment of late life depression. *Advances in Behaviour Research and Therapy*, **6**, 127–139.

Thompson, L.W., Gallagher, D. & Breckenridge, S. (1987). Comparative effectiveness of psychotherapies for depressed elderly. *Journal of Consulting and Clinical Psychology*, **55**, 385–390.

Townsend, P. (1981). The structured dependency of the elderly: A creation of social policy in the twentieth century. *Ageing and Society*, **1**, 5–28.

Treas, J. (1977). Family support systems for the aged. *The Gerontologist*, **17**, 486–491.

Udelaman, H.D. & Udelaman, D.L. (1983). Current explorations in psychoimmunology. *American Journal of Psychotherapy*, **37**, 210–221.

Unruh, D.R. (1983). *Invisible lives: Social worlds of the aged*. New York: Sage.

Vacc, N. (1987). Gerontological counselling grid: Making judgements about older adults. *Counsellor Education and Supervision*, **26**, 310–336.

Vachon, M.L.S., Lyall, W.A.L., Rogers, J. *et al.* (1982). The effectiveness of psychosocial support during post-surgical treatment of breast cancer. *International Journal of Psychiatric Medicine*, **11**, 365–372.

Vandenberg, J.H. (1980). *The psychology of the sick bed*. New York: Humanities Press.

Victor, C.R. (1991). Continuity or change: Inequalities in health in later life. *Ageing and Society*, **11**, 23–39.

Viney, L.L. (1980). *Transitions*. Sydney: Cassell.

Viney, L.L. (1983). Experiencing chronic illness: A personal construct commentary. In J. Adams Webber & J.C. Mancuso (Eds.), *Applications of personal construct theory*. London: Academic Press.

Viney, L.L. (1985). Humour as a therapeutic tool. In A. Landfield & F. Epting (Eds.), *Anticipating personal construct psychology*. Nebraska: University of Nebraska Press.

Viney, L.L. (1986). Physical illness: A guidebook for the kingdom of the blind. In E. Button (Ed.), *Personal construct theory and mental health*. Beckenham: Croom Helm.

Viney, L.L. (1986). The bereavement process: A new approach. *Bereavement Care*, **4**, 27–32.

Viney, L.L. (1987). A sociophenomenological approach to lifespan development complementing Erikson's psychodynamic approach. *Human Development*, **30**, 125–136.

Viney, L.L. (1987). Psychotherapy in a case of physical illness. In G.J. Neimeyer & R.A. Neimeyer (Eds.), *A casebook for personal construct theory*. New York: Plenum.

Viney, L.L. (1989). *Images of illness*. Florida: Krieger, Second edition.

Viney, L.L. (1989). Psychotherapy as shared reconstruction. *International Journal of Personal Construct Psychology*, **3**, 423–442.

Viney, L.L. (1990). A constructivist model of psychological reactions to illness and injury. In G.J. Neimeyer & R.A. Neimeyer (Eds.), *Advances in personal construct psychology*. New York: JAI Press.

Viney, L.L. (1990). The construing widow: Dislocation and adaptation in bereavement. *Psychotherapy Patient*, **3**, 207–222.

Viney, L.L. (1992). Can we see ourselves changing? Toward a constructivist model of adult psychosocial development. *Human Development*, **36**, 65–75.

Viney, L.L. (1993). Goals in psychotherapy: Some reflections of a constructivist therapist. In L. Leitner & G. Dunnett (Eds.), *Critical issues in personal construct therapy*. Malabar, Florida: Krieger.

Viney, L.L., Benjamin, Y.N. & Preston, C. (1988). Mourning and reminiscence: Parallel psychotherapeutic processes for the elderly. *International Journal of Ageing and Human Development*, **28**, 237–249.

Viney, L.L., Benjamin, Y.N. & Preston, C. (1988a). Constructivist family therapy with the elderly. *Journal of Family Psychology*, **2**, 241–258.

Viney, L.L., Benjamin, Y.N. & Preston, C. (1988b). Promoting independence in the elderly: The role of psychological social and physical constraints. *Clinical Gerontologist*, **24**, 71–82.

Viney, L.L., Benjamin, Y.N. & Preston, C.A. (1989). An evaluation of personal construct therapy for the elderly. *British Journal of Medical Psychology*, **62**, 35–41.

Viney, L.L., Benjamin, Y.N. & Preston, C. (1990). Personal construct therapy for the elderly. *Journal of Cognitive Psychotherapy*, **4**, 211–224.

Viney, L.L. & Bousfield, L. (1991). Narrative analysis: A technique for psychosocial research in AIDS. *Social Science and Medicine*.

Viney, L.L. & Bousfield, L. (1992). AIDS and the client "in the fast lane": Narrative construction and reconstruction. *The Psychotherapy Patient*. **32**, 757–758.

Viney, L.L. & Tych, A.M. (1985). Content analysis scales to measure psychosocial maturity in the elderly. *Journal of Personality Assessment*, **49**, 311–317.

Viney, L.L. & Tych, A.M. (1985). To work or not to work: An enquiry of men experiencing unemployment, promotion and retirement. *Psychology and Human Development*, **1**, 57–66.

Viney, L.L., Walker, B., Roberts, T., Tooth, B., Lilley, B. & Ewan, C. (in press). Dying in palliative care units and in hospital: A comparison of the quality of life of terminal cancer patients. *Journal of Consulting and Clinical Psychology*.

Viney, L.L. & Westbrook, M.T. (1982). Psychological reactions to chronic illness: Do they predict rehabilitation? *Journal of Applied Rehabilitation Counselling*, **13**, 38–44.

Viney, L.L. & Westbrook, M.T. (1984). Coping with chronic illness: Strategy preferences, changes over time and related psychological reactions. *Journal of Chronic Diseases*, **106**, 1–14.

Viney, L.L. & Westbrook, M.T. (1986). Is there a pattern of psychological reactions to chronic illness which is associated with death? *Omega*, **17**, 171–183.

Wagner, K.D., Lorion, R.P. & Shipley, T.E. (1983). Insomnia and social crises: Two studies of Erikson's developmental theories. *Journal of Consulting and Clinical Psychology*, **51**, 595–603.

Walker, A. (1980). The social creation of poverty and dependency in old age. *Journal of Social Policy*, **9**, 49–75.

Wallston, K.A., Burger, C., Smith, R.A. & Baugher, R.J. (1988). Comparing the quality of death for hospice and non-hospice cancer patients. *Medical Care*, **26**, 177–182.

Wan, T.H., Odell, B.G. & Lewis, D.T. (1982). *Promoting the well-being of the elderly: A community diagnosis*. New York: Howarth Press.

Ward, R.A. (1984). The marginality and salience of being old: When is age relevant? *Gerontologist*, **24**, 227–237.

Wattis, J. & Church, M. (1986). *Practical psychiatry of old age*. London: Croom Helm.

Weaver, R. (1973). *The old wise woman*. New York: Putnam.

Webster, J. & Young, R.A. (1988). Process variables of the life review: Counselling implications. *International Journal of Ageing and Human Development*, **26**, 315–323.

Weinberger, M., Hiner, S.L. & Tierney, W.M. (1986). Improving functional status in arthritis: The effect of social support. *Social Science and Medicine*, **23**, 899–904.

White, D. & Ingersoll, D. (1989). Life review groups: Helping their members with an unhappy life. *Clinical Gerontologist*, **8**, 47–50.

White, H. (1980). The value of narrativity in the representation of reality. *Critical Inquiry*, **7**, 5–28.

204 References

White, M. & Epson, D. (1990). *Narrative means to therapeutic ends*. London: Norton.
Winter, D. (1985). Group therapy with depressives: A personal construct theory perspective. *International Journal of Mental Health*, **13**, 67–85.
Winter, D. (1992). *Personal construct psychology in clinical practice*. London: Routledge.
Woodfield, R. & Viney, L.L. (1985). A personal construct approach to bereavement. *Omega*, **16**, 1–13.
Woods, R.T. & Britton, P.G. (1985). *Clinical psychology with the elderly*. Beckenham: Croom Helm.
Yesavage, J.A. (1984). Relaxation and memory training in 39 elderly patients. *American Journal of Psychiatry*, **141**, 778–781.

Index